Being Christian after Christendom

Being Christian after Christendom

Where Are We?

How Did We Get Here?

What Went Wrong?

What Is the Solution?

David Rietveld

WIPF & STOCK · Eugene, Oregon

BEING CHRISTIAN AFTER CHRISTENDOM
Where Are We? How Did We Get Here? What Went Wrong?
What Is the Solution?

Wipf & Stock
An Imprint of Wipf and Stock Publishers
199 W. 8th Ave., Suite 3
Eugene, OR 97401

www.wipfandstock.com

PAPERBACK ISBN: 978-1-6667-6298-3
HARDCOVER ISBN: 978-1-6667-6299-0
EBOOK ISBN: 978-1-6667-6300-3

04/11/23

Contents

Foreword

WE CHRISTIANS COULD FEEL sorry for ourselves for we are in BIG trouble. Our message of good news is spurned by those who don't like us. They do not agree that our message is good, nor that such a stale story could be thought of as news. We have lost all purchase on the slippery slope of the prevailing culture. Nicholas Lemann, philosopher and journalist, advised that for any mindset to have traction in today's world, "there has to be a confluence between the ideas themselves, the spirit of the times, and the interests of powerful players who find the ideas congenial."[1] Christian ideas currently seem to lack cogency, the *zeitgeist* or mood of the age is hostile to us, and those typically acknowledged as "influencers" are so uninterested in Christianity that they ignore it.

How did this grave state of affairs come about, where has it left the Christian Church, what's gone wrong, and what can be done about it? Those are the massive questions David Rietveld has set out to begin to answer here. The result? There ought to be a better word than *tour de force* to describe it.

The argument is cumulative. You must read it all, starting at the beginning. You must not fudge it by skipping to the last chapter, for that would be not only to miss the constructive value of the argument, but also to forfeit the opportunity to acquire vast tracts of learning about the origins of our world's cultures.

You will be immediately gripped by the power of David's reasoning: he thinks hard; he thinks logically. He does not want to think for you, but he does want to guide your thinking. He invites you constantly as you read to engage in dialogue with him. The text is replete with such phrases as "Have you got that?," "Let us sharpen the question," "While you are thinking about

---

1. Mallaby, "Economists' Faith in Markets", para. 11.

that," "Of course, we need to nuance this," "Are you sitting down?," "Can you see that . . . ," "You get my point, I trust . . . " It is an approach that keeps you on your toes and nips in the bud any misguided attempt to dodge issues.

No simplistic thinking here. David's respect for the complexity of the modern world compels him to write with clarity and patient step-by-step analysis. He has admirably achieved his goal to make complex social trends understandable and accessible to as many as possible.

Neither is David's thought narrow. It is expansive and adventurous. He is willing to follow the many tributaries of our very complex thought world, and you will be thrilled by what you learn as you explore those off-shoots with him. But he is not an admirer of tangents, the craft of the self-indulgent who wish to avoid facing the real issue. What matters most is how the post-Christian view of the world (PCWV) has achieved ascendency in our culture and how those of us raised in an older Christian view of the world (CWV) paradigm might come first to understand it and then learn how to live creatively and faithfully within it.

The hard thinking here is not confined to the theological, a practice that limits social analysis. The most conservative of Reformed Christians will dissent from none of David's theology. But, alongside it, supplementing it and thus reframing our awareness of culture and society, are the disciplines of the social sciences, especially sociology, psychology, demography, and economics, and the humanistic disciplines of philosophy and ethics. Along the way, David deals with the seminal thinkers who have made us who we are: not only Jesus, Paul, Augustine, Luther, Calvin, and Edwards, but also Plato, Socrates, Aristotle, Descartes, Rousseau, Marx, Nietzsche, Freud, Jung, Foucault, and Derrida. He is not interested primarily in their thought in general. He is not in the business of showing off his knowledge for the admiration of his readers. He is interested only in their thought when it interacts with the present plight of the post-Christian world.

For all the intellectual rigor of this book, it is not the work of the nerd-ish academic. It is rather the work of the pastor academic. David has profound empathy with the grief and bewilderment of those disorientated by the triumph of the PCWV and the collapse of the CWV. He knows how we feel; he feels it as sharply as any of us. Like all good pastors, he does not offer false consolation. It may be that the post-Christian world retains more traces of Christian influence than a purely secular world (whatever that might be). But PCWV adherents have replaced God with themselves at the center of the world as effectually as any secularist. David's pastoral heart is also manifest in his determination to go beyond the sentimental acknowledgement of our hurt, confusion, and desolation. He does not leave us "stuck" in a past we find so difficult to put behind us, but which no longer exists. The pastor's heart is also manifest in his concern for the all-too-common outcome of joining the PCWV groupthink: loneliness, addiction, depression, purposelessness, futility, and meaninglessness.

Christian authors today, addicted to fashions like anyone else, are lining up to confess openly the sins and abuses of churches over the centuries. Confession seems to make some people feel better, and hearing the recitation makes others more defensive, and that is where both parties leave it. This book is not in that genre. The solutions suggested here are startlingly innovative and genuinely liberating. I must not summarize them for you. That would require spoiler alerts and would deny you the responsibility I have already enjoined upon you, namely to read the whole without taking shortcuts. I suspect that what this book does is to give a general theory to explain how Christianity works over the ages. In every age, effective Christians have selected with discernment what they must stand for. In the long history of Christendom, when Christian values aligned with culture, Christian leaders expected to stand against every perceived evil and triumph in every moral struggle. It is sobering to learn that such an outcome has probably always been impossible and liberating to be counselled that in the post-Christian world it is just plain silly to attempt it. This book will guide us to a better way through wiser discernment of which causes to fight for under the banner of the cross, and which to leave to Providence to address in another time and place.

The truly remarkable achievement of John Wesley and Jonathan Edwards in propagating nation-shaping and social reform in the eighteenth century was due largely to their capacity to rethink Christian faith in the thoughtforms of their age. It was an age of reason, enlightenment, and scientific discovery. Wesley and Edwards were fully cognisant of the responsibility of understanding those developments and harnessing them for the more effective propagation of the Gospel. David Rietveld has taken that responsibility upon himself in this age of postmodernism, deconstruction, and secularization. It is a prodigious effort. Happy are congregations guided by pastors such as he, combining faithfulness to the Word with knowledge of the times and sensitivity to the spirit of the age.

Conjoint Associate Professor Stuart Piggin

Director
The Centre for Christian Thought and Experience, 2005–2016
Macquarie University, Sydney, Australia

Introduction

THE GOALPOSTS HAVE MOVED. Something radical has changed. Admitting you believe and follow Jesus weirds people like it never has before. Doing church like we always have no longer leads to the same results. Something is different.

Here is what it looks like. In the past, when you mentioned in the workplace morning tea room that you go to church, the conversation carried on as usual. Now there is an awkward silence, followed by a conversation change. You just broke some social norm. In the past, you could invite almost any family from your children's school to a Christmas carols service. Now you think which ones won't be offended. In the past, when discussing a question of ethics or morality in public, you could offer the biblical view—without quoting chapter and verse—as a possible valid position. It might lead to some debate. Now you are ignored, get odd looks, but no engagement.

Pastors are thinking that our church is running quite well. We have quality programs, gifted musicians on the roster, clear and practical teaching. There are no messy tensions at the moment. In the past, when church was like this, it grew. There was a tangible sense of vitality and momentum. Now, there are few new people, and my regulars are attending less and less.

The children's program has a bring-a-friend morning, and few, if any, come. The youth group books a band and a jumping castle. Attendance is up a bit, but nothing like it used to be when we ran an event like this twenty or thirty years ago. There is a conversation on social media about parenting. Every perspective is validated, except for the Christian one; it is hated on. That is what it looks like.

What it feels like is standing on unstable ground. We feel insecure, uncertain, and confused. The unstable ground is somehow unfair: it's not a level playing field. The odds are not in our favour, and the house is betting against us.

Why is the Christian position so quickly dismissed, even mocked? Isn't our culture supposed to be open-minded? Have I missed something? How come the time-honored teachings and traditions of Jesus and Christianity are now maligned? Christians have started hospitals, funded and volunteered in welfare agencies, championed education for all. Yet, now we are perceived as power-hungry, abusive bullies, arrogant and judgemental.

Things are more than just unfair, it's unsettling. There is something comforting about numbers, about having friends and allies who think like you do. As Christians are increasingly marginalized and isolated, being a public Christian feels like being a BBQ salesman at a vegetarian convention. The natural response is to feel like there is something wrong with us. We ask ourselves, "is there something I don't get, because everyone else is heading in the other direction?"

This sense of being unsettled is not just internal. Doesn't Jesus promise to build his church and the gates of hell will not overcome it? So what are we, the twenty-first-century church in the West, doing wrong? Are we being unfaithful? For some, this may even lead towards anxiety, fear. How come this is happening on my watch? As our forefathers have for centuries, we have to pass on the baton of faith and we want to leave a healthier church than the one we inherited. Why is the church in decline, both in terms of attendance and influence?

If what I am saying resonates with your experience, this is the right book for you. I will help you understand what has changed. I will outline why and how. And I will suggest some ways we can be the people of God in the new world we find ourselves inhabiting.

Perhaps you are not entirely with me. You might be saying something like: "that's kind of true in some churches, but not in mine." Or, "it's true in part of our church, but not in our ethnic congregation." You might be puzzled. Why are the trends mixed? Stick with me. I'll try to help you understand that too.

Or you might be thinking: "yep, I know the problem, and I know the solution. If all churches were more like this, and less like that...", "If only we had done this, and not done that..." Again, stick with me. I'll survey the most popular narratives as to what the problem, and what the solution is. I'll explain why the current discourse about how to do ministry and mission is so tribal. We will explore why there are competing stories about how to be a church. Are all "recipes" for a healthy church equally valid? Do some work better than others? Or are we in a season where having niche market churches, kind of like the seven choices we get at the food court in the regional shopping center, is a strategic way for churches to cater for the diverse preferences of contemporary Christians?

And of course, we have to do some theology, not just sociology and history. How does the church, the bride and body of Christ, find itself in decline? Has God allowed that? Is it our fault? Are there biblical touchpoints to guide us through this troubled season? To foreshadow my conclusions: yes, the Bible contains narratives that align with our current scenario, but they are not the biblical truths we are used to retelling or most often rehearse.

The church in the West has had a long slow, steady advance for about 1600 years. Or at least that is how we imagine and retell church history. We have a long and established pattern of being drawn to passages and interpretations that fit with that narrative. We anticipate more slow and steady growth. But it's not our present experience. It's time for a second look at the history of church attendance in the West.

The story where the church is in slow, steady continuous advance, that world, often called Christendom, has gone. We need to go back to scripture, but approach it with different questions and read it from within a different context. I will take us to some familiar biblical narratives but highlight different dimensions as we reframe how we be the people of God in what some call a post-Christian era.

Before I map the journey, a brief word to various readers. This is a thought-provoking book aimed at educated readers, but it is not an academic textbook. I have tried to write in ways that are accessible, engaging, and connect with experience. To that end, I have kept footnotes and references to a minimum. Just because I have not referenced others, does not mean I have not borrowed and played with their insights.

The heart of this book is not new thought, but integrated thoughts across various academic disciplines in ways that interact with our current context. For those that wish to explore the thinkers whose thoughts I have borrowed, I acknowledge them by including them in my bibliography.

A second consequence of writing an inter-disciplinary book that is "popular" is that at times I must choose to refrain from an in-depth explanation of any one topic, as understood through any one discipline. Historians will at times find my history thin, sociologists will find my observations embryonic, and theologians will find my explanations underdone. If this book is likened to a piece of art, it is an impressionist work that explores the interaction between primary colors, rather than realism that attempts to capture every facet and fine detail.

A word for those readers who are used to reading Christian books. Christian talk normally accounts for social happenings with theological explanations. That denomination shrank because it lost sight of the truth. That person became a Christian because the Holy Spirit convicted them of their need of a savior. If that is your experience, you will find this book unusual and even provocative. This is an exploration of how social, cultural, historical, psychological, and theological perspectives shed light on the present. All disciplines are given equal voice because, after all, all truths are God's truths. I hope you find the inter-disciplinary dialogue stimulating.

A note to readers who might not describe themselves as Christian. Perhaps you have never understood yourself to be a person of great faith. Or maybe your patterns of regular church attendance have ceased, and you now consider yourself a believer in some sort of God, but not a practicing Christian. You may have been given this book by someone else. If that's you, I suggest you approach this book like someone who looks over the neighbor's fence, only to discover they are looking back at you.

This is mostly a sociological book, written by a Christian, for Christians, struggling to make sense of a post-Christian world. As I describe the former Christian view of the world (CWV), the emerging post-CWV, and the assumptions behind both, you might wish to reflect on your assumptions about the state of our culture at present. How do I or we decide what drives us? What do we value most? How do we treat others? Who and how do we determine right from wrong, opinion from absolute? Ask yourself, as I see them looking over the fence describing me, does it resonate? I hear their pain. With the passing of the CWV, they feel they have lost something. Have I lost something too? Not as much as them, but still something. I hope you find this read stimulating, stretching.

So, here is the journey. This book will be in four parts, exploring four questions. They are not just my questions. These are questions any and every culture asks when it finds itself in disruption or transition. Where are we now? How did we get here? What went wrong? What is the solution?[1]

In our shared memory, we have lived through a season of radical social change. We have watched on as church attendance has significantly declined. Churches that have housed congregations for centuries are now turned into dwellings and cafes. Religious affiliation, that is, ticking the box on the census form, has also radically declined and for the first time in history, a new category of atheists or non-religious persons makes up a major block of citizens.

Having said this, church attendance is growing in pockets. Also increasing is religious schooling, as is the not-for-profit sector which is dominated by Christian agencies. While overall church attendance declines and some Christian values are publically eroding, we shall see that

---

1. This phrasing is borrowed from Wright, *New Testament and the People*, 123.

the Christian legacy casts an enormous shadow. Some, but not all parts of Christianity are in decline.

This is to foreshadow a distinction at the heart of this book. Church attendance rates have fluctuated over history. We are experiencing not the end of Christianity in the West, but the end of the West as a Christian culture. In chapter 1, we will explore this. When everyone shared what we might call a CWV, how did society work? What did it mean to be a regular citizen, as opposed to a practicing Christian, who lived as part of an era called Christendom? What did they believe? How did it influence their behaviors?

In chapter 2, we will outline the central values of the West's shared belief system: our CWV, the one we are in the process of losing. We will also consider the church's former role in society, when the shared CWV was stable and widespread.

Chapters 1 and 2 will re-plough fields we know well. This is necessary, as sometimes over-familiarity undermines our capacity to perceive. We will tease out and clarify the contours of where we have just come from. It is foundational work that will give us the perceptive frameworks and tools we need to venture into the present in chapter 3. Here we will consider what has replaced the shared CWV. Finally, in chapter 4, we will explore the status of the church, Christians, and Christian thought, in the post-Christian era.

Part 2 of this book is "how did we get here?" And yes, some of you will already be thinking "I'm not into history. I might skip this section." If you think that, you are such a product of your culture. We Westerners believe we know better than all who have gone before us. We trust our intuition and live in the moment, with only the occasional eye to the future. We see the past as the past, and you can't change it, and we have moved on. To be frank, this view is arrogant. We assume we have little to learn from the past. Worse, we believe the past does not influence the present. We believe we are in control of ourselves and our destiny. We get to define ourselves. We discredit and dismiss the wisdom of traditions, built up over centuries. One of those wise maxims we ignore is "those who fail to learn from the mistakes of the past are bound to recommit them."

Chapter 5 will survey the key thinkers who have contributed to the displacement of the Christian worldview and the content of its replacement. As I just said, Westerners have a type of "we-now-know-better" overconfidence, the flip side of which is ignorance. To counter this ignorance and break out of the binary Christian–post-Christian exchange, I need to introduce some other lenses. In chapter 6, I will briefly sketch some alternate worldviews. What wisdom is there in other traditions? We also need to consider entire coherent traditions, not just cherry-pick the bits we like. To cherry-pick disrespects those traditions. Through these "other" lenses, we can better understand how the West got here, not somewhere else. This is not the only path we could have taken. There were, and are, other options. Having appreciated alternatives, we can now ask, Did we take the best path?

Having dealt with the broad sweep of history, chapter 7 is something of a transition chapter. Even without the type of analysis we will conduct in this book, most people in church have noticed the decline and have theories about why that is. There are presently, within the various Christian "tribes," competing narratives around what mistakes have been made in the past, mistakes that render the church weak in the present. We will rehearse, contrast, and assess each of these accounts. While these competing narratives each get lots of "air time," in my view, they all fail to grapple with the substantial changes that have unfolded.

This brings us to the third of our big questions: what went wrong?

This is a complex question. The ignorance and arrogance of Western culture can be the enemy of insight. Once again, we need some other glasses to get perspective. This is not the first time a predominantly Christian culture has found itself in such decline and was eventually displaced by another worldview. In chapter 8, we will review the growth (from 50 AD to about 800 AD) then the decline (from 800 AD to 1350 AD) of the Eastern (including North African) Church. In addition, we shall briefly survey the British Church (from the Reformation onwards), then the American and Australian Churches. This will allow us to ask the question, Has something actually gone wrong? Was the decline in the Eastern Church their fault? Is the decline in the Western Church our fault? Or are there larger forces at play than just the health of each local church, which leads to the total health of the temporal church in a given culture? And if so, what are they?

At this point, we will find ourselves at risk of confusion or conflation. Stopping the decline of church attendance has not been, I will argue, entirely within our control. The decline of church attendance is of concern. Christians assume that church attendance correlates (but not one-to-one) with spiritual wellbeing. Fewer people at church suggests individual and corporate levels of commitment are falling. However, the decline of church attendance is different from the end of the CWV.

To outline the decline of the CWV will bring a tear to many an eye. In chapter 9, we shall lament its passing. Lamenting will allow us to move on, pivoting towards our last question: what is the solution? If the post-Christian world is different and views Christians differently, what is our place in it? How do we be salt and light in a different context? We will explore this difficult question. It's difficult, not because it's complex, but difficult because we have 1600 years of unlearning to do. That does not happen easily or without pain or lament. Chapter 10 is about lament and unlearning. How did we do evangelism and discipleship in the past? Why might our tried and tested tools not work in the post-Christian West?

This brings us back to scripture. In chapter 10, we will reconsider Elijah and then Daniel and his three friends. How did they cope with the transition from living in a majority God-honoring theocracy to living as a minority in an idol-worshipping pagan culture? What did they have to let go of? How did they reposition themselves? How did they see God's hand move? How did they behave and be in their new worlds? The answers from Daniel will likely be a little different from what you were taught in Sunday School.

In chapter 11, we can finally re-approach the gospels and the early church. Some may think I ought to have started here but walk with me; we will get to the gospels. Perhaps you will be surprised at what we discover as we reconsider our sacred texts with fresh lenses.

In chapter 12, we can close the circle. How do we bring the best of our tradition into the future? Given some patterns we have seen in scripture, what might be possible solutions going forward? I will leave you with metaphors that highlight some green shoots where the kingdom is growing at present and provide some frameworks for thinking about how we can be a faithful, healthy, fruitful church and Christians in a post-Christian world.

My suggestions won't be completely new. There is nothing novel about the idea that Jesus calls and grows disciples. So why read to the end of the book? Because discipleship, or faith, is always embodied. It is lived out in lifestyle, in a culture, in a time and place. Jesus is the same yesterday, today, and forever. Much of following him will be constant but the context has shifted. So, in some senses, must we.

A word about the structure of each chapter, or section. We are dealing with complex social phenomena. Despite this, many people rate themselves as amateur sociologists, kind of like bush lawyers, kitchen-table economists, or lay experts in pandemic management. We analyze social trends and speak quickly and confidently of things too wonderful for us to understand. Quick answers are simplistic. I will often introduce an idea alongside our simplistic analysis of it. Then I will complexify the issue and demonstrate why our simplistic solutions do not serve us well.

But I don't want to leave you there, lost and overwhelmed by complexity. One of my favourite quotes is, "I would not give a fig for the simplicity this side of complexity, but I would give my life for the simplicity on the other side of complexity."[2] My goal is to make complex social trends understandable and accessible to as many people as possible. Here is my pledge to you. I will try my best to leave you at the end of each chapter with

2. Oliver Wendell Holmes.

a simple summary. I would ask that you make this commitment: don't try to arrive at that simplicity by taking a shortcut and skipping the complexity of the body of the chapter. Such effortless simplicity is not worth much more than dried fruit.

Finally, a caution. At times, you will disagree with me. I expect that. We are interpreting complex social phenomena and social trends that are themselves a moving target. Sometimes I write, go to bed, and wake up only to disagree with what I wrote the night before. We are doing sociology, not maths equations. Social commentary and biblical commentary do not hold the same weight. If you disagree, that's fine with me. Use this book—the parts you agree with and the parts you don't—to prompt you to distill how you think our culture has shifted, and what implications that has for us as we follow Jesus and be his people.

PART ONE

Where Are We Now?

An exploration of the beliefs and values of the Christian world-view that is passing, and the post-Christian worldview that is replacing it.

1

What Is the "Christian Worldview" We Are Losing?

IN THE LATE 1980s and early 1990s, I lived with my parents, brother, and sister in Hobart, Tasmania. There were two local branches of the national TV stations, Channels 7 and 9. This was before TV stations broadcast 24/7. There came an hour when programming for the day came to an end. Then, early the following day, broadcasts would resume.

On Tasmanian TV, before the TV shows began or after they ended, there was a "thought for the day." As the wife of a local minister, my mother, together with the local Anglican vicar, used to deliver a short "devotional" that would bring closure to the day's proceedings, kind of like when you were a kid, and your mum read and prayed with you before going to sleep. Every evening, the station close was marked by a Christian thought.

Less than twenty years later, in the mid 2000s, I moved back to Hobart with my wife and four children. Television programming is now around the clock, and the "thought for the day" has long gone.

We enrolled our children at the local state primary school. As Christmas approaches, the teacher asks the students to generate Christmas words for the weekly spelling list. The kids call out words like "present," "holiday," "food," and "family." My son suggests "Jesus" and "angel." The teacher responds in an annoyed voice, saying, "we are not going to make Christmas all religious," and fails to write his suggested words alongside the others she has written on the whiteboard.

That is a classic example of the end of the shared Christian worldview (henceforth CWV); or the end of Christendom.[1] It's an experience we have

---

1. I am using three terms somewhat interchangeably although there are slight technical differences between them. The terms "Christian worldview" and "Judeo-Christian

all had a thousand times over: when the supermarket sells maple syrup on "Pancake Tuesday" and no-one has any idea why; when the major sporting codes use Good Friday as an excuse for a blockbuster local derby; when students are forbidden to pray at schools.

We all experience examples of what we have lost and what is no longer acceptable or politically correct. We know that feeling, that trend. But what exactly is the CWV? Why would my son's school teacher not validate the suggestion that Jesus has something to do with Christmas?

The answer is not that between 1990 and 2005 most of the people in Hobart abandoned their personal belief in Jesus as their Lord and Savior. The decline of church attendance is different from the decline of the Christian worldview and its influence. The church was in attendance decline in the 1930s, but it was not losing its influence. Likewise, the church grew in attendance in the 1950s, but it did not have a boom in social sway.

From the 1960s onwards, within our living corporate memory, we have experienced in Australia and indeed in most of the Western world, the most radical decline of both attendance *and* influence of the church in 1600 years of Western history. We have, for the most part, assumed they are the same thing. But they are not! They are different and while the differences might be subtle, they are profound.

The Christian worldview is not the majority of citizens in a given country professing Christian beliefs. A person can hold to a CWV without actually being a professing believer or follower of Christ.

One such person is the former Associate Professor of Psychology at Harvard and social commentator, Jordan Peterson. He is a passionate activist for the preservation of the Christian worldview, but he is not a Christian. He believes the Bible is no more than a compilation of wise sayings or myths. He does not believe Jesus is the Son of God who died and rose again.

He is an excellent example of my point. You can hold to a CWV and not be a Christian. Historically, in Australia as in most of the West, almost everyone had a CWV, but most were not Christian.

What is happening in our culture is more than just people no longer coming to church or believing in Jesus. It is a culture-wide abandonment of the CWV and it is happening among non-Christians and even some Christians.

Before we progress to consider the contours of the emerging worldview we now inhabit, it is worth slowing down and naming the defining

---

worldview" refer to a coherent set of beliefs and values. The term "Christendom" refers to an historical era when many Western cultures shared and held to the Judeo-Christian worldview.

features of the CWV. So what is the CWV? And how can one hold to it, without being a Christian?

Defining the CWV

Journalist Roy Williams defines the CWV as a belief in three essential components:[2]

1. An all-knowing God who created and sustains the Universe, and who is vitally interested in the thoughts and conduct of each individual human being;

2. An afterlife, in which each of us will be judged by God;

3. The divinity of Jesus of Nazareth.

By his own admission, Williams acknowledges this list is insufficient as a creed. It does not adequately summarize the central beliefs of the Christian faith and too much is missing. But that is not his point, or mine.

In the CWV (or the era of Christendom, from approximately 400 AD to 2000 AD), there was a shared assumed consensus regarding the above. Let's consider each in turn.

In Williams's first point, he affirms that life and the universe are not here by chance. The world was created, or the evolution of it was guided, by the hand of a purposeful God. That hand of God is discernible by humanity, because God somehow inhabits his world. Ethics are a case in point. God has shaped the world so that it has a moral fabric, engineered into its design. Humans have an individual and shared conscience. Intuitively, we know right from wrong.

So it follows that murder is always wrong, kindness is always right, and honesty is the best policy. A person is worth more than their possessions. All human life is inherently sacred. These statements are true, not because they are announced in a sacred text by a religious authority. These statements are, in a CWV, all deemed to be self-evidently true. When we hear them, we say, "yes, that statement expresses a reality about how the universe works that I just know to be true."

Williams adds to his characterization of the CWV that this God both creates and sustains the universe. God has not wound up the clock and walked away. This continuous engagement by God has a focus. God is "vitally interested in the thoughts and conduct of each individual human being."[3]

---

2. Williams, *Post-God Nation*, 12.

3. Williams, *Post-God Nation*, 12.

The Christian understanding and practice of prayer is an excellent example. As our world becomes increasingly pluralistic, it is common to hear experts who inform us that all religions are essentially the same and that prayer is an example of this. Such statements highlight the similarities between religions—and there are similarities. It is in the differences that we find the unique emphasis of each religion.

Muslims pray five times a day, which is perhaps more than Christians do, but they pray in a very formulaic way. They pray facing Mecca because Allah is more there than here. They kneel, reinforcing the central Islamic tenant that humans submit to Allah, and they recite or chant pre-scripted words that focus on Allah.

Buddhists pray. In popular Buddhism, it is more the monks who pray. You pay them, and they pray for your protection. I remember standing in a shopping strip in the capital of Buddhist Cambodia, Phnom Penh. Monks would stop outside the front of every shop. They would politely stand and wait until the shop owner came and made a cash offering. The monks would then pray against evil spirits and for prosperity. I remember thinking that this type of prayer looked more like organized crime running a protection racket than a created human being communicating with their creator god.

In some expressions of Buddhism, there are even prayer wheels. You don't even have to say the words. Just spin the wheel, and this is just as effective in nudging the gods in your favour.

For Hindus, prayer is mostly the chanting of mantras. Prayers are more effective when combined with a sacrifice and recited in a temple.

By contrast, the Christian view of prayer is radically personalized. You can pray anywhere, because God is with you. You don't need a priest to pray on your behalf. You don't have to pray in formulas. You can ask God about personal and private concerns because the Christian God is both all-knowing and vitally interested in each of us. We are called his children, and we address him as Our Father.

The Christian practice of prayer flows from the distinctly Christian view of an all-knowing, loving God. But here is my point. In the era of Christendom, (almost) everyone, not just those who regularly went to church, believed they could cry out and ask God for mercy and help in their time of need because everyone shared a belief in an all-knowing, loving, personal God.

The second of Williams' core components to a CWV is belief in an afterlife, in which each of us will be judged by God. There is a flip-side to holding, even if only vaguely, to an all-knowing God. He knows when you need help, and he knows when you "sin." Combine that with the belief that the universe has a moral fabric, woven into its design, and everyone has an internal moral compass, a conscience.

In addition to being all-knowing, and vitally interested (classically we would use the descriptor "loving"), the CWV's God is also just. He is fair. He does not let evil go unpunished.

Clearly, justice does not always exist in this life. It is God's role to nudge the scales of justice in this life and balance them in the next. This belief gave a culture-wide sense of security, of stability. Justice ultimately reigns, even if not always in the present.

Again, it is vital to get the nuance here. Christian worldview cultures from 400 AD onwards, and we are talking about Europe and their colonies, did not universally accept that every law and precept in the Bible was eternally true. It is perhaps even an overstatement to say that everyone believed that the Ten Commandments were a baseline universal moral standard. Stark notes that in 1551, in the diocese of Gloucester, more than half the priests could not even recite the Ten Commandments, and some did not know Jesus was the author of the Lord's Prayer.[4] We overestimate the levels of practicing faith through the history of the Christian West.

Regardless of how many people actively follow Jesus, we can say this: the shared assumption, the assumed consensus, was that there is a knowable right from wrong, and that God judges individuals according to how they have lived in this life, which will determine their destination in the next life.

An illustration will reinforce this point. Australia was founded as a convict penal colony. Some places, such as Sarah Island on the west coast of Tasmania, were reserved for the worst re-offenders. Life was unbelievably inhumane. This gave rise, on occasion, to something called a murder or suicide pact.

Some supposed death would be preferable to convict life but they had a massive dilemma: the common belief was that suicide was an unforgivable sin that would lead to condemnation and eternal hell. There are documented incidents where two individuals appear to have entered into a murder pact. One convict allowed himself to be murdered by the other. No attempt was made to cover up the crime. On the contrary, the murderer's intent was to be caught, convicted, and hanged. Thus both men got to escape convict life, without either committing the unforgivable sin of suicide.

It matters not if this logic is correct or biblical. What is telling is the shared belief. People agreed that there is a God who sees and judges, there is the hope of an afterlife and the fear of hell, and there is some causal

---

4. Stark, *Triumph of Christianity*, 260.

connection between behavior on earth and one's eternal destiny. These are all facets of the CWV. Even convicts and murderers believed this.

Anthropologists make the same point differently. Anthropology is the study of humans and human behavior. At a macro level, anthropologists propose three types of cultures in the world: honor-shame cultures, such as in Asia and the Middle East; and power-fear cultures, where most African cultures fit. I will expand on these two worldviews in chapter 6. Lastly, there are guilt-innocence cultures. That is us, the West. In such cultures, there is a focus on doing right and avoiding wrong. There is an internal sense of guilt that needs to be alleviated. We all desire to be seen as innocent before God and neighbor. We have a profound inner peace when we know we are without guilt.

This is another way to describe the CWV: a shared belief that there is right and wrong brings an internal sense of innocence or guilt and an eternal outcome of blessing or judgement.

If you hold to a classic view of Christianity, please note what I have not said. I have not said that in the past everyone believed in all of the Ten Commandments. I have not said everyone believed in original sin, or that believing in Jesus' death and resurrection, and repenting and asking for forgiveness is the only way to alleviate guilt. This is what confessing Christians believe. Confessing Christians make up only a subset of citizens in CWV culture.

There is vagueness among the broader citizens about how the intersection of forgiveness, good works, and small, less consequential sins versus deadly sins all come together. Cultures are comfortable with vagueness in certain areas. Ambiguity does not undermine a culture's capacity to be coherent, to knit all of its citizens together.

An illustration. Australia is presently definite about the fact that sexism is wrong, but we are vague about what behaviors are sexist. Is it sexist to encourage your son to play footy and your daughter netball? There are diverse opinions about that, but we are agreed and united that sexism is wrong. Likewise, in the past, there was a shared belief in good and evil, guilt and innocence, blessing and judgement in this life and the next, even if we did not all agree on the details and mechanics.

The last of Williams' list is mention of Jesus. In the CWV, there is a shared belief in the divinity of Jesus of Nazareth. There is something intriguing about Jesus. Even today, he has an enduring appeal. He elicits an unrivalled fascination. His teachings have an ongoing authority and his life sets an exemplary standard. It is almost impossible to over-estimate the influence Jesus has had on Western culture.

Statements like this are not new. Having said that, allow me to flesh out a couple of examples to highlight what I mean. If you watch a movie, chances are the hero reflects something of Jesus. Our superheroes are humble, focused on the good of others, and self-sacrificial. You may say, "Of course they are, aren't all superheroes like that?" No! Greek and Roman gods do not look like that, nor do the recent anti-hero types like Snape of *Harry Potter*, Captain Jack Sparrow, or Deadpool. For the most part, the attributes we respect in our superheroes are attributes that mirror Jesus.

John Dickson makes a similar point in his book, *Humilitas*. Humility is a virtue traceable back to Jesus. The Greeks and Romans despised humility, as it was a sign of weakness. Its place of esteem in Western culture is directly attributable to Jesus.

I am sure you can think of dozens of other examples. But here is my point. The life and teachings of Jesus are normative for all of Western culture. He was, and I contend still is, the most influential person in our culture. Many of the values and attributes to which Westerners aspire originate from Jesus. This was true for the entire Western culture, not just those who had a personal faith in Jesus as their Lord and Savior.

Before we move on, I need to expand on Williams' list. He mentions Jesus' divinity explicitly. My view is that Williams' emphasis on Jesus' divinity reflects his Roman Catholic heritage. Granted, Catholicism has had a significant global influence. However, countries such as America, Canada, England, Australia, and Germany have a more Protestant history. To simply refer to Jesus's divinity is not sufficient when describing his influence in Protestant-dominated countries. Williams makes no mention of Jesus' teachings, nor the wider Bible in which his teachings are recorded. And yet, the Bible is the best-selling and most influential book of all time. We must say something of it.

The Bible, in the CWV, is not God's inspired Word, full of infallible truths. It is that for Christians. For society at large, the Bible is a collection of stories and statements articulating accumulated insights into how life and the universe work.

The teachings of Jesus are the high water mark, but the entire Bible is a well of wisdom and instruction. Consider our previous reflection on morality. Some of the moral fabric of the world is self-evident. The Bible reinforces these parts. Murder is wrong, and this moral claim is both self-evident and reinforced in biblical narrative and commands.

But Jesus, and the rest of the Bible, provides guidance for a moral life beyond what is self-evident. So Jesus says, "Blessed are the meek" (Matt 5:5). As Dickson points out, the notion that meekness or humility was virtuous was not self-evident to anyone else in the first century. Likewise,

Jesus and the wider Bible give instruction around values and the larger purposes in life. Again Jesus says, "It is more blessed to give than to receive" (Acts 20:35). This truth is counter-intuitive. You need to act it out to discover its power. Left to our own devices, we naturally drift to the notion that it is nicer to receive.

This brings us to the heart of how a CWV culture uses and views the Bible. The Bible is a library of accumulated truths, distilled over centuries of experience, trial and error. Jesus is the greatest rabbi and his message, radical in its day, is, loosely speaking, divinely inspired. There is wisdom contained in the gospels that is beyond most mere mortals but it is teaching made accessible to the common person. Anyone and everyone can read it and when they do, parts of it will resonate. People will say, "Yes, that is true! I might not have been able to put it into words myself, or even come up with it, but now that I hear it, intuitively, it rings true."

In a CWV culture, the Bible is the shared repository of our highest wisdom. So let's have a thought for the day to begin and end the day of TV broadcasting. It will bring a pearl to everyone, be they practicing Christians or otherwise.

To summarize, Christendom, or the CWV, was an era in history from about 400 to about 2000 AD. In the West, people shared Christian views about how the world works. These beliefs were assumed to be common to everyone, regardless of their relationship with Jesus.

The key component of this worldview is a belief:

1. in an all-knowing God who is the source of all life; he is personal and loving, and just;

2. that he has created a world with a moral fabric, with good and evil;

3. that Jesus' teachings and life are the highest expressions of the good life;

4. that the Bible contains divine wisdom and following its guidelines will correlate (though not a one-to-one correlation) with a content life;

5. in a God who sees and knows us, and will judge with some combination of grace and justice. His judgement of our life determines where we spend eternity.

That is the CWV. That is the Western way of thinking, of understanding how the world works. It *was* our shared belief system. The obvious questions that flow are: Why did we abandon it? And what have we replaced it with? We shall come to that in chapters 3–5. But I need to take us a step or two further in another direction before we get there.

To understand the CWV, we need to appreciate more than just its shared beliefs. We also need to understand how individual citizens who live in a Christian culture believe and behave.

Joseph Banks as an Example

An illustration will aid us at this point. In Australian and English history, Joseph Banks is a notable figure. He was the botanist/naturalist/scientist on board Captain Cook's ship, the *Endeavour*. Banks was born in 1743 to a privileged family and was educated at Eton and Oxford. He was a standout patron of the natural sciences and part of a wave of Enlightenment thinkers who sought to expand human knowledge through them. He was the president of the Royal Society for forty-one years.[5] His journeys crossing the Atlantic and Pacific Oceans are rightly understood as part of this effort to extend the reach and influence of the natural sciences.

Banks was not known for his religious devotion or behavior. He was a proverbial sailor who had a girl in every port and would frequently share conjugal relationships with the natives on his expeditions. History does not record him as being a practicing Christian.

When Banks encountered cannibalism among the Maoris of New Zealand in 1773, he was disturbed. He noted in his diary that cannibalism is a "custom which human nature holds in too great abhorrence to give easy credit to."[6] Later, he wrote " . . . nature through all the superior part of the creation shews how much she recoils at the thought of any species preying upon itself: Dogs and cats shew visible disgust at the very sight of a dead carcass of their species, even Wolves or Bears were never sayd to eat one another except in cases of absolute necessity, when the stings of hunger . . . "[7]

What is noteworthy here is Banks's logic. He was a naturalist, or a scientist, who was inclined towards natural as opposed to spiritual explanations of phenomena. Yet, he also believed there is a creation-wide order instilled into the universe. Just as animals intuitively avoid eating their own, so too it is unnatural and immoral for humans to practice cannibalism.

At the risk of being too pointed, Banks believed:

1. in a moral Creator God,

2. who has sewn morality into the fabric of his universe;

---

5. This society was formally known as The Royal Society of London for Improving Natural Knowledge.

6. Banks, *Journal*, 212.

7. Banks, *Journal*, 237.

3. that humans and other creatures are obliged to discern and align with this order,

4. and will suffer some negative consequences when they do not, in this life if not in the next.

Banks believed all of this, without being a Christian. Put another way, he held to and was committed to a Christian worldview, without being a committed Christian.

How Shared Belief Outworks in Behavior

Beliefs had implications for Joseph Banks. He believed it was unnatural to practice cannibalism, yet permissible to have extra marital affairs in certain circumstances. What about the beliefs of Average Joe? A regular citizen of Australia, who lived sometime in the fairly recent past—let's imagine the 1960s. Without ever having thought about it a lot, or being conscious of having made a decision, he too holds to the CWV, but he is not a Christian either. How do his beliefs outwork in the ways he behaves?

Average Joe believes in right from wrong, good from evil. Furthermore, Average Joe believes there is a god who sees most things, if not everything. This god has standards and there will be some form of judgement, some day of reckoning. So Joe tries to do the right thing. He thinks it is wrong to murder, steal, cheat, and lie. He avoids these behaviors, and agrees society must punish such actions.

Average Joe works and provides for his family. Family is very important for Joe. He understands his role as a father means he needs to protect, care, and provide for his family. He has a role to play in educating his kids. In part, he lets the local school do this but in part, he does it. He teaches his kids how to play tennis, just as his father taught him.

The behaviors Joe practices are going to work, earning an income, buying a house and car, providing for his family. There are other behaviors, too, which have to do with finding a wife, starting a family, and being a parent. Behind these behaviors are beliefs. Joe understands himself to be both an individual and a person who exists in relationships. He is a father, husband, and a member of an extended family, and an individual in his own right.

Average Joe is married. He loves and is loyal to his wife, though they might not always agree. And married life has a way of, on occasion, becoming ordinary, mundane, even challenging. But Joe understands that one has to make sacrifices for the sake of peace, stability, and the children. Here too, practical behaviors are necessary, such as housework, playing with the children, and quality time with one's spouse. In all of this, Joe is also embodying the CWV. Peace, and even happiness, are found in thinking of others first and making personal sacrifices.

Average Joe describes himself as not really a Christian. His wife describes herself as Church of England, but not practicing. Their children receive religious instruction at school. They go to the school Christmas nativity play. The local vicar gives a talk afterwards. Joe and his wife are okay with all of this. It's a good place for their children to learn values. As an individual citizen, some of Joe's behaviors are interactions with social institutions. His children attend school. He enrolls them, transports them, and provides a uniform and lunch. In some way, the family celebrates Christmas and, in so doing, engages with the church.

Average Joe believes he is morally autonomous, that is, he has free will and is capable of making choices. He obeys the road rules, more-or-less. He pays his bills and taxes. He is civil and polite to his neighbors. So yes, he does make choices. But they are all options within the culturally accepted and shared CWV.

The insight that his choices are CWV choices is likely lost on Average Joe. If his car is broken into, Joe does not suspect it is because he failed to ask or pay the monk to pray for him. He does not consider a holiday to Mecca, or even the Vatican, because a spiritual pilgrimage is part of one's duty. He does not consider bribing his children's school teacher, as one might in an honor-shame culture. He is not polite to one neighbor, but ignores the other, because they are of a lower caste than him.

Average Joe behaves as a citizen who has ascribed to the CWV, whether he knows and understands this, or not!

Slightly outside the average—but still very normal—is Chris, a practicing Christian. She, too, holds to the CWV. Chris and Joe have a shared baseline that includes beliefs, practices, and engagement with religious symbols (both celebrate Christmas), but Chris believes in more. In addition to considering that murder, stealing, and cheating are wrong; she considers coveting as bad, as is thinking impure thoughts.

Both believe in right and wrong. Both think that Jesus was the most upright of persons. Both believe God judges. Average Joe has a sense that his moral intuition, shared by most, causes him to arrive at conclusions that parallel some (but not all) of the Bible's ethical mandates. Yet Chris believes that coveting is wrong, even though it has no immediate negative consequences. She believes in morals that are beyond the intuitive. God has revealed what is right and wrong.

But the essential difference is still yet more profound. Joe believes Jesus is an actual historical figure. If he thought about it, he would suspect the gospel accounts of Jesus are likely part true, part myth. Nonetheless, for Joe, Jesus remains an inspirational figure and an aspirational norm. For Chris, Jesus is that and more. He is still alive. Jesus somehow indwells her by his Spirit. She has a living relationship with him. Jesus not only inspires her, Jesus also transforms her from the inside out.

My point is this. Both live in Christendom, and both hold a CWV. But only one is a Christian.

Average Joe behaves as a citizen who has ascribed to the CWV, as does Chris. In addition, she also has a personal relationship with Jesus. That produces an additional range of behaviors and beliefs, like regular prayer, church attendance, and Bible reading. But none of those other behaviors and practices are essential to being a citizen who has ascribed to the CWV.

Our two archetypes, Average Joe and Christian Chris, inhabit their Christian worldview culture in different ways. And yet, they are both proud citizens of the same society. This is an important distinction. As is the next one. In the following chapter, we need to add another layer of complexity. Joe and Chris have different views of what the church is, and what it ought to be doing and not doing.

A concluding observation and segue. Most Australians have not rejected every aspect of the CWV. They still believe all human life is sacred; that murder, stealing, and lying are wrong. They are both pleased when the church expresses compassion by running social welfare programs for the poor, or English classes for migrants. They have some respect for Jesus, who, in their mind, championed love and compassion.

But most Westerners view Christians a bit like, say, lawyers. If we happen to know a lawyer, our experience is that most of them are actually nice people on their own. If you meet them over coffee or as fellow parents of your kids' sporting team and your interaction is not around the law, they are pleasant. But get lawyers together, disputing law, and it's a different thing. They become like a pack of greedy, selfish hyenas, who fight and scavenge over the misfortune of others.

There are an awful lot of Average Joes out there who know and like individual Christians. But when Christians get together and become the church, when they start talking about religion or ethics, Average Joe has a new-found and recent distaste for the church.

Why is that? We shall come to that. For now, I have attempted to make clear (or explicit) what is normally left unspoken (or tacit) about the following.

Simplicity on the Other Side of Complexity

Western culture held a shared consensus from about 400 AD to 2000 AD. This CWV was held by practicing Christians and average citizens alike. It was widely assumed that:

1. An all-knowing, powerful, good, personable God made the world, on (and hence with a) purpose;

2. His world has a knowable moral fabric;

3. Jesus, who is somehow divine, teaches and lives the good life;

4. The Bible contains teachings from Jesus and other wise people;

5. There is an afterlife. God decides who gets there, based on our moral choices in this life;

6. Average Joe's lifestyle fitted within the acceptable range of CWV behaviors;

7. Whatever has happened in our culture is more than just a widespread loss of personal faith. It is about all the Average Joes abandoning their shared belief in the CWV.

2

The Role of the Church in Society

In this chapter we will reflect on the role of the church. When Christendom was an accepted and stable worldview, what did Average Joe think the church was and ought to be doing? And how was that similar to and different from what Christian Chris thought?

If, as I contend, the West is losing its CWV, then it follows that the type of church that fitted into that previous world is also at risk of losing its place. So does the way the church positions and expresses itself need to change? To answer this question, we need to understand what was. How did the church fit into culture until recently and what has changed? Only once we have distilled answers to these questions can we do the necessary emotional work of letting go of what has been, to embrace what is.

Asking a sociologist how the institution "church" fits into the society "Christendom" is like asking an economist how the "Reserve Bank" fits into a "growing free-market economy." You will quickly encounter different theories about how the various pieces of the puzzle fit together. The Reserve Bank controls some things, like the official interest rate but is also influenced by many things outside its control, like China's rate of economic growth. There are many pieces to the puzzle, and the relationship between the components is dynamic; it's complicated. Different economists have different answers.

I shall offer you a brief introduction in response to a particular question. What role did the church play in a Western democratic society like Australia? Note the word "did." The title of the previous chapter was "What is the 'CWV' we are losing?" In this chapter, we ask: "How did the church fit into the old consensus of the 'CWV' that we are losing?"

Before we go there, we need to do some unlearning and clarification. If we ask Chris, our practicing Christian, what is the role of the church, she will be quick to answer. She may say that what is unique about the Christian faith is the idea of grace, that God loves us, and in Jesus, he freely forgives us. We, the church, are called to be salt and light in the world. We love others, as God has loved us. Furthermore, we invite others to repent and to accept Jesus as their personal Lord and Savior.

That is all good and true. But it answers a different question. It answers a question like: "what role does the local church—the body of Christ—play in any setting that it happens to find itself?" I am asking a different question, one framed in response to a specific context. We find ourselves at the end of the shared CWV and entering a post-Christian era. This is our social historical context, a fast-moving transition between one specific view of the world and the next.

In addition to appreciating the effect of a changing context, we also need to differentiate between what a sociologist might call the institutional church, and what we feel we are a part of—the local body of Christ. From now on, when I mean the church as a broad, nationwide social institution, including all its its neighborhood expressions, I will demarcate it as "the church." When I mean only one gathering of believing disciples who come together in a local church building, I will call it "the local church," or maybe St. James or New Hope.

Now that we have clarified our vocabulary, our specific question, for now, is: "What role did the church play in a Western democratic society like Australia?" It is an important question. My thesis is, given that Western democracies like Australia have changed, the role and function of the church needs to shift. But how do we reposition the church without losing what we understand to be the calling and essence of the local church, churches like New Hope and St. James? That is where we need to land. But not where we start.

What Does a Sociologist Think the Church's Role in Society Is?

The most common answer is to focus on the church's function. A society is a social system of interconnected parts that all form a stable, balanced whole. Each part must play its role. Banks, schools, hospitals, government departments, and the family—all are social institutions and they all have a role or a function. And so we can ask: "What is the church's function? And how does it connect to the other parts?"

Let's use law and order as a case in point, something all societies require. One role of religion then, is to clearly and explicitly articulate morality.

There must be a clear, shared moral code: laws you can either obey, or break. Confusion or vagueness will cause conflict and disharmony.

Furthermore, morality needs to be grounded in something objective, deeper than just intuition, that can be accessed to bring greater clarity. In a shared CWV culture, biblical principles underwrite the law. The church is the expert in interpreting God's Word and applying it to life. The church's function within society is to provide the framework and interpretation of morality that underwrites our laws.

To be specific, it is wrong to lie about your income to the tax department. The government passes laws about what is lying in your taxes and what is not. The police enforce those laws. The Bible underwrites the shared belief that lying is wrong. The church declares this to be a universal truth, with consequences for every level of society.

Another example would be how the church is instrumental in marking social rites of passage. We have a religious ceremony for each significant life-stage change. We move from conception to joining a family through baptism, from childhood to adulthood through confirmation, from leaving our family of origin through to forming another through marriage, and from this life to the next through a funeral. It is the role of the church to perform public rituals that celebrate each change-of-life stage and to validate the transition of status as legitimate.

We could list many other specific functions of the church, and the local church, such as caring for the poor, building community, and so on. Emile Durkheim, one of the three fathers of sociology, was a functionalist. He had a very high view of the role of religion. For him, the point was not to list every single function that religion serves. Instead, in the big picture, religion tells the shared story that is the glue holding a society together. Religion creates an integrated, meaningful web of ideas. People feel connected, as if they belong to something bigger than themselves. They know where they fit, their contribution, and thus why their life has meaning. This is religion's most significant function.

Religious rituals were also crucial for Durkheim. They also have a specific function. They bring people together, remind communities of core beliefs, and they do so in a way that facilitates a shared identity. So Christmas is a reminder that God gave us his son, and we find joy in giving to others. The annual preparation and celebration of Christmas binds families and communities together, prompting us to share and be generous.

Max Weber was the second father of sociology. He, too, had much to say about the role of religion in society. Weber asked why did capitalism occur in Western Europe first? He was not the first to ask this question.

Historians had noted that most of the conditions required for capitalism had existed elsewhere before they did in England.

Weber's seminal thesis was that the Protestant work ethic is unique to Western Europe, which is the crucial factor. Protestantism has within its beliefs the notion that one works hard, as for God. But it would be self-indulgent and greedy to spend all of one's profits on oneself. After all, the goal of life is to store up treasures in heaven, not possessions on earth. Saved surplus funds become capital, available for reinvestment. Investment facilitates innovation and new technology. This, Weber believed, was the exceptional condition that propelled capitalism to evolve in the West.

Weber's most significant contribution to sociology and the understanding of religion was this: ideas change things. Before him, people believed that only social structures (or social institutions) change things. But Weber added the insight that religious beliefs and ideals are a powerful social force that shapes how societies think and behave.

Yet another group of social theorists combine Weber's concern for ideas with Durkheim's focus on rituals. They are known as symbolic interactionists. Their interest is not so much in the ritual per se, but in the deeper meaning attached to them.

For Christians, the cross is our most profound symbol. Two pieces of intersecting timber can stand for love, justice, peace, forgiveness, and sacrifice. Other religions have symbols too: temples, idols, and the like, as do secular cultures. Grand Final days are modern-day religious festivals with associated symbols. For Australians, in cricket, The Ashes symbolize our capacity to overcome our convict past and get one back over the oppressing colonial Poms.

Other symbols are less obvious. Words can have a symbolic aura. Think about the word "gospel" and what it means for an evangelical Christian. Or the word "justice" and what it means for so-called "liberals," or the words "Spirit-filled" and what they mean for a Pentecostal. Beyond religious circles, think of what the word "discrimination" means in Western culture.

Symbols become vessels that carry incredible amounts of implied meaning. The connection between a symbol and its meaning is often deep and partially sub-conscious. It's the type of stuff we have wars over. Try removing the organ from your local church and replacing it with a drum kit. Stop using the common cup at Communion. Try closing down the Scouts program or the local footy club. Suggest we use the word "mission" instead of "evangelism." When you do, you are playing with symbols. You will likely get an immediate, passionate, knee-jerk response. Think of the recent same-sex marriage debate in Australia. It was a public tug-of-war between two views on what the symbol of marriage means. Does it mean love between any two individuals, or is it the foundation on which a mother and father form a family?

For symbolic interactionalists, religion is a web of ideas and symbols that underwrites shared beliefs and practices, such that we attribute meaning to our lives.

Next, there is a group of sociologists called "conflict theorists." Regarding religion, the most famous of these is Karl Marx, the third of the three fathers of sociology. His famous dictum was that "Religion is the opium of the people."[1] Religion is used to reinforce the unjust status quo by promising rewards in the next life rather than in this one. In this sense, religion is used to stop the revolution.

Sadly, religion and conflict have a long and sordid history. The Crusades are a case in point. For a sociologist, whether the conflict is really about religion or something else is tangential. Religions are often used by the powerful to create a compelling and united banner under which to gather an army. For a pure Marxist, conflict is never over religion or religious ideas; it's about competition for limited resources. Religion does not cause conflict, but it is a powerful tool to prevent or perhaps hasten it.

We have briefly surveyed various historical sociological approaches, or perspectives.[2] We need not lose ourselves in the distinctions. For our purposes, it will suffice to conclude that, in the view of sociologists, whichever theory they may ascribe to, all societies require religion. In our case, that means the West needs the church. Religion performs important functions. It is the glue that binds us, its ideas shape us, and its rituals unite us. And they are often flashpoints in times of social dislocation and change.

Debunking a Simplistic Story

What exactly, then, was the role the church played in a Western democratic society like Australia?

As I attended state schools in Australia and New Zealand in the 1980s, the simple view of religion was to explain the things science could not, by reference to God. God was a god of the gaps and religion was a collection of mythological stories and superstitious activities. Religion held sway in the Dark Ages. Since then, through science and reason, we have been

---

1. Marx, *Contribution to the Critique*, para. 4.

2. Sociology is further divided into various branches that focus on particular topics such as political sociology, criminology, or the sociology of religion. Of greater value to us are the lenses that structural functionalism, conflict theory, and symbolic interactionism afford us.

"enlightened." Our need for religion has been superseded. And thank goodness for that, because religion held us back.

That narrative is less influential, less shared than it used to be, for two main reasons. Historians note that the Dark Ages were never dark. There was always a steady march of progress and learning. Historians now talk of the Middle Ages. The phrase "Dark Ages" was coined by eighteenth-century Enlightenment philosophers and historians, as a contrast to their self-belief that they were the enlightened ones. Also, despite the growth in scientific knowledge, globally speaking, belief in God is growing. Even in Western cultures, we remain open to the spiritual dimensions of life, despite recent falling attendance rates at religious ceremonies.

In contrast to the views present during my schooling years, there is an emerging recognition that the CWV offered a positive, progressive, shared story, not an anti-science one. Much energy from various sources is being focused on this question at present. As the West sheds itself of the CWV, several authors have been alarmed into action. Their reflections are like that of the Joni Mitchell song, later covered by Counting Crows, "Big Yellow Taxi": "you don't know what you've got till it's gone." It is as if these social commentators are observing the dying stages of shared CWV and the church attached to it. They feel compelled to write the eulogy and as they rehearse its achievements, they can't but help note the West is recklessly abandoning its heritage, and they implore us to rethink.

Already I have referred to Roy Williams, a respected Australian mainstream journalist. Greg Sheridan is another mainstream journalist who writes in this space. Sheridan, in particular, has no history of writing or publicly reflecting upon the church but both have felt a recent need to lean into this space.

More broadly, Rodney Stark, a leading sociologist and historian, has traced the rise of Christianity in the West from the time of Jesus until now. His book, *The Triumph of Christianity*, demonstrates how and where Christianity cradles the development of all Western civilizations. Tom Holland's book, *Dominion*, is similar.

The Book That Made Your World by Indian philosopher Vishal Mangalwadi offers a multi-cultural approach. Writing against the tide of anti-colonialism, Mangalwadi demonstrates how much that is admirable about India and the West comes from the Bible.

While each book is distinctive, there is a common theme and conclusion. In ways that build upon Weber, each argues that the Christian worldview contains a nucleus of ideas that has given rise to the best of Western culture. It is the CWV that births some combination of the following: universal human rights, especially for women and children; justice; selfless heroism; optimism;

compassion; education for the masses; capitalism; public healthcare; the scientific method; secular politics; morality, and more.

That is an impressive and compelling list, seriously impressive. For those of you who are skeptical, who see that list as wishful thinking by the biased, I shall expound upon just one as a case in point. Why did the scientific method eventuate in the West? Greek philosophers had long speculated about scientific questions. At what speed do objects fall, for instance. Aristotle thought heavier objects would fall faster. But thinking about scientific questions is altogether different from answering them with a scientific method. No ancient Greeks ever thought to walk up Mount Olympus and test the speed at which two objects fall with an experiment.

The Romans discovered all sorts of amazing things, like concrete, and the Chinese discovered gunpowder. Neither did so using the scientific method. There was no systematic process of hypothesis-experiment-analysis-modified thesis and new test. Concrete and gunpowder were discovered by something closer to trial and error, or even by coincidence.

So what preconditions do you need to evolve the scientific method? Several. You need a belief in an ordered universe. Christianity posits a god of order, who purposely creates a world with an order. The Greek gods are erratic, not ordered. Likewise, you need a god of reason, who creates reasonable creatures. Hindu gods are easily annoyed; they are quite unreasonable. Allah expects submission, more so than contemplation or investigation.

Science requires a belief in stewardship, the idea that humanity is charged to care for and utilize the planet's resources. You also need a belief in the sacredness of all humankind. If there is an underclass of untouchables, you don't need to invent a sewerage system and a toilet. The untouchables can remove human waste. In contrast, a belief in the sacredness of all humans drives one to progress and improves all humanity's lives.

In sum, the development of science requires a belief in a god of order who creates an ordered universe, rational humans capable of understanding that order, and a reason to explore that order—in Christianity's case, to improve the dignity of all humanity. All are present in Christendom, so the West was uniquely positioned to give birth to the scientific method.

To step back and look with a broader lens, what each of the authors we have discussed so far is arguing is that there exists within the Christian tradition a nucleus of ideas that have made Western civilization what it is. The West has a shared commitment to values such as human rights, progress, and compassion, all of which are products of a CWV. This unique combination of beliefs exists nowhere else. Other religions, other worldviews have not given rise to a culture like ours.

But before we go there: a distinction. In the last chapter, we noted the shared beliefs of a CWV. Beliefs are ideas or convictions we assume to be true. Beliefs involve faith since they are non-empirical; we cannot test them in a science lab. Beliefs are held as true or false. Either there is a god, or there is not. Beliefs are one thing; values are another. The CWV holds both beliefs and values.

The CWV Values

What are values and which ones are specifically CWV "values?" Values are not beliefs about what is right or wrong; rather, they are statements about what is important. And values can compete. So a culture can value both individual freedom and public safety. We value free speech and respect for diversity. As a culture, we arrive at a shared consensus about which value trumps which and when.

In an honor-shame culture, people value making statements that bring honor to family and leaders above making factual or correct statements. To make an inaccurate statement, but one that protects the honor of a leader, is the right and proper thing to do in Asia. To us Westerners, that is called lying. Western cultures place truth (or at least truth defined as making statements that align with the facts) as a value above personal loyalties.

If the West's accomplishments are built upon our unique beliefs and values, what are the most influential Western values? And are they demonstrably Christian in their heritage?

Let's begin with Article 1 of the United Nations Universal Declaration of Human Rights. This document holds an authoritative status when discussing Western values (despite the irony that it is called Universal):

> All human beings are born free and equal in dignity and rights. They are endowed with reason and conscience and should act towards one another in a spirit of brotherhood.

The inherent value and equality of all human life is arguably the foundational Western value. Is it not universal, shared by all cultures? No, sadly, human rights are not universal, but slavery is. Sexism is also historically commonplace as is discrimination by age, caste, tribe, or religion.

So where does this Western emphasis on human equality and dignity originate? From Christianity. In the very first chapter of the Bible we read that "So God created mankind in his own image, in the image of God he created them; male and female he created them" (G 1:27). Every male and female equally carries a divine spark, and is equally an image bearer.

Some might object. Christians have in the past been sexist and racist and whatever else. I must confess they have but this was never the ideal and it was not how Jesus (who is the ideal type of person in the CWV) lived. The very notion in Christian belief that Jesus is God become human is yet another reason why Christians value human life. God becoming human in some way sanctifies the human condition.[3]

So yes, despite the failings, there is sound evidence that the Western value of the dignity and equality of all human life is traceable to the CWV. Let us explore this idea further. Connected to the idea of the dignity of all human life is the value of freedom. If all are equally dignified, it is wrong for one person to hold another in bondage or slavery.

And yet, slavery is common, even universal. It is endemic in most worldviews. Some Muslims believe certain men receive female sex slaves in heaven. If heaven is the state of perfection, then slavery exists in a perfect world. In both Hinduism and Buddhism, religions that entail the cycle of reincarnation, people of lower castes are lesser because of choices they made in previous lives. Religion is thus used to condone discrimination.

If you are thinking, as did Karl Marx, that religion is the opium of the masses, used by the powerful to oppress, consider this: communist and atheist states have the worst track record. Three states have outlawed religion in history: China under Chairman Mao; Russia under Joseph Stalin; and Cambodia under the Khmer Rouge. Those states have atrocious human rights records. They applied the ultimate form of discrimination and anti-freedom practice: death. Estimates are that, as recently as the 1970s, Cambodia killed about two million people, or one-quarter of its entire population. Regarding Russia and China, estimates are that, directly and indirectly, communist discriminatory policy has led to the death of perhaps one hundred million people combined.[4]

Let us consider the other side of the ledger: not the prevalence of slavery, rather its containment. Only twice in human history has a culture succeeded in systemically ending slavery. Both times it was Christianity, as I shall document in chapter 11.

The belief and pursuit of universal freedom for all humanity is not self-evident. On the contrary, no other religion or worldview has ever stopped slavery. Most endorse some form of it. It is a value that flows from the CWV. God freed Israel from slavery in Egypt. Jesus freed people from slavery to

3. John Dickson's book, *Bullies and Saints*, outlines the ideals as expressed by Jesus that are sometimes lived out by Christians, and at other times Christians go off-script and get it all wrong.

4. Satter, "100 Years of Communism—and 100 Million Dead."

sin and death. It was the cause Jesus was prepared to die for. Christianity is fundamentally anti-slavery.[5]

The Christian version of freedom is more than freedom from oppression. Humanity is endowed with freedom to choose to do the right, God-honoring thing, or otherwise. In the Garden of Eden narrative, Adam and Eve have free will and are given a moral choice. The exercising of their freedom is real, as are the consequences of their choices. In Christianity, emphasis is placed on the free human being as a morally autonomous and responsible actor.

As free actors, humans sometimes make right, as opposed to wrong, decisions. At other times, our choices are better understood as either wise or unwise. As beings made in the image of an all-knowing God, humanity is created rational. The biblical narrative traces characters who make wise and unwise choices. We see consequences unfold. God's sovereignty is not undermined, but humans are invited to love God with their hearts and minds. An entire section of the Old Testament, about 15 percent, is called wisdom literature. It contains advice on how to live wisely, or well, in God's ordered world.

Behind the notions of the dignity of all humanity, freedom, and rationality, sits another distinctly Christian value: individualism. If humans are morally autonomous—if they have a capacity for reason and the ability to make a wise personal choice—then it follows that persons are to be conceived of as individuals.

But not individuals in isolation. Adam is incomplete without Eve. Adam reflects a Godhead where the Father is both one person, but whose being is made complete in relationship with the Son and the Spirit. Christianity affirms a type of individualism, one where individuals exist in relationships with others. "Individuals who are interdependent" is how best to understand the Christian view of personhood.

Combined, the values of the human dignity of each individual, freedom, and reason make up a tight core—a central nucleus of Christian values. Around this sits a second ring of essential values, ones that build upon the inner core.

---

5. At this point others will highlight the Old Testament God-sanctioned practice of Israel committing genocide and ethnic cleansing. My response is to suggest these actions are best understood as God's judgement of slavery, not his sanctioning of it. The tribes Israel displaced were nations that practiced female sexual enslavement. Men would copulate with female temple slaves. Any resulting offspring would be sacrificed. God's command to rid the land of such groups represents his judgement of slavery and child sacrifice, and his warning to Israel that he would judge them similarly should they adopt such abhorrent practices. And in time, being even-handed, God did judge Israel with banishment from the land.

Democracy is an excellent case in point. The ancient Greeks believed in a type of democracy. Their belief in reason, freedom, and human dignity led them to create democratic cities. In these city states, only educated, free, Greek males could vote. Slaves, women, and foreigners could not. Greeks and males, it was believed, had a greater capacity for reason than non-Greeks, women, or slaves. They believed in the equality of some, but not all. The Greeks did not develop what we might call modern secular democracies. Some core values required as a building block of modern secular democracies were missing. You need the entire combination of Christian values to get a modern democracy.

Let's entertain an objection for a moment. Some might push back and say that the CWV does not lead to secular democracy. It leads to an unhealthy church–state relationship, like what we saw in medieval Europe. If this objection seems intuitively right to you, I would suggest you are with me, not against me.

We do find in history, at times, an unhealthy relationship between the church and state, a kind of pseudo-theocracy, but this was at times when the church had become too powerful. At those times, powerful men often used the church as a seat of control, income generation, and self-aggrandizement. Rival powerful Italian families, such as the Medici family, viewed the office of pope as the mafia might view the status of godfather. At such times the conflict theories of sociology (following Marx) offer useful insights into how religion was being used, or perhaps abused.

In contrast, the more profound logic of the CWV is that all humanity is inherently dignified. All citizens, regardless of their gender, race, or even religion, have worth and ought to be granted freedoms—rights and responsibilities—in the society in which they happen to live. Thus a woman's right to vote was pioneered in Christian countries, at times with the backing of the church.

Jesus, speaking to Jews living in a Jerusalem that was subjugated by Romans, was asked about paying taxes to foreign powers. He responded, "So give back to Caesar what is Caesar's, and to God what is God's" (Matt 21:22). Way before his time, Jesus was endorsing living as a responsible God-fearing citizen in a pluralistic society. Christians have a responsibility to give to God via the local church, but they also have a responsibility to contribute to the wider state. In so doing, Jesus implicitly endorsed an inclusive state, where all citizens participate towards the common good. This value is foundational and necessary for the evolution of what we now consider the modern secular democracy. Objection addressed. Let's return to the secondary ring of CWV values.

Along with democracy, progress is also a Christian value. As we have seen, the scientific method flows from the notion that every life is valuable and that, where possible, it is a good thing to improve the quality of human life. Given that God has created us as rational, and his world is ordered, we can explore and experiment within that created order. The often-maligned Puritans pioneered much of modern science. They imagined science as thinking God's thoughts after him.

Progress is part of humanity expressing its dominion over creation. Medicine and later technology, for instance, can be used to extend compassion and overcome suffering. Advances in agriculture help feed the poor. Progress thus allows the church to express another of its core values, mercy, more widely and effectively. Since their inception, local churches and monasteries have doubled as hospitals, centers for farming excellence, and relief centers.

When applied to the workplace, this value of progress, this willingness to use technology to improve life, means the Christian worldview is the one that gives birth to capitalism. Monasteries already had a sophisticated banking system in the ninth century. The Middle Ages, according to Stark, had already grappled with a biblical response to excess capital, long before Max Weber's dating of the industrial revolution in post-Reformation Protestant Europe. The practical outworking of the CWV gives rise to an economic system—capitalism, that lifts the wellbeing of all of its citizens out of poverty more so than any other financial system.[6]

Our legal system, which maintains the rule of law, likewise brings justice to more of its citizens than any other legal system. It too is founded on Christian principles. The CWV views people as a mixture of good and evil. Our leaders may be capable of great things, but we also need checks and balances to restrain the darker inclinations present in all humanity.

Western politicians have the power to make laws but are separate from the police, who have the power to enforce the laws. Police are in turn separate from the judicial powers, who can interpret and apply the law. The system is designed to stop any one group from becoming too powerful, because as (practicing Catholic) Lord Acton wrote: "Power tends to corrupt, and absolute power corrupts absolutely. Great men are almost always bad men . . ."[7]

This separation of powers, designed to minimize the risk of the powerful becoming corrupt, is Christian. The king, the high priest, and the prophet are three distinct persons in the Old Testament. The prophet

6. Stark, *Triumph of Christianity*, 244–46.
7. Acton, *Letter to Bishop Mandell Creighton*, April 5, 1887.

Nathan can challenge King David when he commits murder and adultery. Leaders like President Assad, or Chairman Xi Jinping do not have the checks and balances around them that flow from the Christian perspective of human nature.

Furthermore, in Christian thought, we all bear and can reflect God's image, his goodness. But we are also tainted and tempted by sin. We are all prone to putting self before God and others. So we need a political and legal system that allows people the freedom to prosper and express goodwill to others. We cannot allow power to become too centralized, because the love of power and money leads to evil. Like God, societies must proactively restrain evil and temptation. This requires a rational system of objective law.

Somewhere else in this nucleus of values is education. If God is a rational being and we are made in his image, humans are rational creatures, capable of thought and learning. Education is the discipline of acquiring the body of shared learnings to date. Progress is built on the shoulders of it. Ancient Jewish worship involved the public reading of sacred texts. Christians, who emerged from within Jewish communities, continued this practice. The Christian scriptures are to be read and meditated upon by all. This creates an imperative to teach the masses to read. For much of its recent history, the church, including its missionaries, has been the pioneer of education for all.

To summarize, the CWV gives rise to both a coherent set of beliefs and values such as the dignity of all humanity, freedom of the individual, and rationality. These, in turn, give rise to other values like democracy, progress, mercy, capitalism, the rule of law, and education for all. The church has long championed and embodied these values. These values are expressed across all of shared CWV cultures, not only in the church. The combination of these values has given rise to the many accomplishments of Western civilizations.

So the Role of the Church Is . . .

Now, finally, we are in a position to answer our question: "What was the role of the church in a Western democratic society like Australia?" The church provided the shared story that encompassed shared beliefs and values and gave rise to our society. In short, the story is something like this.

> A loving and just God made you, me, and everything in the
> world. The world has both a moral fabric and a sense of purpose.
> The human task is to live within God's world in ways that align
> with the God-given moral fabric, to live in ways that reflect the

life of Jesus, who fulfilled this task better than anyone else. That means being kind, honest, thoughtful of others, law-abiding, hardworking, and faithful to one's spouse, family, friends, and country. If you live a decent life, things should go well for you in this life. That means owning a house, putting food on the table, enjoying family and friends, avoiding excessive trouble and suffering, and living a comfortable life. As for the afterlife: well, God will somehow notice and honor your efforts in that life too.

But I stress that not all citizens, scientists, teachers, or plumbers who ascribed to these values were believing Christians. There were, of course, institutions other than the church that did public good and contributed to the public conversation. Nonetheless, it is specifically and uniquely the CWV that gives rise to a set of beliefs and values that gave birth to and cradled and nurtured Western culture. It was the church that told the stories where those values were embedded: stories about how the world was good and ordered and it was our task to care for it; stories about how when we fail to listen to God and instead walk outside his guidelines, things fall apart; stories about how slavery and brokenness is a consequence of living for and trusting self; stories about how, when individuals or families repent and trust God, he blesses them with land, crops, peace, and children. The main character of this story is Jesus, who trusts and obeys God as his father, is compassionate toward the poor and outcast, and gives his life sacrificially for the good of others. Jesus is a rabbi and a healer, and so it follows that the church will build schools and hospitals. Biblical narrative underwrites western beliefs and values, and it is the church's role to rehearse, retell, and remind us of our story.

The story not only informs us of what we value, but also of what we loathe. The church also provided a temporal and eternal framework that sought to deter evil and encourage good. Religion is in part about prodding people to be the best they can be. Put in Christian-speak, faith encourages people to repent and turn from evil and selfishness, to do unto others as we would have them do to us, to reflect God's image, and to be transformed into the likeness of Christ by the power of his Spirit.

Somehow, deep in his psyche, Average Joe, who lives in the era of a shared CWV, appreciates the critical role the church played in the evolution of Western culture. He may not attend church or believe Jesus rose from the dead, but he takes some comfort that the church tells and re-enacts the stories that underwrite his culture. The church reminds us of our core values and prompts us lest we fail to practice them as often as we should. It is within this shared cohesive story that Average Joe finds his sense of connection and belonging. It is the story he is a part of.

Christian Chris also sees herself as part of the Christian story. By this, she means belonging to her local church, which is connected to a denomination, which is somehow part of a wider religious movement. This movement has a long and (mostly) impressive history. When Chris holidays in Europe, she visits cathedral after cathedral. She wishes she lived in a time when they were full. Her living experience of her local church is that it is not as full as it used to be, not as respected as it used to be. She imagines a past when everyone went to a church and respected and trusted the church.

Strangely, the reality is that those cathedrals were rarely full. Take the Middle Ages for instance. Church attendance was seldom. Services were in a dead language no longer spoken or understood by the general public. Biblical knowledge was poor. Godlessness was common. Christian Chris feels a profound sense of loss. She mourns the passing of a church that perhaps never was.

Part of Christian Chris' anxiety is misplaced. It was the church that was most prominent in Western history: the church as an institution, Christianity as a view of the world. The local church—St. James or New Hope—may never have been that impressive. But that is not what she feels, what she believes, what she mourns. She has conflated, or fused together, her understanding of the local church and the church. She assumes that when everyone held a CWV, everyone went to their local church, but they did not. She hopes that if we could reclaim, or at least maintain our CWV, people might return to their local church. This assumption is flawed. I will argue (later, in chapter 12) that Christians like Chris ought to focus their efforts elsewhere other than in trying to maintain the influence of the CWV.

For now, we note your Average Joe Western citizen has changed his assumptions. His intuition now tells him something different. He used to subscribe to a CWV where a divine God had made a good world with a discernible moral fabric. He believed Jesus lived the superlative version of the good life and his teachings carry clues for how we might do the same. He believed the church had a function, a role to play as the storehouse and communicator of the values that make for a good life. He believed in justice beyond this earthly life. He believed in an afterlife where a just, manifestly Christian-type God would reward the upright and noble.

However, in a remarkably short period, this shared consensus has been swapped out for a new consensus. What has the CWV been replaced with? (Chapter 3) And what is the status of Christians and the CWV in this new consensus? (Chapter 4)

Simplicity on the Other Side of Complexity

1. Sociologists think about religion from within different "schools." All agree that societies require religion. Some focus on religion's function as the social glue that holds a society together; others how religious ideas shape the culture; others how it carries and reinforces our systems of meaning and significance through symbols; and still others how it is a factor in conflict, change, and social evolution; and some how it is a factor in all of the above.

2. In addition to beliefs, cultures have shared stable values. Beliefs are assumptions we hold to be true. Values are things we hold to be important, and they flow from our beliefs. Values often compete with each other. Like beliefs, they are simultaneously shared and mostly unspoken.

3. Christian worldview values include humility, the dignity of all humanity, freedom of the individual, and rationality. These, in turn, give rise to other values like democracy, progress, mercy, humility, capitalism, the rule of law, and education for all.

4. Average Joe, not a practicing Christian, subscribes to the CWV beliefs and values. This allows him to be a connected, productive, and stable member of his culture. Average Joe was happy for the church to function as the affirmer of the shared CWV beliefs and values. He was, that is, until very recently.

5. Christian Chris feels things differently. She assumes the previous higher levels of influence of the church were because of higher levels of participation in the local church. She conflates the widespread decline of personal belief with the loss of influence of the church, and the shift away from the widely held CWV.

6. This is a flawed assumption. Western culture has held a CWV with Christian beliefs and values, but the actual numbers of Christians who believe in Christ as their personal Lord and Savior have likely always been lower than what Chris suspects.

3

The New Consensus

IF AVERAGE JOE NO longer holds a CWV, what does he believe? What are his new assumptions? Intuitively, what will seem right to him, and what will seem wrong? And why? Are there underlying beliefs and values that act as a foundation to his new house of knowledge?

The simplistic answer would be to focus on the fact that most Average Joes have simultaneously moved on from Christian assumptions. God is no longer needed to explain things; science has displaced him. Such an answer fails to appreciate what belief in God has been replaced with. Put another way, cultures need a coherent and shared story, one that is widely believed. Without such a story, people lack a sense of belonging to something that is going somewhere. There is no reason to participate in anything, or outlaw anything.

So what are the new shared beliefs and values of Average Joe? These are critical questions and difficult to answer because they are tacit. That is, they are the opposite of explicit. Tacit means unspoken, never articulated out loud. These questions are not only tacit, but they are also emerging. In this chapter, I will give examples and even a few reasons for what Average Joe now believes. Further, I will try to draw out some underlying patterns or principles to this new way of thinking.

In short, if Average Joe has abandoned or moved on from his CWV, what is the shape of a post-CWV? Average Joes and Joannes haven't just changed their minds on a few topics. The transition is much more profound than just a switch from being anti- to pro- same-sex marriage and moving away from Sunday as a day of rest. We are living through the changeover of worldview. Hold on to your seats; this kind of stuff only happens every couple of centuries. It can be quite a roller-coaster ride.

In an attempt to get some handles on this new emerging worldview, let us work from the known to the unknown. In chapter 1, I outlined the key components of the CWV (or worldview). It is a belief:

1. in an all-knowing God who is the source of all life; he is personal and loving, and just;

2. that he has created a world with a moral fabric, with good and evil;

3. that Jesus' teachings and life are the highest expressions of the good life;

4. that the Bible contains divine wisdom. Following its guidelines will correlate (though not a one-to-one correlation) with a content life;

5. in a God who sees and knows us, and will judge with some combination of grace and justice. His judgement of our present life determines where we spend eternity.

Rather than trying to map out the PCWV from the get-go, let's play with the ideas by contrasting them with the preceding worldview: the CWV.

PCWV Beliefs

Does Average Joe still believe in God? Let's get a little hard data from the Australian Census. In 1966, 88 percent of Australians defined themselves as Christian. By 2021, that number had dropped to 44 percent. Over the same period, those who self-reported as having no religion increased markedly from 0.8 percent to 39 percent. Younger people are far more likely to tick the no religion box. Within the same timeframe, other religions grew from 0.7 percent to 8 percent. These statistics and trends mirror those in New Zealand, Canada, and the United Kingdom.

Fascinatingly, the trends in the USA are quite different. America has much higher rates of regular church attendance than other Western Protestant countries, roughly four to five times higher. The decline in local church attendance is slower in the USA. Conversely, rates of religious affiliation among those who don't regularly attend remain high. This is not a book written from within the American religious cultural landscape. From a distance, one can observe that while segments of contemporary America remain highly traditional and conservatively Christian, one can still discern a substantial move away from a shared CWV. For example, it is now illegal to hold organized prayer in most US state schools. The US Federal Court in 2015, has, in effect, legalized same-sex marriage in all states.

This shift away from shared CWV assumptions is unfolding even while church attendance remains higher in the USA. This is the flip side of my premise: the decline in the influence of the CWV is different from the decline in church attendance. In Britain, Canada, Australia, and New Zealand, both church attendance and church influence are in decline. In the US, church influence is declining faster than church attendance is.

To return to imagining Australia as the home for Average Joe, 60 percent of Australians self-report as believing in God. Or should I now say "god." Since 1966, the world has shrunk. "Globalism" has changed the landscape. Nations are much more multi-cultural. International travel is common. Over four billion passengers took an international flight in 2017. Our TVs now have free-to-air multi-cultural dedicated channels, not to mention the pay TV and social media choices.

All of this means that when you mention "god," the obvious question is now which god, or whose god. To claim one God as above others is seen as naïve. Culturally insensitive. Arrogant. We now know better.

In the CWV, God was knowable through his word, the Bible; through his Son, Jesus; and through the church, the present expression of the continuous "people of God." This is no longer the case. Now, the Bible and the Christian tradition is but one way to access "god." Muslims have another, as do Buddhists, and Hindus, and so on. Then there are the religions of the past, like Zoroastrianism, or Vedism. Our Western intuition tells us they were likely onto something too?

In the PCWV, god is knowable indirectly. God is now accessible through the multiple lenses and experiences of divergent religions. But god is only knowable second hand, mediated through the frameworks of others. In other words, religions make claims about what god is like, but those claims may tell you more about the religious persons than about the god they claim to be making statements about.

Of course, most religions claim to have direct knowledge of god, a hotline to god. But when a person or a religion claims to know the truth about god, that is now interpreted as like saying food from my country is the best-tasting food in the world. Sure, Thai food is great, but so are French, Japanese, and Middle Eastern (let's just group all those countries together and call them the same!). Taste is a matter of personal preference, mediated through culturally shaped experiences and frameworks. Exclusive claims about god, morality, and meaning are now seen as overstated culturally driven preferences.

This idea is often captured in the oft-repeated metaphor that all paths lead to the top of the mountain. In the CWV, the dominant metaphor (borrowed from ancient cities) was that heaven had a massive set of gates with a locked door. Inside the city walls, one found safety and refuge. The shared belief in the CWV was that Jesus was the one key that unlocked the door to eternal life. In the PCWV, do we now say that every key opens the door? No, that does not quite work. In any case, modern cities no longer have gates. So instead, we have changed metaphors. We have reverted to another ancient image, one of the mountain top as a spiritual place. Our new metaphor is that all paths lead to the top of the mountain.

What are the consequences of changing metaphors away from one key and towards many paths? Let us return to analyzing multiculturalism through the lens of food. I can sample numerous nations' cuisine and do my own fusion cooking that suits my palate. Instead of meat and three veg for dinner, I can combine my vegetables, fry them in a wok, and cover them in oyster sauce.

I want to suggest that we treat big topics like knowing god, ethics, and finding meaning in life much the same way. We have retained some parts of the old CWV, like a piece of stand-alone steak. But we have changed other parts of our diet under the influence of globalism. To be explicit, my first point is this: the emerging post-CWV (henceforth PCWV) is not a wholesale abandonment of every feature of the prior, more Christian views. Instead, we have retained some of the assumptions and beliefs of the previously shared worldview and modified others.

The second consequence of changing metaphors is that God becomes knowable only in a vague, shadowy way. If all religions have some truth, and there are many religions, you could taste test them all if you like. Then you could imagine your own picture of God by drawing on various elements of all religions. A few people try this, but most don't.

It is here that the PCWV hits a dilemma. How do you find out about "Allah" or "Shiva?" Through the religious texts and beliefs of their followers. But those who claim to know god directly are single-minded and zealous and those who make exclusive claims about their one true god are now perceived to be flawed, prejudiced messengers. When those messengers make truth claims like "we know god, and you should believe us, and obey him—or else," such claims are dismissed as naïve and power plays.

In avoiding the dangers of becoming like a single or narrow-minded religious zealot, Average Joe has to admit that he is not an expert in any one approach to god. To return to my cooking metaphor, while Average Joe might like the taste of pad thai, falafel, and lamb kofta, and has an aversion to steak tartare, in practice, he does not cook an authentic version of any. Perhaps he buys some mass-produced version of this dish at the food mall or a pre-packaged version at the supermarket.

Similarly, it is now, in any real sense, impossible to know with any certainty much about god. Having a profound experience of any one god requires a sustained religious devotion that is beyond most. Instead, we taste test small, mass-produced, digestible bits of religion like the meditation or yoga of Buddhism, the idea of a spiritual pilgrimage (but not to Mecca) from Islam, and the golden rule from Jesus.

But to know god with any intensity is not possible (not to mention excessive and dangerous). That is what Average Joe's intuition tells him. That is the new consensus. Therefore, Joe believes that objective knowledge of god is not feasible. You can only know god in a second-hand vague way. If there is a god, one can be forgiven for being confused about what he is like, or how to get to know him intimately.

Not only is knowledge of god at best vague. God's will cannot be known with any certainty. There are too many competing interpretations (from those flawed interpreters) about what is right and wrong. We cannot discern the moral fabric of the universe by looking back to the religious traditions. They disagree!

Sure, Jesus was a good guy, but so was Buddha, and Gandhi (a Hindu), and most people suspect there are some upstanding Muslim leaders out there too, though they never bother to go and investigate. But the same problems remain. How do you know precisely what Jesus or Buddha said? How do you get past the noise of extremists and find out if there is some good in Islam? And how do you combine the insights of all the great sages to understand the essence of life? The experts who try don't agree on that either.

So if we can't work out what to learn from the great ones, and if we can't discern the moral fabric of the universe, then we can't be held to account. That is only logical, so Average Joe concludes.

Each of the five central tenets of the CWV has been deconstructed. At the risk of being too definite, of overstating the uniformity and the clarity around the new shared consensus (because the shared consensus is most powerful when it remains tacit), here is my attempt at the old versus the new:

1. An all-knowing, personable loving God has become a vague divine force;

2. A created moral fabric world with good and evil has become a place where old-fashioned morality is seen as a power play, and we are beyond being made to feel guilty;

3. The concept that Jesus' teachings and life are the highest expressions has become Jesus was but one expression, and we can't necessarily trust what religious zealots tell us about their opinions of what their leaders stood for;

4. That the Bible contains divine wisdom leading to a content life has become many books contain wisdom, but the Bible also contains bigotry, and misogyny, and false binaries, and we need to be selective in how and when we refer to it;

5. A God who sees and will judge where we spend eternity has become "it isn't clear; nobody can know for sure, so I can't be held to account."

Have you got that? Now we need to take another step. What I have just outlined is not the new consensus of the new worldview. It is the new consensus about how we deconstruct the old worldview; how we step away from the frameworks and obligations of the past. How we absent ourselves from previous responsibilities. Those former ways have been tried, tested, run their course, and culture has moved on. We need not feel guilt, or perhaps even loss. They may have made sense in the past, but it's a new day—or so Average Joe thinks.

Does the emerging worldview or shared consensus have anything definite to say about now? Does it offer any alternative constructs and frameworks? The standard answer that a historian/sociologist will give to this question is that it's too early to tell. Social change moves gradually. And it is best understood and evaluated with the clarity that comes from hindsight.

Allow me to reinforce this point by borrowing and extending a metaphor known as Neurath's boat. Imagine we are on a boat at sea. We are trying to understand this boat, but we can't get a wider perspective on it. There is no helicopter to board and no land from which to get a vantage point. If we stand on the bow, we can't see the stern. Wherever we stand, we can't see anything below the waterline. How can we understand the contours of our boat? Only when we board another boat can we look back at our old boat and see most (but still not all) of its parameters.

Interpreting culture is an exercise bound by the same constraints. As we look back at the boat called the CWV, most people deconstruct it as an arrogant, power-hungry, moralistic, misogynist, leaking old rust bucket. Others, like Stark, Sheridan, Williams, Holland and Mangalwadi, whom I referred to earlier, disagree. Their message is something like: that boat, that view of the world, got us where we are today. Our progress is attributable in large part to being on that particular boat. No other boat has afforded its passengers similar levels of comforts and progress.

Whichever view one holds, the dilemma is that we are now on another boat. As a culture, we are scrambling to make sense of this new boat, while we are on it. We can't see below its waterline. We can't see the bow and the stern at the same time. We have no other vantage point. (I will argue somewhat to the contrary in the next chapter, but, for now, go with me. This insight has explanatory value.) Our assessments are partial and incomplete.

Having acknowledged this constraint, I still feel what the French call *l'appel du vide*, the call of the void. For me, being made in God's image means that humanity is rational and called to express some sense of dominion. Like God, we desire to bring order out of chaos, to step into the void and try to make sense of it. So my view is yes, in an emerging sense (this boat is new and being modified while under sail) we must attempt to define the core features of the PCWV. Here is my current best effort to expose them.

Outlining the Contours of the PCWV: Its Beliefs

Let's begin with God. If you are a Christian who has been born and bred in a CWV, it can feel like the new playing field is not just post-Christian, but is anti-Christian. In some ways, it is. I will explain why in the next chapter. But just because our world is anti-Christian does not mean it is now secular and atheist.

People who live in Australia, Canada, New Zealand, the UK, and most of Western Europe are not predominantly atheists. There is no common shared assumption that there is no divine god or spiritual dimension to life; there is only physical matter and nothing more. While measuring rates of atheism is difficult due to the challenge of definitions, studies report atheism runs at between 7 percent and 20 percent in the West.

If the West is not predominantly atheist, does this mean there are more agnostics? Technically and historically, this term designates someone who believes that knowledge of god is inaccessible, leaving God essentially unknowable. Our senses allow us to access this physical or phenomenal world. But the noumenal "heavens" are on the other side of a gap that we cannot traverse.

I do not read most Average Joes as being agnostic in the above sense of the word. Instead, I describe Average Joe as post-Christian. Most Average Joes believe there is a spiritual dimension to this life. Most believe that Christianity and other religions have tapped into something real. Echoes of the divine can be accessed through the natural order, intuition, and a high level comparison of the best of religious traditions.

Furthermore, Western culture still believes in rights and wrongs. Just because Average Joe no longer agrees with all of the Bible's moral standards around sexuality, or the need for a day of rest and worship, does not mean he has abandoned morality. Discrimination, homophobia, judgementalism, and sexism are all wrong, absolutely wrong. There is still a discernible moral fabric to this universe. Here is the key point: these wrongs are considered absolutes because they have a divine "oughtness" behind them, in the minds of many. As the philosopher Immanuel Kant (1724–1804) argued, there is a shaft of light that originates from the transcendent. It breaks through the noumenal gap, such that our morality is more than just a shared opinion. The above-listed evils are absolutely wrong.

It is an odd combination to believe in a divine god who is knowable only in a vague second-hand way, and yet being absolutely certain that specific things are wrong because they oppose his divine order. Yet this view is common among the Average Joe and Joanne. My attempt to capture this dynamic is to use the term post-Christian. The prevailing worldview, I suggest, is not an entirely new worldview, built from the ground up without reference to god. It is not secular in that sense.

I am not alone in suggesting this. Deist (but not Christian) historian, Tom Holland, concludes that "The West . . . had become skilled in repackaging Christian concepts for non-Christian audiences."[1] Holland acknowledges that in terms of allegiance, the West is post-Christian but in terms of underlying conceptual frameworks, the West has a modified, repackaged, but still identifiably Christian fabric.

Another recycled feature of the PCWV is founded upon a belief in a (semi-knowable) god: human rights. The PCWV holds that all life is inherently precious, even sacred. Two documents capture this thinking, and express it with eloquence. One, as we have seen, is The United Nations Universal Declaration of Human Rights. Here we read, "All human beings are born free and equal in dignity and rights. They are endowed with reason and conscience and should act towards one another in a spirit of brotherhood."

The second is the United States Declaration of Independence, which reads "We hold these truths to be self-evident, that all men are created equal, that they are endowed by their Creator with certain unalienable Rights, that among these are Life, Liberty and the pursuit of Happiness." Note the religious underpinning, which gives this assertion an objective "oughtness."

As I argued in the previous chapter, the belief that all humans are born free and equal is not universal. Try telling a Palestinian who lives in Gaza he has equal rights. Try telling a Rohingya who lives in Buddhist

---

1. Holland, *Dominion*, 505.

Myanmar, or a female in Afghanistan, that they are equal. Try telling a Bangladeshi who works on a building site in the Middle East, or an untouchable from the Dalit caste in India. Human dignity, equality, freedom, and rights are not universal or self-evident. They never have been. Under the Roman Empire, 20–25 percent of the entire empire were slaves. The evidence is unequivocal. Discrimination and slavery are routine; self-evident human rights are not.

Where human rights have been most self-evident, most intuitively taken to be the case (though sadly there are significant and heart-breaking exceptions), is in Christian and post-Christian countries. If you search the Human Freedom Index of 2017, historically Christian countries make up twenty-two of the top twenty-five ranking countries, with the other three being colonized by Christian nations at some point in their history. Conversely, historically Christian countries are absent from the bottom of the list. I am tempted to say more on this topic, but it is not the concern of this book. For now, we note that the appreciation of all human life as equal, sacred, and dignified is a distinctive feature birthed in historically Christian countries. The PCWV has de-coupled this belief from its Christian foundations and adopted this belief as its own.

Yet another feature of the PCWV is a suspicion of the powerful, particularly those who function as corporations or institutions. I have noted above something of the deconstruction of religious knowledge. Deconstructionism as a lens through which to understand how social phenomena are widespread. High school English students are taught to deconstruct texts, authors, and their original cultures as a core skill. But nowhere is this lens more the default framing tool than when it comes to understanding power. Power is a dangerous means, used by the privileged to perpetuate control and influence, usually to ends that are in the self-interests of the already powerful.

Hold that thought. Let us jump back to the belief that the individual is dignified and has inherent rights. Also, jump back to the fear that religious leaders, previously the privileged, can't be trusted. Instead, we now believe intuition is the best way to know good from evil. Mix those together, and you get this: *You can't trust corporations and institutions; they abuse power for self-interest. Instead, let us empower individuals, who can listen to their inner intuition, exercise their freedom and rights, and their decisions will be what is best for them and for all.* The belief that the individual is a free agent, able to and best positioned to make decisions for themselves is a core PCWV conviction.

When this personal freedom is practiced in morality, we tend to call this moral relativism. You can decide what is right for you relative to your needs, desires, and past experiences. This, too, is a central feature of the PCWV. But we need to add to this the qualification that there are a few absolutes. For instance, discrimination and domestic violence are absolutely and always wrong. The PCWV individual might be free, but he cannot choose to be racist, abusive, or sexist.

How does our culture arrive at shared absolutes? If not from the Bible, how do we know something is universally wrong? There is an appreciation that we have arrived at a shared intuition that certain evils are absolutely wrong. We shall trace where this shared intuition is grounded in the next section. For now, we note the consensus that there are certain absolutes. We all know better, although a few are lagging, and it is not apparent to them just yet. Our culture now holds to moral relativism, with some unquestionable absolutes.

If moral relativism means the individual can choose what is right for them, this begs another question. By what measure do persons choose? Against which criterion? The new textbook (or should I say Facebook-acceptable) answer is that it is up to you. You do what is right for you. This vague answer will suffice in almost every social setting.

Closer observation indicates that a new shared yardstick is also emerging. There are now few positive moral absolute virtues, beyond giving others the right to self-autonomy. Previous altruistic virtues and pursuits are giving way to personal pleasure as the new default yardstick. Our culture is drifting towards the idea that if it feels good, it is good in as much as it brings about personal fulfillment, improved feelings of self-confidence, and self-esteem. If I feel good about me, my self-confidence will allow me to believe in myself, give it my best shot, and achieve my potential. When I am the best version of me I can be, the world is a better place. Therefore anything that makes me feel good is good and begets better.

If personal happiness is how we measure what is good, we can also use this yardstick to measure what is not good. Preventing others from making autonomous choices, restricting the freedom and rights of others—that is evil. It prevents them from experiencing pleasure, growing in self-respect, and becoming their best selves.

Second, and this one is new, suffering is now bad. In the past, suffering may be a path to growth, being stretched in new directions, and cultivating resilience. We spoke of "redemptive suffering." What did not kill you made you stronger. Increasingly, suffering is seen as unnecessary, or even evil. If I don't want it and it does no good, I should not have to endure it. If achieving my potential is my chosen path to self-growth, suffering is an obstacle that I have the right to have removed. Now, what does not kill me weakens my self-esteem and my capacity to be me.

At the pinnacle of the things our culture most believes and values is that the autonomous individual has a right to choose their path to self-actualization. Furthermore, the new shared belief is that nowhere can you express the deepest, most core elements to your chosen identity than in your sexuality. For in consenting sexuality, pleasure, choice, and individual uniqueness, free from the constraints of the previously powerful, is where our core self finds its most celebrated expression.

We have covered some ground. At the risk of reducing the complex into dot points, I will attempt to summarize the emerging worldview contrasted with the previous worldview.

When contrasted with the CWV, the PCWV is a belief that:

1. there is a god, partially knowable through intuition, the natural order, and the best of religious traditions;

2. there is a moral fabric to the universe, best discerned by individuals. On core issues, there is a coming together, a shared intuition that reflects a deeper morality;

3. all individuals have inherent dignity because everyone carries a divine spark;

4. individuals have rights, and when given freedom, are the best positioned to make fitting choices for themselves;

5. personal happiness is an appropriate yardstick by which to make choices, given that it leads to personal flourishing;

6. when we all flourish as individuals, the world is a better place;

7. suffering is a negative stimulus that is undesirable, unproductive, and where possible, we have the right not to have to endure it; it has the opposite outcome to flourishing;

8. one's sexuality is the preeminent realm in which much of the above can come together in a symbolically powerful way and is to be celebrated.

As I read this list, I sense it as close to the PCWV, but somehow it falls short. Why? Because I wrote this list as a counter to the order and logic of the CWV. So, if the CWV is founded upon the belief in a God as an all-knowing, personable, loving God, then my counter is that in the PCWV, knowledge of the divine is vague and second-hand.

But that is not the right place to start describing the PCWV. It is not founded upon God. He is not the cornerstone from which all other beliefs, like morality or purpose, are referenced.

The PCWV starts where Protagoras (490–420 BC) starts: man is the measure of all things. Individuals are the cornerstone and the key reference point of the PCWV. Here is my attempt to re-order and express the (still tacit and emerging) PCWV in a way that Average Joe would say, "Yeah, that's actually what I believe!"

1. I am unique and special, as is every other individual. I have my own unique combination of passions and gifts.

2. I am the expert on me. I can look inwards, through personal intuition, and understand myself better than others can. My passions, gifts, and my sexuality, combine to form my sense of self, my identity.

3. When I am in touch with my true inner self and give expression to me through my choices, I am being authentic. I am being true to who I am. I will feel positive about me. Actions that cause me to feel better about my "self" are morally good in their outcome. My self-esteem will be healthier, I will be even more empowered to reach for my highest, and become my best self. I will flourish and thrive.

4. Others have a way of contaminating my sense of self. Their own self-interest biases them. Individuals and institutions that seek to influence me towards their ends deny me freedom.

5. When a person does not have the power to make choices that express their true self, this is unjust. They are being denied their human rights. It is just to speak up against and oppose those who abuse power. Likewise, when a person chooses to try to fit in with the crowd and not be true to themselves, this is being "fake" or "inauthentic." Both are a sure path away from wellness.

6. Those who have experienced systemic discrimination—those who have been denied the capacity to be authentic—may struggle to express themselves. The previously discriminated against may be timid and lack self-confidence. They need our support and encouragement. Former powers-that-were need to hear their voice. The one-time powerless need to listen to their own voice too. It is right and just to champion and celebrate the cause of those who are coming out against previous prejudices.

7. Moral discussions now center around empowering individuals to express themselves, as long as they do that in a way that does not impinge on the freedom of others to express themselves. Do no harm.

8. Suffering is also harmful. It causes me to feel worse about my self; it lowers my self-esteem and ability to be authentic. I have a right to protect my "self" from negativity.

9. Anything that causes me to feel better about me, anything that is procreative, is good, and I can choose to bring that influence into my life and to allow my "self" to be defined by that. If I believe a spirituality enriches me, I embrace it. [Religion is forced on people by the powerful. It claims to have the authority in "God." Spirituality is self-referential, not God-referential].

10. When I am being my best me, and everyone is being their best selves, we will naturally express concern and care for others. Self-love precedes other person love. When my tank is full, I can fill others.

That is my best attempt to define the core beliefs of the still-emerging PCWV. In addition to beliefs, the PCWV's values have also evolved. Remember, beliefs are about right versus wrong, whereas values are about what we think is most important. To remind ourselves of the previous set of values, I suggested that the CWV ascribed to values such as dignity, individual freedom, and rationality. These, in turn, give rise to other values like democracy, progress, mercy, capitalism, the rule of law, and education and health for all.

The Contours of the PCWV: Its Values

Again, the PCWV is still in its infancy and its values set is still unfolding. These are matters best seen with the wisdom of hindsight. Here are my suggestions about the values that Western culture now considers as most important.

The PCWV has stepped back from valuing rationality and truth to the extent that previous generations did. Instead, in line with turning inwards, your sense of being in touch with your passions and feelings are increasingly esteemed. We are encouraged to look inside our hearts and discover what is most important to us. Put another way, the subjective dimension to knowing has been raised, whereas external and objective claims to truth are viewed with increasing suspicion. Rationality is still important, but feelings and intuition are more prized and pursued.

Following on from this, if someone believes something to be true for them and is passionate about it, then being loving now means accepting them without qualifications. Love is increasingly synonymous with acceptance, tolerance, and respect.

As with beliefs, the PCWV holds onto some values from former CWV, but has modified and redefined them. In the CWV, to love someone is to be in a deep relationship with them where the goal of your friendship is to want the best for them. In this context, the best means to become more like Jesus, who expressed humanity par excellence. Life has a purpose, a direction. Creation is somehow orientated towards its creator. So to love someone involves helping them become a better person: more compassionate, more thoughtful, more self-controlled, more patient, more honest, less selfish. At times, love means saying the hard things and speaking the truth in love.

Love has been redefined. If people now define their "self" by looking inwards and expressing their passion, this can be tenuous. How can you be sure you made the right choice? Individuals, as social animals, require affirmation. Sociologist Charles Cooley calls this "looking-glass self." When we make a choice, we imagine how others perceive us. We look for clues that our actions have caused others to think more of us, not less. If we believe others will think more of us, our self-esteem increases and we feel better about ourselves.

The modern world values the right to choose more than making the right choice. However, individuals who select out-of-the-ordinary choices can feel isolated and judged. So the loving thing to do is to affirm, to validate, to like. The outcome of love is now that the chooser feels validated in being true to themself. Love is now any action that causes a person to feel better about themself, not better as in more like Jesus.

Related to this is how the PCWV redefines what is just. Justice used to mean our best attempt to bring fairness between persons, reflecting the loving, fair, all-knowing God. Justice was restoring order so it realigned with the natural laws of the universe, making sure people receive what they deserve. There was something objective to justice, in that God established order and fairness. Justice is about returning matters to their God-intended state.

Now, justice is preventing the abuse of power by the powerful, who exploit the weak. The aim is not so much to achieve order or fairness, or to prevent exploitation. Rather, justice is about giving the oppressed a voice and the power to make self-determining choices.

In both the modified definitions of love and justice, there is a pact of mutual self-interest. If I don't criticize you, but instead affirm your right to choose, then you are obliged to do the same for me. Love as tough love in your best interests has been demoted, whereas love as the empowerment of the other to make their own choices is promoted.

The CWV value of progress has also been not discarded, but modified. In previous generations, there was something pioneering about humanity using progress to overcome hunger, disease, poverty, war, etc. There was altruism around making the world a better place for all. Together humanity was a pioneering race. Think of the mission of the original *Star Trek* series, which began in 1966. "Space: The final frontier . . . To explore strange new worlds; to seek out new life and new civilizations; to boldly go where no man has gone before." This was research and progress for its own sake.

This pioneering spirit has been re-orientated, I suggest, such that now progress is a path to personal prosperity, and prosperity is again a path to empower individuals with resources so they can make self-expressive choices. Education has experienced the same shift. We value education for the doors it can open for our children. We invest specifically in their education so that they can prosper and realize their potential. If you happen to have a friend or family member who is a lecturer or academic, I am sure you have heard them bemoan the fact that science for the sake of science is gone, and that universities are now businesses.

In a related way, ethics have also lost some of their potency as a positive force for good. Here is a very quick history lesson. Much of Western and indeed Christian ethical thinking is indebted to Plato and Aristotle. Both talked about the virtuous person who does what is right regardless of the consequences. The contemporary expression "What Would Jesus Do" (WWJD) is an example of this, in that it focuses on the character of the actor. Historically in virtue ethics, happiness is not a goal, but a by-product of a virtuous life.

Consequentialist ethics have largely displaced virtue ethics. The best-known example of this is utilitarianism: the greatest good for the greatest number. In this formation, consequentialist ethics still make proactive, positive choices for as many as possible. Our culture is moving away from a utilitarian consequentialist approach towards an individualist one. What is the greatest good for me, as I define "good?" Ethicists call this egoism. Alongside egoism sits not a positive ethic towards achieving the greatest good for others, but increasingly an "avoid the negative." Being ethical is less about doing good and more about doing no harm to others. Do not interfere in their self-determination.

Some at this point may think I am being harsh, even unfair. Does not the research suggest that the next generation of youth has a social conscience? They desire to make a difference for good. True. My argument is not that we are seeing an abandonment of virtues such as concern for others. Rather we see a modification, which initially sounds virtuous, but often ends up being a dilution. Concern for others now comes a clear second to concern for myself first. If I don't care for my self first, so we are told, how can I have the energy to care for others? If my tank is not filled, how can I fill others? In my observation, Gen Y and Z can be genuinely other-focused but it tends to be brief, sporadic, easily distracted, and involves more social media rhetoric than real interpersonal action.

Globalism has given rise to yet another emerging value: open-mindedness. As opposed to being judgemental, where my way or my tradition is correct, open-mindedness embraces the new, the different. This embracing goes beyond traditional dualisms, such as right versus wrong, or truth versus falsehood. It goes beyond outdated binaries. An open-minded person can live with ambiguity, appreciate the "both-and," or a spectrum. This emerging value has to some extent displaced our value of the truth as hard realities we need to face up to, no matter what the consequences.

Before I proceed to exploring and defining where the PCWV is taking us, I ought to say something specifically about the meta-shift that has taken place. Behind each of the particular beliefs and values listed above, a more fundamental shift has taken place. Marvel with me at the significance of the seismic shift that has unfolded.

From a God-Centered Universe to a Self-Organized Life

The CWV begins and ends with God. He is a God who made the world and everything in it, and yet remains interested in me. I carry his divine spark, live according to his moral compass, and am returning to him. We could call this a theocentric universe. To use a metaphor, history is a divine drama that is telling the story of God. Our part in the story is as extras; we are the people of God called to reflect his glory back to him and be a light to nations or the world. If the drama has a leading actor, it is Jesus, the brightest light.

In the CWV, God is seen as the author, the director, the audience, and God the Son is the leading actor. We find our rightful place in the dramas as extras, whose role is to shed light only because we carry a divine spark from God, because Jesus' Spirit is in us, allowing us to imitate and point people to Christ.

To stretch the analogy to its limits, the theater is also enchanted. God's Spirit animates all actors in this divine theater company. God is present everywhere. He is on stage, side stage and backstage, sustaining this drama at every level so that it continues to reveal his narrative faithfully.

Then came the Enlightenment (seventeeth to eighteenth centuries), which emphasized human rationality. Two fundamental assumptions changed. Increasingly, humanity believed that God was one step removed from the drama, an absent director. God left us in charge. Given that we were created as actors (in God's image), humanity continued to improvise, believing we were coming of age as enlightened actors in our own right. We imagined a more significant role for ourselves in the plot. Second, we discarded the notion of an enchanted theater. There was no magic backstage, which enlivened the actors and the plot. The only thing that counts is what can be seen or heard on the stage: things we have direct control over.

Despite the observations above, I suggest that the Enlightenment remained more or less on script within the CWV. What remained was a commitment to right and wrong that aligned with the mind of God, a belief in the dignity of all because everyone bore God's image, a commitment to progress because God was a God of order, whose kingdom was coming, etc.

What I am presently suggesting is that we are living through an even more significant seismic shift. If the Enlightenment made God a hands-off director, the PCWV makes God simply an extra. It rejects the divine initiation of a God who propels the universe towards its purpose, the divine image-bearing nature of humanity, and the divine authority that judges and draws the universe towards its goal. Instead, in its place is the self, or billions of selves. Humanity is now self-referential, inhabiting its own anthropocentric world.

To express this shift within the metaphor, the Western PCWV has decided that if there ever was a director, he has been absent so long, and the show continued just fine without him, that we should take over the theater. Furthermore, we can change the direction of the plot. If the leading actor is absent and we have been improvising with success, we imagine the drama is now an autobiography where we get to tell our story. Actors look to their own spirit, supposing it is theirs to interpret and express. The story is now about us and not God. We are no longer extras. Instead, each of us squeezes out our own drama about the real me that I imagine I am becoming.

It is in our minds where each of us conceives and constructs our personal scripts. We have become the leading actor, our personal script-writer, director, audience, and critic.

You can see where this leads. Actors who write their own scripts are limited only by their conceptions and imagination. Individuals are freed from the constraints of God's narrative, the realities of his created order, and the culpability of being held to account. In this new world, actors can dream. Some imagine themselves to be females trapped in a male body. Despite having the biology of a man, some feel they are wired to act out the story of a woman, and when they live that story, they are being authentic. The notion that I exist to tell my story, where my world is anthropocentric, can lead to radical outcomes.

It would be a mistake to suspect that only LGBTI+ people construe a world where imagination trumps reality. I am suggesting everyone who lives and breathes inside the PCWV is prone to thinking that we get to organize our own lives as we imagine them to be, that we are the autobiographers of our story.

Have you heard the phrase, "don't let that define you?" Don't let your past, or your mistakes, or your occupation, or your body, or your ex define you. This statement supposes that your mind operates as a filter with the capacity to allow some things to define you and not others. You are above being impacted by others and experience. What impacts you is what your mental filter decides is allowed to shape you.

Some actions you carry out are not the real you, but others are, and you get to decide which is which! What you do with your able-bodied arm is the real you, but what you cannot do with your disabled arm does not define you. Does that make sense? I am not sure it does! But it is the rhetoric of our culture.

What is more disturbing is I hear Christians talk like this. I can sin, but my vice does not define me. I can hang out with the wrong crowd, but they are not influencing me. I can watch movies or listen to music with ungodly themes, but I do not allow those media to shape me. My sin has no consequences, and it is me who gets to decide that it does not. Really?

The so-called prosperity doctrine can also be anthropocentric. God exists to bless me and to hold back the forces of evil in my life. So can the forensic gospel. The forensic gospel focuses on the legal and personal aspects of salvation. God loves me, I am fearfully and wonderfully made. Jesus died to save me from my sin, so I get to be free and enjoy a special seat at his eternal banquet.

When Christians talk like this, it betrays that they have absorbed an anthropocentric post-Christian worldview. Even though Christians believe in God, the Bible, the cross, Jesus and his return, PCWV Christians are prone to believing they are still the director, the scriptwriter, and the lead actor. As strange as it sounds, we can twist the gospel so that it is no longer God-centered, but me-centered. Variations of this twist abound. Where does it lead?

The Contours of the PCWV: Its Social Outcomes

Trusting your intuition, looking inwards, becoming your best self: these are the values and beliefs of the PCWV. How might these values find expression in our culture? If the former Christian values gave rise to democracy, the rule of law, and health and education for all, what will the PCWV's values lead to? What will be the social trends we experience? As I said earlier, it is problematic and premature to predict what kind of social phenomena will settle. But, let's step into the void again; here is my take on the early signs.

The first is consumerism. If the individual expresses and finds themselves in their choices, and the yardstick of choice is personal happiness, people will choose to experience and own more things. I detect an evolution here too. We own bigger houses, filled with more toys and more clothes. We travel to more exotic locations, seeking an adventure, a pilgrimage, not just sight-seeing and rest.

Consumerism can take on a life of its own. Take food as an example. No longer is food just a means of fuelling our bodies so we can work and live. Mealtimes now become an end in themselves. They are a gastronomic experience. Somehow it tastes better if you "share" it with others on social media, and they "like" it. If I am not eating gourmet food, I am missing out. This creates an opportunity in economic terms for food producers to sell us more exotic and expensive cuisines. Speaking personally, I see this in my children. They cannot accept that it's okay to bring a peanut butter sandwich to school. The other day for lunch, my daughter took two omelette burritos. That is, the wrap was made of omelette, not flour. She took two so she could swap one with a friend. He brought creamy chicken pasta. To eat anything less is not only dull, it is social suicide.

Consumerism is also evolving. It may initially take the form of: I will be happy when I own a . . . European car, the latest iPhone, a Swiss watch, or (insert your choice here). Of course, the initial feeling of euphoria that comes with owning an object of desire soon fades. This does not lead Average Joe to the conclusion that stuff cannot make one happy. Instead, consumerism evolves into a cycle of desiring, choosing, possessing, enjoying, becoming bored, desiring something else, and choosing again. The continuous act of expressing one's self by making more niche or novel choices becomes the essence or narrative of existence. And the multi-nationals oblige. There is always a new must-have accessory about to be released that is just so you.

Linked to this is the result that life will become more and more fast-paced. People will be searching for the next big thing and multi-nationals will be competing against each other to produce it, market it, and sell it. Science and technology are increasingly the servants of industry (and not progress) to increase sales. Can you hear that university lecturer complaining again?

These two trends, expressive consumerism and at a faster pace, will have other social structural implications, such as the capacity to purchase 24/7; the increased wastage of a throwaway society; the challenge of recycling; and the environmental consequences of over-consumption.

Is the PCWV Delivering? Are People Happier?

The emerging worldview would like to think that its most significant upside would be individuals with greater self-esteem who are therefore happier. Given the focus on resourcing and empowering individuals to make self-fulfilling choices, this expectation seems reasonable.

Are we happier? A claim such as this is difficult to prove or disprove, especially with the recent complications of COVID-19. So I will quote pre-COVID statistics here to exclude lockdowns as explanations for falling rates of mental wellbeing.

In broad terms, suicide rates are growing in Western countries, particularly among middle-aged, white males. In Australia, suicide rates have risen slightly in recent years, but the longer-term trend goes up and down. This is despite the concerted efforts to increase support for those dealing with mental health issues. While indigenous and remote persons are more likely to take their own life than the general population, so are middle-aged white males.

In the USA, suicide rates by whites between 2000 and 2017 have grown by 40 percent. In the UK, between 1981 and 2017, suicide rates have fallen. In Canada, suicide rates have also fallen over the same period, but there is a recent slight increase. New Zealand is similar.

Beyond suicide, in Australia between 2000 and 2012, self-harm rates that have resulted in hospitalization have increased by 40 percent. Teenage females are most at risk. In the USA between 2001 and 2015, self-harm rates increased by 50 percent. In Canada, there was decline from 1994 to 2014, of about 40 percent. However there was an increase among females from 2010 onwards. New Zealand trends are similar to Canada, with a lesser decline, then a significant jump among young females: 20 percent from 2014 to 2017.

Depression and anxiety rates are notoriously harder to track, because they are less objective. You do not measure deaths or hospital presentations, but rather diagnoses. The recent increased awareness and destigmatization of depression and anxiety may have led to increased presentations seeking medical support and diagnosis. Conversely, you can argue that Western nations have recently invested more resources in mental health awareness and prevention, so we ought to expect rates to fall.

As I understand matters, depression and anxiety rates are likely stable in Australia and Canada over the past few decades, but increasing in the UK, USA, and New Zealand. One study, focusing on General Anxiety Disorder, involved 147,261 adults from 26 countries. They found that in poorer countries, rates of anxiety were at 1.6 percent of the population, whereas in higher-income countries, 5 percent were diagnosed. It is the more impoverished people within wealthier countries who are most likely to suffer from anxiety.[2]

To refocus our question, given its focus on individuals enhancing their own self-esteem, has the PCWV generated higher levels of wellbeing? The evidence is that this is not the case. In fact, among white middle-class males and adolescent females, mental wellbeing is declining. And yet, these are two social groups that would appear to have access to resources and freedoms such that they can make self-fulfilling choices. Contrary to expectations, the data informs us that measures of mental health have either been stable or in decline over the recent decades.

My interpretation of all this is that the PCWV creates the expectation that people will feel more fulfilled. The CWV revered Jesus who came not to be served, but to serve; who taught us that it is better to give than receive. Joy comes as a by-product of focusing on others, whereas the PCWV informs you to love yourself first. You must fill your tank first, then focus on others. The statistics suggest the PCWV's shift has not delivered.

Another claim of the PCWV is that it engenders a more inclusive and relational society. It is argued that if we are less closed-minded, less committed to the exclusive truth of one narrative, we will be less judgemental and more accepting. People will, in general, be more empowered, and feel more affirmed to be themselves. Add to this the technological advances that facilitate social interaction, and we ought to expect a more cohesive all-encompassing society.

There is evidence once again to the contrary. Social isolation or loneliness is rising. The UK has become acutely aware of this. Again, these statistics are pre-COVID. Among the aged, half a million older people go at least five days a week without seeing or speaking to anyone at all (in 2016). Two-fifths of all older people (about 3.9 million in 2014) say the television is their primary source of company.[3] Britain now has a government Minister for Loneliness.

Social media, which can be a tool for social connection, is also clearly a tool for bullying and hate speech. Studies reveal most teenagers have been exposed to cyber-bullying and cyber-hate. Studies also show high rates of correlation between depression, loneliness, and social media use. Decreased or limited use of social media correlates with increased levels of wellbeing.

Regarding social media, this new platform has led to the emergence of a new social anxiety: FOMO. That's Fear Of Missing Out, for those of us

---

2. Ruscio et al., "Generalized Anxiety Disorder Across the Globe," 465–75.

3. Hewings et al., "Facts of Loneliness," para. 2.

who are not up with the latest acronyms. Yes, it's a real thing. Psychologists study it and publish papers on it in respectable journals. What is the world coming to?

Yet another social outcome of the PCWV is a decline in resilience. I am guessing most readers have come across Google Books Ngram Viewer. It's very cool. It plots the usage of a word over time. Its search engine researches millions of books and it makes allowances for the fact that there are more books in print today than before. If you put the word "resilience" into Ngram, you discover its usage has almost tripled between 1960 and 2000.

As I write this chapter, I live in the state of Victoria, in Australia. The local government schools all have core values they proudly display on signs near the entrance gates. Over the past few years, I have noticed more schools including "resilience" as a value. Research reveals the current generation of youth and children lack resilience. Over-protective helicopter parents have shielded their children from pain, hurt, loss, and negativity. At the end of the season, everyone gets a trophy. No one misses out on an invitation to the birthday party. This reflects the PCWV's belief that suffering is avoidable, whereas success and inclusion breed healthy self-esteem. It turns out that disappointment and suffering breed resilience, a core skill needed to cope and succeed in life. Jesus was onto something when he talked of gain for those who would deny themselves and take up their cross.

My final observation regarding the type of social outcome flowing from a PCWV relates to politics. In elections across the globe, we see a shift to extremes. In recent European elections, voter turnout was up. For the first time in 40 years, the two classic centrist parties do not hold the majority. Why is there a shift to extreme positions, both to the left and the right?

The CWV had its foundations. The prevailing beliefs about right and wrong and what constituted a good life came from an agreed, unchanging text: the Bible. In addition, the philosophical milieu of yesterday, the Enlightenment, supposed knowledge was built upon the firm foundations of science and reason. Rightly or wrongly, the previous era offered certainty and stability.

The post-Enlightenment and post-Christian mind has deconstructed this former house of knowledge, such that reason and religion are now viewed with suspicion. In its place, I suggest, the PCWV has not offered its citizens a replacement house. Instead, within the bounds of not limiting the freedom or autonomy of others, individuals are told they are free to construct their own unique personal dwellings, fit for themselves. Everything is possible, little is off-limits. All this comes with a severe downside.

My own private unique house of knowledge that helps me make sense of my life, which allows me to create my sense of meaning and purpose, is built on a foundation of personal opinions. If there are no over-arching religious, moral, or objective narratives that underwrite our shared view of the world, we are sailing close to what philosophers call nihilism. That is, the conclusion that all things are ultimately meaningless.

In response to this lack of foundations, many are searching for external affirmation. How do I know I have made the right choices for me? Answer: if you have made the right choice, you will flourish. What does flourishing look like? Answer: it looks like you being the best at your chosen passion, best as in amazing, better than everyone else. People will like you doing your thing on Facebook.

High-rating reality TV programs are built on the same logic. If food is your thing, you can flourish in the kitchen on *MKR*. If your passion is singing or dancing, enter *The Voice* or *Britain's Got Talent*. If your gift is renovations and styling, sign up for *The Block*. If you achieve external approval and therapeutic validation, you will know you have found your passion, expressed your inner self, and discovered where you will thrive.

In addition to searching for external affirmation, many people are searching for absolutes. Extreme positions offer absolutes. What is wrong with the world, so the left announces, is human over-consumption; it is the new sin. Renewable energies and sustainable living are the new saviors. Greenies and vegans alike can be militant advocates with devout zeal for their sacred mission. On the other wing, what is wrong with the world, so the right announces, is excessive immigration, particularly ethnic and economic refugees. They take our jobs, dilute our cultural traditions, and tear apart our social fabric. Right-wing populist nationalists are equally convinced of their diagnosis and solution for current ills.

It turns out a libertarian anything-goes approach to culture gives rise to its own antithesis, both on the left and the right. Ironically, the progressive inclusivists try to maintain the inclusive society—by excluding the exclusivists.

So Things Are Slowly Getting Worse?

As our culture has abandoned its Christian heritage, things are slowly getting worse—is that my conclusion? I have just made a series of observations that suggests this is the case. Some commentators go further. Carl Trueman, Christian theological and ecclesiastical historian, suggests that everything in Western culture has been in slow decline since the Reformation.[4] Do I agree? No, I do not. Some, perhaps even the greater part, of cultural fabric is being

4. Trueman, *Rise and Triumph of the Modern Self.*

torn with negative consequences. But not all. The rise of the post-Christian era has been paralleled with some positive social movements.

I began this section by tracking the recent rise of suicide. Many others do likewise. It has risen since about the year 2000. Between 1915 and 1935, male suicide rates were about twice what they are now. Suicide rates among both males and females fell drastically in the 1940s but jumped in the 1960s to higher than current rates. Suicide rates are currently lower than previous peaks. Likely world wars and economic depression were triggers for high suicide rates. My point is this, the CWV is not an antidote that resulted in low suicide rates.

Let us consider war. It is estimated that from 1900 to 1970 something like 200 million people died in war, and about another 100 million died due to some war-related genocide. That is about 0.075 percent of the global population. War has been an ever-present part of human history. Europe, the center of the CWV, has been a hotspot for the bloodiest, longest wars. Since 1970, global wars have sharply decreased. In the twenty-first century, about two million people have died in war, and the global population has doubled since 1970. Presently about 0.03 percent of the global population die in war. The post-Christian era has been one of less warfare.[5]

The PCWV, with its emphasis on protecting the vulnerable, has seen a growing opposition to domestic violence. Likewise our culture now takes steps to protect children from abuse in ways it previously did not. Abuse and domestic violence are not new; they both happened during the CWV. The social good of opposing these evils has increased on the back of the social conscience of the PCWV.

Likewise moves to recognize first nations people and right previous wrongs have gained momentum under the PCWV. Australia, New Zealand, and Canada have all experienced a combination of apologies, native title claims, compensation payments, and discussion or action around constitutional recognition of their indigenous peoples.

Other examples of the positives that have unfolded during the rise of the PCWV could be cited. Then again, further social negatives of recent social changes could have been cited too. And as John Dickson demonstrates, Christians have behaved as both bullies and saints at every stage of history.[6] We need to step back from the detail to get a sense of the bigger trends. I acknowledge the social good in parts of the PCWV and the social wrongs that persisted during the CWV. Nevertheless, in my summation, I

---

5. Roser et al., "War and Peace," paras. 1–9.
6. Dickson, *Bullies and Saints.*

interpret the transition from the CWV to the PCWV as a greater step away from the good than towards it.

This is as close as I can come to describing, at an accessible level, and at the moment, the beliefs, values, and social outcomes of the emerging PCWV. At the risk of taking the complex and reducing it to a benign series of dot points, I will conclude this chapter with my customary summary.

Simplicity on the Other Side of Complexity

The PCWV is a belief that:

1. I am unique and exceptional, with distinct passions and gifts;

2. I am the expert on me. I understand myself better than others do. My passions, giftings, and sexuality, combine to form my sense of self, my identity;

3. When I express my true inner self through my choices, I am being authentic. I am being true to who I am. I will feel positive about myself, and my self-esteem will be healthy. This will empower me to become my best self. I will flourish and thrive;

4. Other people may undermine my sense of self. Driven by self-interest, individuals and institutions may seek to influence me and deny me freedom;

5. Everyone has the right to express themselves. To deny this is unjust. It is right to speak up against any abuse power. Likewise, trying to fit in with others and not be true to self is "fake," or "inauthentic." Both move us away from wellness;

6. Those who have experienced systemic discrimination—those who have been denied the capacity to be authentic—may struggle to express themselves, and lack self-confidence. They need our support and encouragement. Everyone needs to hear their voice. Giving former minorities voice is a just cause;

7. Morality is about empowering individuals to express themselves, in a way that does not impinge on the freedom of others. Do no harm;

8. Suffering is also harmful. It lowers my self-esteem and ability to be authentic. I have a right to protect my "self" from negativity;

9. Anything that causes me to feel better about myself is good. I can choose to bring that influence into my life and to allow my "self" to be defined by that. If I believe a spirituality enriches me, I embrace it.

[Religion is forced on people by the powerful, who do so claiming the authority in "God." Spirituality is chosen by me]

10. When my tank is full, I can fill others. My best self naturally expresses concern and care for others. Self-love precedes other-person love.

The PCWV esteems values such as:

1. intuition and feeling; looking inwards as the path to enlightenment;

2. truth as subjective and affective (the truth moves you to action, it is more than ideas);

3. the freedom of the autonomous individual to make choices;

4. love as the non-judgemental acceptance of the other, who can make their own choices;

5. justice as empowerment; giving people back control to make their own choices;

6. self-expression or self-actualization; making choices towards your chosen identity that will increase your self-esteem, allow you to become your best self, and achieve your unique potential, which is good for you and has positive consequences for others;

7. the market is a neutral space that provides a never ending diversity of consumables.

Initial trends that can be observed as flowing from the PCWV include:

1. a plateau or decline in personal wellbeing;

2. a fear that my choices are just my opinions (technically, close to solipsism);

3. a related fear: the fear of missing out (FOMO);

4. social isolation and loneliness;

5. low resilience in the next generation who have been protected from suffering and been told they can achieve anything they set their hearts to;

6. a search by some for absolutes and certainty, often in extreme positions;

7. the ongoing concern for individuals, focused around the previously marginalized, has facilitated some positive trends including protecting the abused and vulnerable.

4

What Is the New Status of Christians?
The Church? And Christian Thought?

OVER THE PAST THREE chapters, we have tracked various social trends. What is happening in our culture is more than just the decline of church attendance. There was this collective idea that I am calling the CWV. It was a society-wide shared set of beliefs and values. It was consistent and coherent, and it underwrote Western cultures for about 1600 years. In the past few decades, Average Joes have abandoned, or at least radically modified, this shared, accepted CWV.

In its place is arising what I am calling a PCWV. This new worldview, I suspect, is still in what we might call its emergent phase. That is to say, it is still adolescent, like teenagers defining themselves against their parents. What key things it stands for, how those beliefs and values translate to social structures, and what this means for the world's inhabitants is yet to become completely clear or fixed. History will tell, hindsight will bring clarity, and future speculations are not the fodder for this book.

What we shall consider in this chapter, then, is the status of the old worldview. What role does the church play in the new and emerging landscape? What is the status of Christians? What about the social function of religion as bringing objectivity to morality? In a new worldview, how does the up-and-coming consensus interact with the old one? If I can push my metaphor a little further, how are the teenagers who are becoming young adults interacting with and viewing their parents? With honor and respect? Or as if Mum and Dad have become geriatrics?

This will be the last chapter in the first section of this book: where are we now? In the next chapter we shall transition to our second frame: how did we get here?

The Status of Christians?

How often have you heard the frustrated complaint from Christians that, far from us being judgemental, we are now the ones being judged. That Christians are now demonized in ways that amount to something close to discrimination? As I write, it is 2019, and the Israel Falou post on his social media page about how hell awaits sinners, including homosexuals, has been a big story. Why is no one getting upset about what Anthony Mundine posts on his Facebook page? He is an anti-vaxxer. He calls for the reinstatement of the death penalty against paedophiles. As a Muslim, he criticizes the Christian view of a triune God. There is no widespread backlash against his posts.

Australia, England, Canada, and New Zealand now have various legislation forms that prevent pro-life or anti-abortion demonstrations around abortion clinics. These areas are demarcated as an exclusion zone. The right to protest is denied. Recently, there was a case in Australia where vegans demonstrated against a café with goats that patrons could pat. The goats were stolen and the café had to shut down. This incident captured media attention, but militant protesting, including illegal activity such as trespassing, closing down workplaces, stealing livestock, sit-ins at major intersections in cities, are on the rise. The levels of prosecution of anti-abortionists and anti-carnivores are unequal. The media coverage is at times and on various channels sympathetic to the vegans, but never the anti-abortionists. Is this not a form of discrimination?

And what about the mainstream media's portrayal of Christians? There is an evident and widespread attempt to normalize the presence of gay persons and the gay lifestyle. Most TV shows now have an obligatory same-sex person or couple. We regularly hear calls in the political arena to bring greater equality to women or people from ethnic minorities into public life. Christians are usually portrayed as either judgemental, or simplistic, or both. In 2001, Ned Flanders from *The Simpsons,* made the front cover of *Christianity Today* as the most visible evangelical Christian.[1] Flanders is a two-dimensional, bland, uninspiring caricature of a Bible-believing, church-going Christian.

Christians are now a minority, not just numerically, but more so in terms of influence. Our position of privilege in public debate has been displaced. We are but one voice among many. Yet various other voices on the margin, such as Islam, the LBGTI+ community, or the Greens, are often given a profile beyond their size. The West often champions the cause of the marginalized. So if Christians are now a minority, why is it socially

---

1. See this cover at https://www.christianitytoday.com/ct/2001/february5/.

acceptable to hate on Christians, but not gays, or Muslims? Isn't this evidence that we are discriminated against? How has our culture concluded that some minorities need to be honored and heard, whereas others can be dismissed and discounted?

There is a logic that our culture follows. In *The Rise and Triumph of the Modern Self*, Carl Trueman comes the closest I have read to articulating it. This book is a solid read, and now has a second more popular level version, *Strange New World*. For most Christians, the unfairness of it all remains a mystery. As I have said already, such things are often left unspoken, tacit. For the sake of clarity, I will try to articulate out loud the thinking of our culture. I will attempt to make the logic and reasoning of our culture explicit.

Discrimination is now one of the biggest sins. Discrimination is despised because it attacks the individual's freedom based on their arbitrary external qualities. Somehow because of gender, or sexuality, race, or beliefs, an individual is denied the capacity to make autonomous choices.

Remember that individual freedom and the empowerment of others are two of the West's new strongest held beliefs. The PCWV's answer to the questions "where are we now?" and "what is wrong?" is that certain groups of people have long been subject to discrimination. The next question that follows is "how did we get here?" How is it that we have a history as a culture of systematic discrimination against certain minorities? Who has been denying these individuals freedom and empowerment? Who are the judgemental people who are telling others what to do?

The answer is: the group that was most recently in power. The group that used to its power to outline a morality that suited its own interests, and to perpetuate the powerlessness of those who were being discriminated against. Remember that the PCWV is schooled in deconstructing power, particularly when held by faceless corporate institutions.

So, if the question for Western culture is "how did we get here?," here being a society where some have experienced ingrained discrimination, the answer is that the powerful and judgemental church of yesteryear got us here. Homophobia, Islamophobia, sexism, turning a blind eye towards pedophilia, the downplaying of male-perpetrated domestic violence, the abuse of the environment because it's all damned anyway—these are all products of the CWV. It is the fault of the Christians and the church of the recent past. They are to blame. Intuitively, this argument seems fair and accurate to Average Joe.

When Christians Speak Up Like They Used to

When a Christian speaks up for what they believe to be moral or true, what happens then? This transpired with Australian Rugby great, Israel Falou. Falou, a Pacific Islander by heritage, was initially asked, on social media, his views on the eternal destiny of homosexuals. Later he posted on Instagram an image that reads: "Warning: drunks, homosexuals, adulterers, liars, fornicators, thieves, atheists, idolaters—Hell awaits you—Repent! Only Jesus saves." Besides this, Falou wrote, "Those that are living in Sin will end up in Hell unless you repent. Jesus Christ loves you and is giving you time to turn away from your sin and come to him." After this, he quoted Gal 5:19–21. Falou's warning list is drawn directly from 1 Cor 6:9–10.

Here we see a clash of worldviews. Falou holds to a version of the traditional CWV. To complicate matters, Falou was born in Sydney, to Tongan parents. He is an Australian, raised and living in a Pacific Islander sub-culture. He attends an Islander church, and is married to a New Zealand-raised Samoan. Falou holds to a CWV that is part Pacific Islander, part old-school Western Christianity. Falou believes the Bible is still true and authoritative. And he believes it is appropriate he affirms biblical truths when asked.

What is relevant to the thesis of this book is to focus on what happens when mainstream Australia believes that an advocate of the former CWV asserts that the Bible is still the moral authority for all cultures. Falou was branded a homophobe in the media, sacked as a rugby player, publicly disowned by his code and many of his former teammates and other sporting professionals, and hated on social media platforms.

The treatment of Falou was unsophisticated. It lacked nuance. So did his post. I believe Falou's posts lacked prudence, but that is not my concern at this point. The Instagram picture that was most referenced named eight sins. Falou did not single out homosexuality but no one was offended by his warning to drunkards, liars, or thieves. Second, Falou was quoting an entire Bible passage. The Bible is a Western cultural text that has been respected and considered trustworthy for 1600 years. Within Falou's Islander sub-culture, the Bible is still taken as reflecting the mind of God. Third, Falou would argue the warning is precisely that, a warning that people loved by God might find forgiveness. It is reported Falou has gay friends.

This is a complex issue, and I am not trying to say all that can be said on this topic. I am simply using this social incident as a phenomenon we can analyze to track societal changes. My concern is this: How does Average Joe (who now subscribes to the PCWV) view Falou's behavior?

Average Joe thinks Falou's post is hate speech directed at a formerly discriminated against minority: same-sex attracted persons. People are not leaping to the defence of drunkards, liars, and thieves. Why not? Because there is no shared perception that drunkards, liars, and thieves have been the victims of sustained discrimination. There is no word in our vocabulary for someone who has a pathological fear of liars or thieves. We don't label Falou a pseudophobic or a kleptophobic.

But homophobia is in the mind of Average Joe a real and dangerous thing. According to Google Ngram, the term homophobia was nonexistent before 1970 and its prevalence has since sky-rocketed. We now use this word about five times more than claustrophobia, and one hundred times more than any other phobia.

Homophobia is considered dangerous for layers of reasons. It attacks the individual's freedom to make an empowered choice that expresses their core identity and allows them to self-actualize. Homosexuality now carries deep symbolic meaning.

Recall that for sociologists, symbols are important. Individuals and cultures invest meaning into their symbols. They become the sacred vessel that represents a cluster of deeply held core values. The right for a same-sex attracted person to choose a homosexual lifestyle now has its own symbol, a rainbow. The symbol of the pride rainbow encapsulates the values of individualism, freedom, choice, self-expression and actualization, love as acceptance and affirmation of the other to be other, and self-satisfaction as the path towards increased self-esteem and personal growth. If I can be me, then I will flourish.

In a word, the pride rainbow is the new symbol for love. It is a symbol for same-sex attracted love in the first instance, which expands into an affirmation of a broader all-inclusive definition of love. Love is accepting that the other knows what is best for themselves, respecting choice, and empowering others to seek self-fulfillment as they follow their dreams. This new symbol of love—the pride rainbow—is displacing the previous symbol of love—the cross.

In the CWV, the cross captures God's love for us in that he sent his son to die for us. Jesus so loved us that he willingly endured the shame of the cross and separation from his father, so that he might make reconciliation possible between God and humanity. The cross captures the sense of sacrifice that love sometimes demands. It captures the willingness to submit oneself to God's will and definition of love, not our own. It holds in place the tension between love and justice. The cross both affirms that justice matters—sin demands a high price and affirms that love prevails—when the judge takes the judgement upon himself and pays that price with his life.

In the previous CWV, it was appropriate, even caring to remind others of God's standards and judgement. Now, such reminders are deemed to be born out of fear. Homophobia captures a cluster of new evils such as judgementalism, the denial of the empowerment of the other to be themselves, a desire to abuse power and control, and a patriarchal arrogance.

In short, the pride rainbow and the cross are two symbols that represent love, but from two different views of the world. What is playing out here is a values or worldview clash, and Falou has stepped right into the thick of it.

For Average Joe, Falou was attacking the core symbol of Joe's new, more enlightened worldview. Falou killed the sacred cow, or burned the enemy's (rainbow) flag. In so doing, Falou took the low ground and was being judgemental, denying others their rights to choice and self-empowerment, seeking to regain or retain the power of the dark past, abusing that power, and being arrogant.

In the process, Falou added fresh insult to the already discriminated-against gay community. Average Joe now believes they need our affirmation, our validation. As a previous minority, the public dialogue needs to be therapeutically supportive of LGBTI+ people.

If you did not before, can you see why Rugby Australia believed they had to act? They thought they were caring and standing up for the downtrodden, standing up against the previously powerful bully, who needs reminding that he does not get to make the playground rules anymore. I am not saying Rugby Australia got it right. Using sociological lenses, I am simply trying to explain why Falou's tweet pushed so many buttons and why Rugby Australia's response made intuitive sense to many Average Joes.

Am I arguing that Average Joe hates Christians? No. I previously suggested that Average Joe is likely to view Christians like lawyers. Joe is cautious and suspicious of Christians. They are like throwbacks from a previous era. If he meets them one-to-one at a party, Christians can be friendly, pleasant people. But get Christians together, or speak to one on the wrong topic, such as morality, sexual morality in particular, and Joe's newfound distaste for Christians emerges. Joe believes Christians have a hypocritical judgemental inclination, a morbid fascination with sexuality, and a mistaken belief they still have a right and power to tell others what is right.

The Status of the Church

In the previous chapter, I noted that the post-Christian era is inclined to deconstruct. To be fair, whenever there is a transition of worldview, a certain amount of unpacking "the things we could not previously see but have now become clear" occurs. Such conversations and insights are used to justify the need for change. They help people let go of the past and embrace the future. I contend that in this particular transition, we are more schooled at deconstructionism than previously. I will argue this in the next chapter as part of how we got here. For now, I highlight that our new shared narrative is formed around a deconstruction of the past.

Average Joe is suspicious that institutions somehow cause their most strident advocates to be blindly loyal and push for decisions and outcomes that bring more power and influence to their given organization. There is a type of group-think that kicks in among the faithful, which means they must sustain and enhance their "thing" by whatever means.

Let's take politics, for instance. English, Australian, American, and a few other Western democracies are driven by a two-party conservative versus democratic/labor divide. Whether you listen to a politician from the left or right, the narrative is oddly similar. The best thing that can happen is that my party is re-elected with a majority. The worst thing that can happen is that the other side gains power.

Power is an addictive drug. We have noted Lord Acton's saying, "Power tends to corrupt; absolute power corrupts absolutely." What is different now is that the PCWV sees that institutions are the curse of society in that they are the ones who have a drug-like addiction to power. Politicians abuse their parliamentary privilege or their allowances and entitlements. Banks abuse their right to charge fees. Unions abuse their power to hold developers or importers to ransom, or to force employees to pay fees.

But the institution most perceived as being addicted to and abusive in using its power is the church. The most obvious example of this, the one that affirms for Average Joe that his suspicions are correct, is the occurrence and handling of child abuse and sexual abuse in particular.

That child abuse ever occurs is abhorrent, but there is something about the power of the church, something about the traditionally respected office of priesthood that attracts or breeds predatory behavior. Like the priesthood, there is also something about the authority of being a religious brother functioning as a school teacher, which gives one access and control over vulnerable school children within a Catholic or church school.

To add insult to injury, not only does the church have a track record of allowing systemic abuse to happen on its watch, but when the church hierarchy becomes aware of exploitation, it has often failed to stand up for and protect the weak and abused. Instead, the church historically protected its own, failing to prosecute the perpetrators. The wrong was swept under the carpet, in an attempt to preserve the reputation of the church.

When such matters come to light, the church continues to behave in deplorable ways that betray its infatuation with power. The church can be obstructionist, and perhaps even a bully to victims. Furthermore, the church has resisted financially compensating victims, despite the widely held belief that the church is an incredibly wealthy institution that has long used its power and influence to amass considerable means.

On this "evidence" alone, many Average Joes dismiss the church as a power-hungry, self-serving organization. Australia has just concluded five years of a Royal Commission into Institutional Responses to sexual abuse that have regularly brought abuse cases into the mass media. New Zealand is in the midst of something similar. The UK has had various independent inquiries. The social media #MeToo campaign had its origins not in the church, but against Hollywood producer Harvey Weinstein. It has been followed by other campaigns, namely #ChurchToo and #SilenceIsNotSpiritual. Average Joe has no trouble finding evidence to affirm his intuition.

The evidence that the (male-dominated) church is power-hungry spreads beyond this subject matter. I need not dwell on them, to list them will suffice. Average Joe would view the church as systematically discriminating against women. Females are denied access to religious offices, the pulpit, and the board rooms of many churches. In marriage, they are told to submit. The church appears to have a morbid fascination against homosexuality (and other LGBTI+ people), and interjects its opinions into the private sexual preferences of others, behaving like a bully. Given its own moral failings, the church's desire to speak on certain moral issues is seen as hypocritical. Since the pope suppressed Galileo, the church has been selectively against science and progress to bolster faith and scripture as the highest authority.

Having said all this, Average Joe would be happy to acknowledge that the church does much good on other fronts. The church runs many welfare agencies, hospitals, aged-care facilities, and the like. Average Joe would happily acknowledge this. Many Average Joes and Joannes are comfortable sending their children to a Christian or church school. Attendance at such schools is growing. In Australia, 35 percent of students now attend a private faith-based school. This number has doubled in the past 30 years.[2] Most people, governments included, are happy for churches to continue to run these institutions. I sense that people believe churches do it well, and they can tap into a large pool of volunteers and benefactors. Churches and Christians drive much of the not-for-profit sector (NFP). In 2014, four of the top five charities were faith-based. Using their volunteer base, churches deliver great bang for your buck.

---

2. Australian Bureau of Statistics, "Schools."

All this is to say that Average Joe is not against the church per se as long as we do not discriminate in our running of schools, hospitals, and welfare programs. As long as the local church functions as a club of the like-minded, they can do their thing. Average Joe is conscious that the church can't seem to help but go back to its old bullying ways on specific topics. If some people continue to frequent church, that is fine, but it is safer for society if the church is powerless and peripheral.

Instead, power is more safely invested in individuals, not in institutions. Individuals understand themselves and their needs. Individuals can make choices that will allow themselves to flourish. Individuals are not subject to the mischiefs of groupthink. Empowering individuals who do not harm or discriminate but rather respect other individuals is intuitively understood as the best way to order a society.

What does all of this mean for morality? Is it totally up to the individual to choose as they see fit? Is morality now totally relative? In the CWV, one of the church's social functions was to underwrite a shared morality so that it had objectivity beyond just opinion. What of this social function? Is it not still needed? Even if Average Joe has dismissed the church as hypocritical and power-hungry, a risky contributor to public ethical debates, is there still a place for the accumulated wisdom of centuries of Christian thought at the table, thinking that is founded upon the teachings and exemplary life of Jesus?

The Social Function of the Church

To move beyond the vague sense that the role of the church is somehow now defunct and only of interest to a few, let me break down these questions as much as I can, and consider them one at a time. Does expressive individualism lead to the conclusion that I can do what seems right to me? Is it now the case that we no longer need moral guidance from a divine source, or from the church who represents the divine? Don't we still need an external divine being to bring moral objectivity to our culture? The answer is: it appears not in the particulars.

In practice, our cultures do not leave all morality to personal choice, yet we no longer reference God as the source of right and wrong. The first absolute moral qualifier of the PCWV is that I cannot do something that harms another. As I argued earlier, ethics have retreated from being a positive virtuous drive to do good to the lesser "do no harm." Do not discriminate, or impinge on the freedom of others. Even this "lesser" ethic brings some parameters, some boundaries: I can't steal, I can't assault, I can't lie if it discredits another person, greed is wrong if my profits come on the back of exploiting another person, and so on.

Okay, beyond that, can individuals do as seems appropriate to themselves, so long as it does not hurt anyone else? One of the apparent realities of the PCWV is that some behaviors are evil. Wrong, in the absolute sense of the word. Their immorality is not just a matter of opinion, even shared opinion. I like to give this phenomenon an ironic title. I call this cluster of absolute evils the new seven deadly sins.

You will know them: homophobia, pedophilia, domestic violence, Islamophobia, discrimination, racism, hate speech, fundamentalism . . . This list is not fixed, nor is it exactly seven. It's not engraved on tablets of stone. But you get my point. These sins are perceived to be worse than others. Somehow they are of a higher order. The question I ask as a sociologist is, why are these actions considered worse than others? And where does this ordering of wrongness find its grounding if not from God, or his word?

The new seven deadly sins are, I suggest, considered more toxic than others because they attack a minority that has experienced ingrained discrimination. They judge people based on arbitrary external characteristics. They do not empower the authentic other to choose, to express self, and to flourish.

I will return to the new seven deadly sins in a moment. To be fair to the PCWV, Average Joe would also claim he and culture stand for positive things. He is not anti-homophobia. Joe would say he is pro-choice, pro-love, and pro-freedom. There remains a shared consensus around positive things that culture ought to stand for. If we polled people, values like fairness, kindness, generosity, justice, respect for others and our environment, the sanctity and preciousness of children, access to health and education would consistently come at the top of the list.

The dilemma for the PCWV is not its inability to stand for anything positive. It does. The dilemma is twofold. First, nowhere is the list codified (listed as an explicit set). There is no equivalent to the Ten Commandments. Second, it is not canonized. It is not recorded in a sacred text with the authority of God behind it. Rather, this list of positives remains vague and disparate.

This creates another dilemma. If it's not codified and canonized, what is to stop Average Joe from saying he disagrees with the list? Or that he accepts only part of the part? Or saying he agrees but then disregards the list? Where is the deterrent for breakers of the new norms, and the encouragement for conformers? Social media—shaming and liking on feeds—is that all there is? The wealthiest person in the world at the moment is Jeff Bezos, followed by Bill Gates. Before their divorce, Bill and Melinda Gates gave away billions of dollars. Jeff Bezos's divorced wife is also generous. But Jeff himself apparently donated little to charity until recently.[3] Can he just decide that for himself? Is hating on him on social media the only tool we have to encourage his generosity?

Back to the seven deadly sins. Let us road test the morality of the PCWV. We will focus on the negative side. Can we arrive at a consensus about what is (right and) wrong? If Islamophobia is discrimination based on religion, why do we not get as upset about Hinduphobia? Answer: because Hindus have not experienced systemic discrimination like Muslims have. The West did not hold crusades against Hindus. If the abuse of children is wrong, why do we not get as upset about the abuse of seniors? Why is more attention given to violence by men against women, than by children against their siblings? Why is abuse by a priest more likely to make it into the news than abuse by an uncle? The answer has to do with power. When a powerful person abuses a marginalized minority, this is a greater evil. My point is this: there is a certain logic to how things make it onto this list.

Where then does this ordering of wrongness find its grounding? To be honest, I am not sure I can provide a credible answer. As I listen to politicians and social commentators, I cannot detect a cogent or coherent answer to this question. What we tend to get is: "We now know better . . . ," or "It's 2023; nobody still believes . . . " There is an assumed moral progressivism, meaning we have moved on from certain juvenile naïve assumptions, and are now more enlightened.

This answer does not constitute an argument. It does not explain why in fifty years we won't think something else again. Progressivism does not naturally lead to absolutes. Nor does it explain why we have decided some previous sins were never wrong, but other previous sins remain sins. Why for instance, is vandalism still wrong? If you intentionally scratch my new European car, I am certain evil has occurred. But no person was harmed.

The only argument that I hear that makes sense of how our culture arrives at a shared view of why evil remains evil, is the one mounted by historians such as Holland. His thesis is that our present moral code and its underpinnings are a remnant of the former Christian way of thinking. Sure, we have chipped away at a few parts we no longer like, such as seeing some sexual preferences as less moral than others, now condoning pre-marital sex and cohabitation, and so on. Holland contends that the West currently holds to a modified version of the CWV, but never publicly admits that.

Fundamentally, I agree with Holland's assessment, but it raises two other questions for me. First, if we have detached profoundly biblical

---

3. Sandler, "Jeff Bezos Just Gave Away," paras. 4 and 6.

values from the biblical story that underwrites them, how long will that scenario last? Who knows, but it is a precarious place in which to be. Second, is there a discernible pattern to which bits the PCWV has modified? And what is the shape or logic to the new narrative by which these modifications are justified?

The grounds on which good remains good, and evil is pronounced as evil, is vague, to me at least. In the past, the CWV served to objectify morality, and named good from bad. Then it encouraged the good and deterred evil. If this is no longer the role of the church, can Christians bring the wisdom of Jesus' teachings into the public conversation? Surely in a democracy, we can speak?

Not on most topics. Why not? Because, as I have argued, people are suspicious that public Christians have alternate motives to reclaim power and use that to tell others what to do. Whose role is it then to interpret and reinforce the new morality?

As I read culture, three groups are claiming this vacant space as their own. Only a subset of one of those groups tends to use anything that resembles traditional Christian wisdom. The first is politicians and social commentators. Be they from the left, the right, and even a few from the middle, some public figures use their profile to virtue-signal to the rest of us. Prominent examples include Canada's Justin Trudeau, New Zealand's Jacinta Ardern, and Australia's Penny Wong.

The second group is comedians. The new breed of comedian such as Adam Hills, Charlie Pickering, or Hannah Gadsby is different from Jerry Seinfeld or Barry Humphries. They have a political leaning and agenda that drives their commentary. Part of their humor revolves around ridiculing others, usually traditional conservatives. Apparently, it's acceptable to poke fun at white, male, Christian boomers (like Tony Abbott), but never gay, ethnic females (like Penny Wong). Jokes about Abbott are entertainment. Jokes about Wong are hate speech. Comedians are in many ways the new preachers of our culture, though they are never so honest as to tell us that is what they are doing.

The third group is celebrities, sporting stars, and even sporting codes. Kanye West's support of Donald Trump was counter-balanced by Meryl Streep's and Tom Hank's damning of Trump. What makes the views of actors or musicians on candidates for president relevant?

In 2016, American NFL quarterback Colin Kaepernick knelt during the singing of the national anthem in protest against racism. In 2019, Indigenous Australians would not sing the anthem during the State of Origin rugby league game. Many sporting codes now hold an Indigenous round, where team jerseys have artwork that celebrates first people cultures. In this sense, sport is functioning as public religion. You can be part of something bigger than yourself.

In 2019, Liverpool defeated Barcelona in a football (soccer) game, and went on to be crowned European champions. Afterwards, the crowd and the players, arm in arm, sang a rousing rendition of Liverpool's club song, *You'll never walk alone*. Search it; it's very moving. The message is clear. Following a team brings you into a family. You can now trade with Liverpool FC cryptocurrency. If sports are emerging as public religion, is it the place to contest and combat racism? And is a sportsperson also now a social commentator? Being good at kicking or catching a ball has little to do with being virtuous or contemplating, articulating, and living the good life.

Whether sporting codes, celebrities, comedians, social commentators, or politicians can adequately replace the traditional role of the church remains to be seen. I have my doubts. But again, I am trying to make a point here. The public function of the Christian religion as underwriting and announcing good from evil is passing. Even if most of our values are historically Christian, Christians can no longer stand up and publicly affirm them. Others are filling that space. When Christians, like Israel Falou, or the church, attempt to reclaim this responsibility, we are judged, maligned, and misinterpreted. Our presence is largely unwelcome. We do our reputation harm. Is the public debate still a place where God calls us to speak up, or has that day gone?

Before I end this chapter, I cannot help myself but come to the defence of the church and present a more balanced history. And also poke a few holes in the emerging PCWV.

Is the Dismissal of the Church and Christians as Power-Hungry Fair?

In short, our culture has dismissed the church as power-hungry and hypocritical. It has dismissed Christians as remnants of a bygone era who occasionally try to resurrect their former influence. The West disregards Christian thought as the source of the ethical frameworks and absolutes that underwrite our shared public morality. All these assumptions follow a line of reasoning. Is it fair?

Again, let's take those questions one at a time. Is the church power-hungry and inclined to use power for self-gain? The answer is yes and no. Yes, in part, some sections of the church have sought to amass power and wealth for their own ends. The church's recent handling of sexual abuse and the practices of popes in the medieval Catholic church are clear examples of this.

But none of this is new to the CWV. As I highlighted earlier, within the biblical narrative is the account of the prophet Nathan challenging King David. Our tradition recognizes that people can be good and bad, and the powerful can act abusively. Individuals abusing power are not new, and such incidents did not prevent the church from becoming an agent for much good.

The more remarkable story is that, on balance, the church, following the example of Jesus, more often uses its power for the good of others, as Stark, Sheridan, Williams, Holland, and Mangalwadi argue. Each writer tells story upon story of how Christians helped the widows, the poor, the sick, females, abandoned children, the uneducated, those without the right to vote, the masses in the workforce, slaves, the untouchables, and so on.

There is something unsophisticated about the PCWV's critique of the CWV. It claims institutions only seek power for selfish gain. This is a pessimistic assessment of human nature, contrary to the evidence of Christian history. Jesus says he came not to be served, but to serve (Mark 10:45). Christianity at its best mirrors this virtue. People's motives are always mixed, and their report card reveals these flaws. But the evidence is that over the long run, and when compared to every other tradition, the church has been a force for much good.

What about homosexuality? Is it fair to suggest that the church has a morbid fascination with the private sexuality of others in general, and LGBTI+ people in particular? Has not this morbid fascination been a breeding ground for homophobia? Again, the answer is yes and no. Yes, some Christians have drawn more attention to sexual sins than to others. I suggest to you that humans of every persuasion have a morbid fascination with sexuality.

Has the CWV bred homophobia? No. I contend the evidence is to the contrary. Let me argue my case by an anecdote and then evidence. I attended an all-boys high school in New Zealand of some 1200 students in the 1980s. It was a testosterone-charged hothouse. The most envied thing you could do at my school was make the first fifteen rugby team. If you did, you got a special blazer. In that era, calling someone a "poofter" was about the biggest insult you could muster.

There was a boy in my class who had some "gay" mannerisms. He was fair game, as were others like him. The principal of our school was an overt practicing Christian. He was even a lay preacher at the local Brethren Church. Whenever he became aware that students were mocked because of their potentially effeminate traits, he would call an all-school assembly and tear strips off the entire student body. It was not because he was socially progressive. On the contrary, he was not. He was socially and theologically conservative. Nor was it politically correct to stand up for gays. It was not— not yet anyway. He did it because his Christian faith affirmed values like compassion, tolerance, and respect. (Those words meant slightly different things then than they do now.) As I recall my high school days, it was usually Christian teachers and students who were the most pleasant to those for whom the label "poofter" seemed to stick.

I contend this trend was not limited to my school. Let us use gay or same-sex marriage legalization as an objective measure of where gay rights are most prevalent. As of 2019, same-sex marriage is legal in twenty-eight countries. Of that list, sixteen are historically Protestant countries, and eleven are formerly Catholic. Only one is non-Christian: Taiwan, and that was at one point a Dutch colony. This statistic is impressive. Only one predominantly Buddhist country, no Islamic, and no Hindu country presently permits same-sex marriage. Conversely, of the eleven countries where homosexuality is punishable by death, all are Muslim.

There is something about the heritage and values of the CWV that means that a country is far more likely to legislate rights for same-sex couples. What is it? Christians believe that everyone is made in God's image. Christians value the freedom of the individual. Christians affirm the right of others to hold a different view and that one day all will be held to account for their own choices by a loving and just God.

These are specifically Christian values, and they lead to respect for others. From here, additional steps are required to arrive at a PCWV that is pro same-sex marriage. But it is the post-Christian worldview, and not the post-Islamic or post-Hindu worldview that gives birth to gay rights. Working backwards, the PCWV is a daughter of the CWV. So it follows that something within the Christian worldview is less discriminatory against gays than other worldviews.

Or consider the story of Henri Nouwen. He was born in Holland in 1932 and ordained into the Catholic priesthood aged 25. While he initially studied theology, he transitioned to studying psychology. He became a famous speaker, author, academic, and professor of pastoral theology at Yale and Notre Dame, and lecturer at Harvard.

As a person, he struggled with self-doubts and loneliness. Nouwen is perhaps best known, not as an academic, but as a spiritual guide who spoke to people's lives through his lectures and books. Consider this quote: "Our life is full of brokenness—broken relationships, broken promises, broken expectations. How can we live with that brokenness without becoming bitter and resentful except by returning again and again to God's faithful presence in our lives."[4]

At his most recognized, Nouwen stepped back from public life and began serving in a residential community for the intellectually disabled called L'Arche. Nouwen was paired with a man with severe developmental disabilities named Adam. Nouwen wrote a book about the experience: *Adam: God's Beloved*. Reflecting on that relationship, Nouwen noted: "It is I, not Adam, who gets the main benefit from our friendship."[5]

Nouwen also struggled with same-sex attraction. Nouwen never went public about this, but he did confide in others, write about it in his private journals, and allude to it in his writings. There is no evidence that Nouwen broke his vow of chastity.

Nouwen is an example of a man who lived with same-sex inclinations during an era that might now be considered homophobic. Yet the church neither shunned nor excluded him. Rather, he was embraced into a community of religious orders, allowed to flourish, and granted leadership, profile, and voice.

If I am right, the Christian community has, at its best, accepted, shown compassion, and tolerated (by which historically we mean sought to understand and include despite real differences) those of same-sex attraction. Why does our culture suspect the anti-gay sentiment has its roots in Christian judgementalism? Why does Average Joe's intuition tell him discrimination is the church's fault?

Something occurs at the changeover of worldviews. If a culture used to believe something (such as homosexuality is an invalid lifestyle choice), and then it changes its mind (homosexuality is now a valid lifestyle choice), that creates a tension, an internal conflict, dissonance. How is it that what we now think of as right was within our living memory viewed as wrong? How do you resolve that conflict? A palatable and standard answer is you blame the previous worldview.

It was Christians who encouraged us to be judgemental. Now that we have freed ourselves from the shackles of the CWV, we are less critical, and more enlightened.

It's not just on the topic of same-sex marriage that we see this pattern of blaming the previous era. Take the treatment of Indigenous Australians as another example. Ask Average Joe why the first European settlers treated the Indigenous Australians so poorly, and I suspect the answer will include blaming Christians. There was something arrogant about European

4. Nouwen, *Life of the Beloved*, 123.
5. Cited by Yancey, "Holy Inefficiency," 80.

culture that thought it was more advanced. Christians took indigenous peoples off their land and put them into missions to teach them how to read so that they could read the Bible.

I am not saying this is all inaccurate. Sadly, regrettably, there is some truth to this hunch. But the greater truth is that white pastoralists shot and killed indigenous people. Christian missionaries started mission camps as a way to save indigenous peoples from extinction. Some indigenous languages remain primarily because missionaries translated parts of the Bible into their native language. The belief that European culture was more advanced and that Australia was *terra nullius* found more of its origins in science: in Darwinian evolutionary theories of the day. The first peoples were considered as not yet evolved to the status of being *homo sapiens*. These stories are the more significant part of explaining what happened, yet these details are less told. Why? Because they don't fit with the guilt-relieving narrative that the previous colonial Christian worldview fuelled racism.

The pre-eminent version that a half-truth validates the new worldview by discrediting the old one occurred over 200 years ago. As medieval Europe was coming out of one era into another, two phrases were introduced. Scholars including Voltaire (1694–1778), Hume (1711–1776), Rousseau (1712–1788), Diderot (1713–1784), and Gibbon (1737–1794) started calling the previous era the Dark Ages, and the emerging era the Enlightenment.[6]

The classic story that mocks the superstitious, in-the-dark, people of blind faith as inferior whereas people of science are evidence-seeking, non-religious, and enlightened is the famous account of Galileo. So the story goes, Galileo and Copernicus concluded via science that the earth was round and not at the center of the universe whereas the pope and the church loathed science and believed in a flat earth. The pope had a vested interest in keeping the Bible and not science as the highest source of knowledge. Once the West threw off religion, science and reason could flourish. This is the so-called Copernican Revolution.

Google "spherical earth." The Greeks theorized that the earth was round four hundred years before Jesus. This theory was not lost but became one of two competing theories. Christian history is filled with leaders and thinkers who believed the world was round, including Ambrose and Augustine (fourth century), John Scotus (ninth century), and Aquinas (fourteenth century).

We find the round-earth theory present in popular medieval art and literature. Dante's *Divine Comedy* (from the fourteenth century) has a spherical earth. One historian notes that no author who had studied at a medieval university (usually born and housed in monasteries) thought the earth was flat. Klaus Anselm Vogel says that, since the eighth century,

---

6. Stark, *Triumph of Christianity*, 252.

"no cosmographer worthy of note has called into question the sphericity of the Earth."[7] The oldest physical round globe we have is from 1492, and Galileo wasn't born until 1564!

Did the three popes of Galileo's era believe in a flat earth? Yes, it appears two held to the flat-earth theory. The third seems to have been open to Galileo's research. Galileo was asked to present a more balanced case for both a flat and round earth but he publicly caricatured Pope Urban VIII as *Simplicio* [a name meaning simpleton]. The popes were powerful men from politically savvy Italian families and were not used to being ridiculed. That insult, as much as anything, landed Galileo in prison. How long was he in jail? One day! Then he was transferred to house arrest.

Historians no longer label the Middle Ages as "Dark." Progress, reason, technology, and invention continued to evolve throughout this entire era. As I have previously noted, the scientific method is born within the CWV, not after it. Voltaire, Rousseau, Diderot, Hume and Gibbon made the classic and arrogant mistake of undervaluing the past by calling it the Dark Ages and over-rating the importance of their own era. They imagined they knew better, and others from the previous generation who went before them knew little. Hence they called themselves enlightened.

Richard Dawkins, Christopher Hitchens, and Sam Harris are contemporary versions cut from the same cloth. There is nothing new about the subsequent worldview legitimizing itself by discrediting the previous one. These blame narratives have a way of sounding plausible and rendering the previous one even more implausible.

We find ourselves at a time in history where the narrative that Christians and the church are judgemental, power-hungry, and hypocritical seems plausible and intuitive and is shared by most Average Joes and Joannes. Christians and the church are seen as most to blame for the discrimination experienced by minorities and the inaction against domestic violence and abuse. The church is perceived as anti-progress and anti-progressive.

This narrative is widely held, well-rehearsed, sounds plausible, and fits the cited evidence. This narrative is assumed to be correct but, for the most part, it's untrue. How did we get here? We shall come to that.

Simplicity on the Other Side of Complexity

1. In the CWV, the church had an important social function: to rehearse the shared moral code, and affirm its divine underpinnings. This gave morality objectivity.

7. Vogel, "Sphaera terrae," 19.

2. In the PCWV, the church is seen as power-hungry and self-serving. When the church assumes and expresses its long-held role and provides public moral commentary, this is interpreted as arrogant, a power play, and an attempt to regain the influence it once had.

3. Average Joe is happy for the church to run schools, hospitals, not-for-profit organizations, and church services for those who still need them. Yet he believes that the church is, on certain topics, dangerous. The church pursues its own interests in part by marginalizing and demonizing others. This is the new shared narrative. The church is dangerous and at times needs to be suppressed.

4. The PCWV maintains many of the assumptions of the previous CWV without acknowledging their Christian heritage. However, the PCWV is a hybrid. It has new parts and new symbols.

5. Love used to mean Jesus giving his life for us, dying in our place, and forgiving our sins. Sin mattered. Love and justice are indissoluble. God's demand for justice necessitates a penalty. On the other side of forgiveness, love means Jesus wants the best for us and the best life is a God-and-others-orientated life. Love now means I accept and affirm your right to choose the path you believe is right for you and you allow me to do the same.

6. The church has lost its social function as the one who affirms good and calls out evil. Politicians, comedians, celebrities, and sports stars and codes are stepping into this void.

7. While the church has a reputation for abusing power, less noted is its track record for using its power to serve the common good.

8. Post-Christian, not post-Islamic or post-Buddhist nations, grant same-sex couples the greatest rights. I contend this is evidence that PCWV, as the daughter of the CWV, has recycled particularly Christian beliefs and values such as the dignity of all, tolerance, and freedom.

9. The pattern of blaming the previous worldview for the current sins is well-established. The most striking example is the so-called Copernican Revolution. The idea that Galileo and Copernicus were open-minded early scientists who discovered the earth was round and orbited the sun and that the church and popes opposed science is a myth, constructed by Enlightenment thinkers.

PART TWO

How Did We Get Here?

The PCWV has displaced the CWV. Belief in God, a world with a God-ordained discernible moral fabric and an afterlife used to be standard. It no longer is. The default core beliefs are now that "I am a unique individual, I am the expert on myself, and I am the best person to decide how I will thrive." How did this transition happen?

5

How and Why Did the West
Displace the CWV?

CHRISTIAN BELIEFS AND VALUES have been the foundation of European and Western civilizations for some 1600 years. They were widely held by all citizens, be they Average Joes or Christian Chrises. They facilitated Western cultures to become the most advanced on earth in terms of levels of and access to education, medicine, housing, political stability, just legal systems and human rights, technology, and food security. And yet, the West is abandoning its Christian worldview heritage. How and why has the West moved on?

Even if we break down history into shorter eras: the classical era or antiquity; the (early, high, and late) middle ages; the modern era (or renaissance, enlightenment, post-modernism), however you map it, we are living through the midst of a radical social transition. And, as opposed to previous transitions, we are doing it at warp speed.

A comprehensive overview of how and why we got "here" is beyond this book, and quite frankly, probably beyond me. It is essential, therefore, I focus on the concerns of this chapter. Previously, I outlined the major contours of the emerging PCWV. In this chapter, I shall restrict myself to explaining the dominant causes that sit before each defining contour. Even as I write, I am frustrated. History is better considered as a long and continuous line or interwoven lines, rather than stages, one-off events, and distinct pieces. Still, I believe this chapter, even with its curtailed aspirations, helps us understand our social and historical context to make informed decisions about how to be and do Christianity and church in our new setting.

Trusting and Expressing My "Self"

The thought that we humans are at the center of our universe, and not God, is not a new one. Protagoras in the fifth century BC proclaimed "man is the measure of all things." But where to begin tracing the thread of modern individualism is a vexed question. For now, we shall begin where most historians begin, with René Descartes (1596–1650).

Descartes was a mathematician and a natural philosopher. He combined his two loves and attempted to prove the existence of God using logic and natural philosophy. His famous dictum: "*Cogito ergo sum*—I think therefore I am" is fundamentally individualist. It is an individual who thinks.

In addition to Descartes focusing on the "I," he introduced a subtle but profound shift. Instead of asking what does the Bible say, he asked what can I be certain of? In so doing, he shifted the discourse from truth as revealed by God, to certainty as it can be known in the individual's mind. In essence, I become the knower, the repository and evaluator of knowledge. And I am seeking certainty in my own mind.

The shift sets some kind of precedent. What else can humanity decide? First truth, next morality, good and evil, or the purpose of life? Some people will rush ahead of themselves at this point, declare that this is the thin edge of the wedge, or the beginning of a slippery slope, and we can see where this inevitably will lead. With Aristotle, I am not a fan of the slippery slope argument. All one needs when faced with a slope is a good set of brakes.

More to the point, Descartes did not contend that man gets to decide truth. Truth remains outside of man, grounded in God. Descartes contended that rational man, created in God's image, can use God's gifts of natural law and logic to access God's truth. Then, in his own mind, man can be certain that he now knows God's truth. Nonetheless, a step had taken place, and Rousseau would take a further step.

Jean-Jacques Rousseau (1712–1788) was born over a century after Descartes. Following the Reformation, huge political shifts were afoot across Europe. Popes and kings had less power and elected governments had more. Rousseau was born in Geneva, the very city where John Calvin spent most of his ministry. Rousseau was first a political philosopher, exploring the relationship between the people and the state. Before Rousseau, theorists had prioritized the state's authority over individuals, given the state is the provider of safety, stability, and the protector of human rights.

Rousseau disagreed. His opening line in *The Social Contract* is "Man is born free, and he is everywhere in chains." Modern societies have a way of enslaving, not protecting. The proximity and competition for scarce resources that are part of living in towns and cities cause people to see themselves in rivalry. Greed, pride, comparisons, the desire to overcome, and keeping up with the Joneses are all consequences of modern life that enslave. Society's impacts on individuals are harmful; they lead us away from our true selves.

By contrast, for Rousseau, man is born free. Our natural state is that we are born with intrinsic self-love, and a concern to alleviate the suffering of others. People have an innate sense of justice and virtue. The role of the state and education is to allow these innate virtues to flourish, and to protect children from the negative comparative and competitive influences of society.

Briefly, though less our concern, is what this means for politics. According to Rousseau, nation-states should remain small so that all citizens get a voice. People will come together, bringing their best self-love and innate concern for others, enter into a genuine dialogue, and arrive at a shared mind or "the General Will," as Rousseau calls it. A conclusion is reached where everyone wins.

Still on a tangent, but of more interest to us, is the void between the state and the individual. Rousseau imagined an ideal world in which there were no interest groups. He was nervous about freedom of association, where like-minded people congregate. Interest groups can pre-align or caucus before the meeting, undermining genuine dialogue. Where social institutions exist, their purpose is to facilitate dialogue so that individuals can flourish.

Rousseau envisaged the ideal social order as having only two levels: the individual and the state. He had a deep aversion to gatherings of like-minded groupings lest they become political establishments that engrain a sense of "us" and "them." Once established, he feared, these associations can use their influence to protect the powerful and take advantage of minorities. Rousseau's fears regarding voluntary associations have become the mainstream critique of the church.

Let us return to Rousseau's view of "self." Social interactions have a way of corrupting the self, causing people to become selfish and prideful. We should not define our self by looking around and making comparisons. Instead, we should look inwards to our natural and innate loves.

That idea is dynamite. First, individuals subjectively appropriate certainty (Descartes). Now they subjectively follow their intuitions to clarify and express their personhood (Rousseau). Given we were in the eighteenth century, most will still believe this innate intuition has the fingerprints of God through creation all over it. But another step has been taken.

For now this thought is contained to Continental European Political Theory. These ideas must be popularized and spread around the English speaking world. And they were, through the Romantic poets Wordsworth, Blake, Shelley, and Keats.

Romanticism is a late-eighteenth-century/early-nineteenth-century movement. Following Rousseau, it emphasizes the beauty of nature, the uncontaminated and innocence of children and youth, the pursuit of ideals, emotions, and personal, authentic feelings. This was contrasted with the cold, rational, exploitative, and controlling monarchy, church, and industrial cities. The battle lines between the haves and the have-nots, the exploiters and the exploited, the victimizers and the victims are being drawn. The Romantics were anti-establishment and gave voice to the poor "chimney sweeps," "fallen" women, returned soldiers, and the insane. Marginal individuals matter.

The Obsession with Power

The reasoning of Rousseau and the Romantics plants another seed. Expressive marginalized individuals (the dominant theme) must be protected from the powerful (the lesser theme). Power as the key theme, as an obsession, finds its sharpest expression in Karl Marx, and those who follow after him. Marx (1818–1883) was a German philosopher and economist who became one of the three fathers of sociology. Remember that for Marx, history is driven by competition for limited material resources.

Marx was the champion at dividing history into stages. History begins with an ideal stage Marx called "primitive communism." Imagine a hunter-gatherer tribe, where no one owns anything and everyone shares everything. Not unlike Rousseau, Marx idealized the simple and natural. One day, this tribe bumps into another tribe, they compete for berries, and eventually they have a war. One tribe wins and enslaves survivors from the other tribe.

Now, and at every future stage of history, there are two groups of people. Those who have control of the material factors of production and those who do not. Those who control labor (slave owners) and those who do not (slaves). Then something happens to upset this equilibrium. Someone works out we can farm and herd animals. This gives way to the next stage: feudalism. Feudalism also has two groups: landowners and serfs. Feudalism is followed by capitalism, where we have factory owners (a.k.a. bourgeoisie), and factory workers (a.k.a. proletariat). Marx imagined two more stages: socialism and communism. By now you have the idea. Two groups in a stable pattern (the thesis), then a new competing factor causes transition (the antithesis), which gives rise to a new order, the next stage (synthesis or new thesis).

Marxism was incredibly influential in the early and middle parts of the twentieth century. Two factors saw its downfall. The first was the growth of the middle class. This phenomenon did not fit neatly into Marx's binary scheme. It was a third class, neither working class nor ruling class. The second and final nail in Marxism was the failure of Communist Russia, or the USSR. Under Mikhail Gorbachev, socialism imploded in 1991, and we got, not communism as the final utopia, but instead fragile capitalism. This simple and yet profound theory lost its credibility.

Or not. Before its demise as an economic theory, Marxism influenced other academic disciplines because of its simplicity and explanatory power. In historical discourse, it became common to read all history as a series of unified and connected stages. In social change, the Marxist (actually he stole this part from Hegel) framework of thesis–antithesis–new synthesis became a standard lens to frame and interpret transitions. This brings us to the ongoing influence of Marx in philosophy.

Two thinkers in particular who interacted with Marxist thought are of interest to us: Jacques Derrida (1930–2004) and Michel Foucault (1926–1984). Both became critical drivers in an influential period of French philosophy in the 1960s. All I shall comment on is the important legacy of these thinkers. Derrida is the father of deconstruction. He sought to show that history, indeed words and their meaning, are all built upon the condition of "repeatability." To understand what I am saying, you must assume that when I use words, I mean something similar by those words as I did when I previously used them. But "repeatability" is an abstract notion, not actually present in this moment. Oddly, deconstructionism rules any philosophical position invalid because it fails against its own criterion. All we have is constructions built on words and assumptions. But they are a façade, which cannot be trusted as fitting this moment or transferable to the next.

Foucault's focus regards knowledge and power. Knowledge is never alone and neutral. In his words "Knowledge is not for knowing: knowledge is for cutting." Knowledge is an instrument used by a person on another. I tell you something because I desire to influence you with that knowledge.

Put Derrida and Foucault together into a Marxist mould, and you get something like this: all knowledge, all use of words and language, all systems of thought are constructs of the powerful. They are using words, ideas, and knowledge to maintain the status quo to their advantage. It is power, not the material factors of production, that is the key to understanding history, power that is expressed through narratives and ideas and abused by the powerful to perpetuate the exploitation of the masses.

At this point, you may think this is philosophical nonsense. Arts students at university may debate this while sharing a joint, but nobody in the real world thinks like this. The problem is that what Arts students think today, everyone thinks within less than a generation.

What about the gender debate? It is argued that the construct or word "male" is created to exclude "females." Even worse, the binary of "male–female" is created to exclude LGBTI+ people. Now the Bible says, "So God created mankind in his own image, in the image of God he created them; male and female he created them" (Gen 1:27). In this text, so it is argued, words and ideas are fashioned, normalized, and then used by the powerful to exclude and discriminate.

Other words do the same thing. Good and evil, creator and creation, white and colored, chosen and those under judgement, heaven and hell. They are all words and ideas that are remnants of the now-debunked CWV. They were always a power play, but we now know better.

Does Average Joe get all this? My teenage daughter certainly does. She told me recently that the categories of parent and child only exist so that parents can make biased decisions in favour of themselves. The words "parent" and "child" are mere constructs. They are power plays. I immediately call to mind the concrete realities of procreation and biology, years of changing nappies, feeding, of paying for clothes and schooling.

My daughter thinks this way, in part, because this is how she learned to read and interpret texts in high school English. Shakespeare saw things the way he did because he was a product of the sixteenth century. My views are a product of my culture and my desire to maintain my interests. But we no longer think that way because we now know better. Average Joe vaguely gets this, but his kids are coached in this way of thinking.

Can you see how deconstructionism and a neurotic fear of power function as a critique? Its insights have become loosely accepted. Some of us may wish to push back: aren't words and ideas, including the words "construction," "deconstruction," and "the powerful," also a construct/power play? Derrida would agree but at this point, you will have lost Average Joe.

The Inward Turn

In addition to its obsession with deconstructing the previously powerful, our culture has also experienced a decided turn inwards. Once again, we can hear the echoes of Descartes and, most loudly, Rousseau. The inwards turn is also a turn away from reason, logic, and historically held arguments. Instead, trust your intuition, feelings, and get in touch with your unique passions. From where has this come?

In the CWV, while there is a consciousness of both the inward and outward (think about Paul in Romans 7: a wretched man struggling with two inner voices), the orientation was more outwards. God made a real physical world with a discernible moral fabric. Jesus' life and the Bible are concrete repositories for wisdom and the good life. One finds direction by looking out towards them. The CWV also had a shared belief in a God who judges with love and justice, and our choices in this life determine our eternal destiny. Motivation for living the good life was found by looking outwards and towards the future.

None of this is to deny that the CWV affirmed a place for introspection. It was believed that God had set eternity in the hearts of humanity (Eccl 3:11). The Apostle Paul talks of how even "Gentiles, [those] who do not have the law, do by nature things required by the law" (Rom 2:14). Augustine wrote the first self-reflective text in about 400 AD. Humans have an innate intuition about what constitutes "good," but these could be both verified and clarified by reference to the external objective source—God's Word.

The balance has shifted. In the PCWV, one looks inwards first. How did this shift take place? The sentiment is present in Rousseau, and popularized in the writings of Wordsworth, Blake, Shelley, and Keats, authors who were common in generations of high school texts.

The emergence of psychology enhanced the inward turn, following Sigmund Freud (1856–1939) and Carl Jung (1875–1961). Modern psychology began in the mid- to late 1800s. Freud was its first famous practitioner, though not the founding father.

Freud likened the human mind to an iceberg. On the surface, we have conscious thoughts and perceptions. Below the surface, we have a vast mass of subconscious and unconscious thoughts and feelings. These are the more significant part of the mind, and they drive the greater part of behavior.

One part of the unconscious mind Freud called the "id." These are our instincts or drives. Freud is most known for postulating that sexual instincts propel much of human behavior. Besides sexual drive, aggression is the other unconscious instinct. These base instincts are controlled or mediated through different parts of our personality. Namely the "ego," which seeks to fulfil the id's desires in socially acceptable ways, and the "superego," which is like a moral, socially responsible parent. It sometimes says no, or wait.

Freud saw life as developing through a series of stages and relationships. Later, Jean Piaget (1896–1980) became the champion of stages of development psychology. We will come to him; he is also significant. For Freud, various things needed to happen at each stage so a person will mature into a functioning adult. Things such as falling in love with, then out of love with, your parent. If something goes wrong at one of these foundational stages and a person experiences repression or denial, this will play out later in adulthood as a dysfunction.

Another critical element of Freud's work is the importance of dreams. This is the space where our subconscious thoughts come closest to the surface where we can access them. Our dreams expose our desires, or what Freud calls "wish fulfilment." The analysis of dreams involves understanding how the various elements of "self" interact. Is this part of my dream the instinctive id speaking? Or the restraining ego? Or the responsible superego? Having brought these elements into the conscious realm, the individual can then make lucid decisions about moving out of the repressed state and into expression.

Jung's theories are similar to Freud's. He agreed we are like icebergs. He agreed we have generalized energy that motivates all human behavior, but he did not limit it to sex and aggression. He agreed that the unconscious is a large and significant part of the mind and a storehouse for repressed memories. And he agreed past experiences shape present and future behaviors.

He is different because he believed our storehouse of shared memories is not just personal experiences (as Freud did). Jung also believed we have something called a collective unconscious. We share these thoughts and feelings with all humanity. They originate from our ancestral and evolutionary past. Think of our instincts, or fear of snakes or heights as an example.

Jung identified constant patterns present in all individuals that flow from our collective unconscious. He called these "archetypes." These include concepts such as the shadow, the dark but creative side of our self; the anima, the yin yang pull we feel towards the opposite sex; the tree of life, which we unknowingly continue to celebrate annually in Christmas trees; and the self, the notion that I am a unified bundle of thoughts and experiences that makes a person. Vocal new atheist Sam Harris's latest book, *Waking Up*, is a recent rehash of this type of thinking. He frames the human inclination to spirituality as innate. Different religions are merely historical collective responses to that innate human inclination.

Combined, Freud and Jung underwrote three features of the PCWV. The first is that the path to enlightenment is an inward path. Having phrased it like this, you might think that this sounds like Buddhism. Isn't Buddhism the great faith of enlightenment through introspection? Yes, but Buddhism is about the enlightenment of the human condition and its relationship to suffering, desire, and the end of desire as the end to suffering. Freud sets you up to understand yourself, your sexual drives, your wishes, and their relationship to your experiences, memories, and subconscious.

Freud combined with Jung means that some of your concerns are more common, more shared, not just your own. Somehow, within you, that combination of the universal shared memory and the unique makes you an individual. A good part of that memory and identity, for Freud especially, has to do with sexuality. The path to enlightenment is an inward path.

Second, Freud and Jung explain the motivation to act. Many psychological theories focus on exploring what a person does. Most struggle to explain why we do anything at all. Freud had an answer for that. We have a deep innate drive to have sex, to procreate and ensure the survival of our gene pool. Or, as it is now put, to express our sexual identity. Conversely, aggression is the counterpart instinct, often directed at those we view as rivals. Jung's answer includes our sexual drive, but imagines a more generalized energy beyond the sexual.

Third, Freud and Jung provide a framework that begins to explain morality without reference to God. For Freud, it will take us down a path of how one must behave in public to be able to fulfill one's id-driven desires for sex. For Jung, it will take us down the same path, and simultaneously, a wider path that gives expression to our deeper collective unconsciousness. This will provide clues and frameworks for how we construct a corporate morality.

A more contemporary expression of this thinking would be Richard Dawkins' book, *The Selfish Gene,* which explores the concepts of "social Darwinism." Humanity, as a species, has a shared memory that if we look out for each other, we all fare better. Cooperation is a virtue that evolves between persons as a kind of mutual selfishness.

Self-Actualization as a Worthy Ambition

A third discernible dimension, yet still following Rousseau, is the shift in the PCWV towards finding and expressing oneself as a path to flourishing. Though somewhat technical, we shall use the term "self-actualization" to capture this idea. In the CWV, people follow the path of Jesus, who came not to be served but to serve. Self-actualization is frowned upon because of its egotistical focus. It is in loving God and our neighbor that we find ourselves. Feelings of self-fulfilment are not wrong, but they are not the primary goal. Rather they are a by-product of serving God and others.

From where does the justification for our more recent desire for self-actualization come? How is it that our culture now views self-actualization as a worthy ambition, and not just as selfishness with a fancy name?

Let us return to Freud. He proposed a natural progression through various stages that each individual must pass through to become a fully functioning adult.

Jung expressed similar ideas. The collective unconscious gives a series of symbols and archetypes we must engage with to grow to maturity. We must all move away from darkness towards the light. That path is highlighted if we listen to a wise older woman or man, who is often in the vicinity of the tree of life. We must all pass through seasons of death and rebirth, symbolized with the waters of floods and/or baptisms. We are incomplete for this journey without our biological other.

To this I will now add the work of Piaget, the developmental psychologist. Piaget theorized that all children must pass through four stages of cognitive development. The precise details of Piaget's stages, and what alterations subsequent psychologists may have made to his theory, are not pertinent to us. It is what we have done with Piaget that is relevant.

Young aspirational parents buy parenting books that outline the stages of development. They then observe their children to see if they are age-appropriate, or advanced. Parents even become intentional about crafting pre-school learning opportunities to create as many neural pathways as possible in their children. The assumption here is that children have an inherent potential. It is the task of the parent to ensure children achieve their full potential. The actualization of full potential is seen as a success, whereas anything less is a failure.

Self-actualization is taking this thinking one step further. If my parents invested in me to help me achieve my potential, and if that is a worthwhile goal, does it not make sense that I continue to invest in myself to reach my full potential?

The Market as a Neutral Space That Provides Choices

Earlier, I suggested that one Western value is that the market is a neutral space. Purchasing, consuming, amassing goods is neither good nor bad. It is simply an expression of our choices. The function of the economy then is to provide a never-ending diversity of consumables. We now find ourselves in economic theory.

Behind such ideas sits the economic theories of Adam Smith (1723–1790). Smith is known as both the father of capitalism and the father of economics. Being a Renaissance man, he dabbled in more than just one discipline. His first published book was actually about moral philosophy, mutual empathy in particular.[1]

Smith's second work considered the opposite side of the coin. Here he argued that individual self-interest drives the economy. "It is not from the

---

1. Smith, *Theory of Moral Sentiments.*

benevolence of the butcher, the brewer, or the baker, that we expect our din-ner, but from their regard to their own interest. We address ourselves, not to their humanity but to their self-love, and never talk to them of our own necessities but of their advantages."[2]

Smith called this notion "the invisible hand," and this part of his think-ing has received greater emphasis since the 1950s. When both consumers and producers are allowed to act out of self-interest, the free market has a way of setting a price for goods and services, and simultaneously stimulat-ing productivity. This is the so-called "invisible hand" at work. Self-interest boosts productivity and sets a market price.

Broadly speaking, such approaches to economics are called economic liberalism. Neoliberalism, which places even more emphasis on the pri-vate sector than government spending, has been popular in most Western economies recently. Key advocates of this approach include Ronald Reagan, Margaret Thatcher, John Howard, and Peter Costello.

In the previous CWV, and oddly also the Marxist view of the world, we had an obligation to share limited resources with the other, with our neighbor. In the neoliberal approach, there are no negative consequences or side effects to my choice to consume. If anything, the harder I work, the more I choose and consume, the better it is for both me and the entire economy. A rising tide lifts all boats.

Globalism

I have previously mentioned globalism. In the past, cultures were more isolated from each other. Each culture was more self-contained. When the CWV held to a shared consensus that something was self-evidently true—that everyone agreed on this topic—we tended not to encounter those who thought differently. Now we are increasingly aware that ours is but one perspective from which to look at things.

Let's consider a couple of examples. As Westerners, we are concerned with time and with punctuality. If you travel overseas, you soon become aware that other places run on "African" or "Island" time. In Island time, things happen when they happen, not at a pre-determined hour or minute.

As Westerners, telling the truth is important for us. Lies are statements that don't align with the facts. It is wrong to lie. For most Asian cultures, the correct answer to a question brings honor to one's elders or family. Truth is more about honoring relationships than facts.

2. Smith, *Wealth of Nations*, 17.

The World Wide Web is also a significant factor in globalism. In the past, we lived in more homogenous, insulated communities. Now, on the internet, you can find evidence for almost anything and everything. Accepted facts are questionable. The views of the fringe can be made to appear mainstream and plausible. The internet provides a place where people from a shared narrow perspective can meet and reinforce each other's preconceptions. There are online communities for holocaust deniers, for climate skeptics, for both pro-anorexia and pro-obesity persons.

Globalism and the internet sit behind three phenomena of the PCWV. The first is relativism. Less and less is absolute, and more and more things are just opinions. The second is fragmentation. We can retreat into tribes, an echo chamber or thought bubble, where we talk to and hear from people with similar views to our own. Combine opinions with tribes, and you get "fake news." On certain topics, like climate change, the risks of vaccinations, or the origins of a pandemic, the search for one objective truth is often abandoned. Instead, we settle for the reality that partial knowledge is held by rival groups, all of whom offer competing truth claims. Complete truth is elusive.

Christian to Post-Christian Drift

Apart from my initial reference to Descartes, I have outlined influences and ways of thinking external to Christianity. I have detailed how forces such as globalism, free-market economics, psychology, and deconstructionism have come from the "outside" and challenged the CWV.

Having said this, I subscribe to the view that core, perhaps even the most defining, features of the PCWV are precisely that: post-Christian. They are a drift or evolution of thinking birthed from within the CWV, but they have moved beyond it—a daughter who has forgotten her mother.

As we saw in chapter 1, central to the PCWV is the notion of a free and autonomous individual who can make choices, to choose to live within God's moral fabric. To see Jesus as some type of a role model and try to imitate his values. At this moment, I wish to ask, free and autonomous from what or who?

If you were not conversant with history, you might think the current push for freedom is about freedom from power. Perhaps the strongest holder and worst abuser of power has been the church. So freedom is about being free from the moralism of the church. This, I suggest, is the image of freedom deep within the DNA of Western culture. It is the assumption of Average Joe. He imagines two opposites: either I decide, or the church decides what is right.

Are religion and individualism enemies? Will restraining religion's voice and influence result in increased empowerment of the individual?

History would answer, no! Evidence demonstrates that anti-religious thinking does not lead to valuing the individual. There have been four recent attempts at anti-religious states. Following the dictum of Marx, that religion is the opium of the masses, all four were communist: China under Chairman Mao, Russia under Joseph Stalin, Cambodia under Pol Pot, and North Korea under Kim Il-Sung. None of these countries championed the rights of the individual. On the contrary, all abused them. Conversely, the USA is the most individualistic country globally, and it has high rates of Christian affiliation.

From where does our appreciation of the free and autonomous individual come? Anthropologically thinking, it is common to place individualism on one side of the spectrum, and collectivism on the other. In this sense, individualism focuses on the "I," and collectivism on the "we."

Let us conduct a thought experiment. What type of cultures fundamentally understand or arrange people as individuals, as detached persons? And what sort of cultures understand themselves as tightly knit extended family networks, which so happen to have people in them?

Geert Hofstede's cultural dimensions theory follows this approach. In 2013, his research found that the top six ranking nations indexed as individualistic were (in order): USA, Australia, UK, Canada, Hungary equal with the Netherlands, then New Zealand. Predominantly Protestant nations made up sixteen of the top twenty ranked countries.[3] There is an obvious, undeniable link between individualism and (historical) Protestantism. Put another way, it appears that individualism somehow connects to a belief in God, or at least the Protestant emphasis of God.

If you know something about the history of Protestantism, this fits. Martin Luther (1483–1586) chose to stand up against the collective authority of the Catholic Church. He championed beliefs such as the individual being saved by grace; that individuals can directly approach God direct through Christ, not through a priest ordained by the church; that God's Spirit indwells, empowers and enlightens individuals. Those individuals can interpret the Bible; this is not the sole domain of the Catholic Church or its councils or popes. Church councils (a collective) can err.

Luther was put on trial for such teachings and excommunicated from the Catholic Church. His often quoted (but disputed) response to the charge

---

3. Hofstede et al., *Cultures and Organizations*, 95–97.

of heresy was, "Here I stand, I can do no other, so help me God." Whether or not Luther actually said these words is a tangent, as are debates as to the extent to which Luther himself could be called an individualist.

The critical point here is that Luther and his fellow Protestants emphasized the biblical theme of the individual, made in God's image, as morally responsible and capable of autonomous actions. Protestant European nations, and the countries they have colonized, absorbed this core belief of the individual as made in God's image, capable of making a stand for what they believe in (even against the church) as central to their ideology. The equality and dignity of all humanity and autonomous individualism originated in CWV beliefs and values.

The Protestant Reformation facilitated a shift towards individualism in a second way. Before the Reformation, everyone belonged to the one Catholic Church. Afterwards, you could be Catholic, or Lutheran, or in time Presbyterian, Baptist, or even a non-attender. Religious affiliation became a consequence of personal convictions and choices.

Descartes was a Christian thinker. He moved to Protestant Holland, where he could be free from persecution for his ideas. The faith status of Rousseau is questionable, remember he was born and raised in Reformed Calvinist Geneva. His views align with many facets of the CWV beliefs and values.

What type of individual freedom did the CWV give rise to? It is a freedom to act and choose. It was a freedom from either the social collective or even the sovereign God who pre-ordains everything. It was a freedom from a life of simple submission to the will of God (as in Islam), or constantly trying to appease God (as in Hinduism, popular Buddhism, and most basic animistic religions). Sure, there are boundaries. Specific choices are declared out of bounds. But within these bounds, freedom is vested in the individual to choose.

Marriage is a great example. There are boundaries. Christians ought not to marry their parent, siblings, people who are already married to others, people of another religion, or persons of the same sex. But beyond that, there is freedom. God does not choose for you, nor do your parents, nor the village religious leader/matchmaker. The individual chooses a life partner for themselves. Christian marriage is something "voluntarily entered into." The Western Christian marriage liturgy enshrines the right of the individual to consent.

The CWV of freedom is freedom within boundaries. The PCWV has taken another step beyond this. Individual freedom means the right to stand up against the church and the established norms and values. The center of human dignity remains invested in the individual. Reference to a divine spark or the image of God as a grounding for this dignity is waning. Precisely why and how the individual continues to be dignified is unclear, to me at least. It is just taken to be self-evident.

What I am arguing is this. The prevailing Western worldview, the one assumed by Average Joe, believes in free and dignified individuals but the foundations for why individuals are dignified, and why they deserve freedom has not come from some new external source. I am aware of no new argument explaining why individuals are dignified, or ought to be free.

In the CWV, choice is esteemed because God gives humanity the freedom to choose him. Loving, worshipping and obeying your creator is the highest and most valid expression of being a free creature. Why is choice important in the PCWV? Who cares if I choose an iPhone or Samsung, if I choose to be vegetarian, vegan, or carnivore?

I contend that the PCWV now emphasizes *who* gets to choose, not *what* they choose. Empowerment of all, especially the previously victimized; freedom to choose anything so long as it does no harm; self-expression of my inner passions, leading to authenticity and increased self-esteem—these are the highest ideals that a modern society needs to enshrine and protect.

This shift from freedom to choose (the what) within bounds was the CWV value; to freedom for everyone (the who) as empowerment is the modified PCWV freedom. Does the new modified freedom measure up?

Let's test this with another thought experiment. If I am free to choose, imagine my passion is playing Fortnite or another online game. What if I decide that being an expert in online gaming is the best expression of my identity? What if I choose to spend all of my disposable income purchasing Fortnite skins? Are those valid choices? Intuitively most will say, no! On what grounds? It is my passion. It does no harm. I can make a living from it. I am not sure how the PCWV argues against the Fortnite fanatic.

This is my point. Freedom and human dignity are Christian values, which have been modified and brought forward into the subsequent worldview. But in this PCWV, these values remain somewhat unhinged, disconnected, and non-focused.

I would argue that the values of progress and reason are similar. Christianity has within it the idea that all of human history moves from God and returns to God. Jesus talks about bringing the Kingdom, or about God's will being done here on earth. There is a moral "oughtness" that fits within the CWV. Progress was part of humanity using its freedom, its God-given, God-imitating capacity for reason, to bring peace and order to as many people as possible. Progress and reason were integrated into an entire worldview package.

Progress and reason remain as post-Christian values in our post-Christian culture, but it is unclear why they remain, and how they now fit with other parts of culture. For example, we agree screening for early stages of breast or prostate cancer is a good thing. Older people like that part of technology. But in the next breath, they may bemoan having to do electronic banking to function in the modern world. Can I choose not to immunize my children? Can I choose not to have a work email address? What if I then buy a watch that receives emails; is that progress? What if I like this watch, but my spouse does not? Why can't I teach my children to do maths on an abacus? My point is that we still believe in reason and progress, but lack a coherent shared story that helps us work out which new things are a step forward or backwards, and why.

This shall suffice as a preliminary list of the influences that drive the PCWV. Externally, the phenomena of globalism, free-market economics, introspective psychology, and deconstructionism have displaced the traditional Christian narrative. In its place, no new intellectual frameworks underpin our emerging worldview. Having said this, much of PCWV is precisely that: Post-Christian. Many of its features are the remnants that linger from the CWV, such as individualism, freedom and autonomy, progress, universal health and education, and reason.

What I have not done is tracked how these forces operate together. For instance, if you add individualism and free-market economics together and remove moral oughtness, you get Ikea. I can spend my hard-earned money on whatever I want, and no-one can tell me I can't. If I want to update all my furniture every eight years and cause excessive waste, I can.

If you add freedom and individualism and introspective psychology together, you get very liberal views of assisted suicide. If I can't see any hope or point in my future, and I have the right to choose what is best for me, then who are you tell me what I can and cannot do? I will leave you to reflect on your insights as to what various combinations of the above can produce.

Thus far we have seen that our culture deconstructs the church as power hungry and has found alternate philosophies to undermine parts of the previous worldview and underwrite the modifications. Yet some CWV values remain, in ways that are disconnected from their Christian scaffolding.

All this leads to an obvious question. What have we lost? What happens if you kill off parts of the CWV and maintain other parts but fail to underwrite those parts by retelling and subscribing to their grand narrative? What happens when you remove God from the story? Do you free humanity? Or do you unleash the beast? Let's consider this question through the eyes of Nietzsche.

Nietzsche: What Happens When You Declare God Is Dead?

Friedrich Nietzsche (1844–1900) was a German philosopher whose most famous quote is "God is Dead." When we hear this quote, we assume Nietzsche was a forerunner of Dawkins, Hitchens and Harris, that he was an early version of an atheist who argues for the death of God. Then when he reaches that conclusion, he pops the champagne and celebrates. This is untrue, and unhelpful.

Instead, Nietzsche announced that God is dead because science has outgrown superstition. We now know the world follows the patterns of natural laws. We no longer view events as the result of divine providence or intervention. God as an explanation of events is unnecessary. The enlightened world will leave God behind as a child leaves their teddy bear.

The opposite of religion for Nietzsche (this is the really important bit) is not atheism, but nihilism. What you risk losing when God is declared dead is meaning. If there is no God, life has (or perhaps risks having) no meaning or direction, there is no morality, and reason is an unhelpful human invention. Big calls. Let us unpack each claim.

If there is a God, and we come from him, and we are moving towards him, human actions have consequences for our relationship with him. Our destiny is with him, or apart from him. If all that is true, then life has a purpose. God is at the beginning as the author and the end as the father who welcomes us home. All the parts in between find their bearings within that grand movement. An action is moral if it aligns with God's intended purposes and moves us towards him as the ultimate good. Likewise, reason is reasonable in as much as it aligns with the God who is all truth.

If there is no God, then the reference points are removed. If there is no original author, then there is no theme to the story. The story just is. It is not coming from or going anywhere. It is meaningless. Actions just are. They are neither good nor bad, moral nor immoral. Actions are just the outworking of evolutionary instincts or personal opinions. What we assume to be reasonable or logical is merely the view of the dominant group that happens to have survived. However, survival and truth/logic are not the same thing. Future survival might be aided by the dominant group being deceptive.

For Nietzsche, religion is like blinkers on a horse. They focus the horse so it runs in a particular direction, free from distraction. In one sense, the horse is better off without the blinkers because it can see things it could not previously see. But who knows where the horse will go once you remove the blinkers? Why bother finishing the race or even agreeing to the idea that we are in a thing called a race? Why can't the horse stop and eat grass? Do as it pleases? Or choose to do nothing at all?

Nietzsche's analysis of the dilemma for any post-religious or post-Christian culture is astute. He powerfully and insightfully cuts to the heart of the matter. The CWV was a coherent entity that had the capacity to make sense of meaning, morality, and reason. What happens if you dissect parts and try to keep them as separate? Can they be sustained apart from the source?

This is a big question that many people are trying to answer. Stark, Sheridan, Williams, Holland, Trueman and Mangalwadi agree with Nietzsche; the CWV did offer meaning, coherence, and more. Whatever we do, let's not discard it lightly.

The PCWV offers other answers. The response of Marx and the political left is to affirm religion as the opium of the people that prevents them from seeing and makes them addicted to the status quo. Rise up, comrades! Embrace the next utopia called socialism! We don't need God (or the church claiming to speak for God) to tell us and then co-opt us to care for each other. Sharing will flow naturally out of our human nature; we do not need coaxing.

Rousseau made similar claims. If we could just lay aside our greed and competitiveness, come together and listen, engage in genuine dialogue, listen to our inner voice of self- and other-person love, then we would rediscover something close to the ideal state of nature.

Derrida and Foucault agreed that power is abused by the powerful. This is the greatest of evils. Power is at its most dangerous when it is in the hands of the institution. Whatever else may come, we must disarm power-hungry institutions like the church.

The death of God potentially opens the door to nihilism. But Jung believed we can secure a collective morality, meaning, and truth by another means, by reference to our collective unconscious, by our primal need for and response to the fundamental archetypes.

Freud agreed that religion is a collective expression of the superego (internalized cultural norms). We have a human need to control, belong, and survive as a species. Religion organizes and legitimizes our superego but does it in a dangerous, inclusive-versus-exclusive way. Freud was a Jew who lived in Germany through the rise of Nazism and anti-Semitism. For Freud, we are better off thinking about morality as an internal struggle between the id and ego. It is more accurate to view the search for meaning as the outworking of wish fulfillment.

For Neo-Freudians, if we express ourselves, which is essentially a sexual self, we will find happiness and contentment.

You can see how the responses of Rousseau, Marx, Freud, Jung, Derrida, and Foucault to the dilemma posed by Nietzsche capture much of how the PCWV has sought to navigate around the obstacles one faces when you leave God out of the picture. Has it, or is it working?

Is the PCWV Working?

Before I address this question, I offer two qualifiers. The primary purpose of this book is not to critique the PCWV. Instead, it is to describe and explain it so that you can understand it. Then you can make informed decisions about how to live as a Christian, be a Christian parent, teacher, or youth leader, be the local church, or the church as an institution, given we now inhabit a different world. I have thus far restrained myself from critiquing the PCWV. I will briefly do so now for one reason.

As I shall argue later, discipleship is not as simple as just teaching the gospels and telling people to follow Jesus. When youth were raised with the CWV, they were socialized to believe in a loving, caring, just God; in right and wrong; in the good life, best exemplified by Jesus; and in an afterlife. Being a practicing Christian meant taking this stuff seriously: being full on, having a living relationship with Jesus, reading God's word, regularly gathering together with other followers of Jesus to encourage one another.

Those raised within the PCWV are being socialized to believe that there is likely some vague spiritual dimension to the universe. The new consensus is that you need to look inwards to decide what is true for you. You should not follow another, but instead follow your internal compass and chase your dreams, because it is in this space you will flourish. If and when you sense that Jesus's example or teachings will help you on this journey, then you can decide to include that in your journey. But it's your journey, and others are on theirs. You ought to respect and empower others' journeys, and we will all flourish and get along, and the world will be a better place.

Discipleship now has new challenges. The baseline Christian assumptions on which discipleship was built are no longer widely held. We cannot assume that youth hold to the basic building blocks such as there is a knowable God, who defines right and wrong, who reveals himself, and who is a loving yet just judge. Nor can we assume that the children and youth we are presently trying to disciple have not absorbed the new post-Christian assumptions. Discipleship into the future will need to teach an entire cohesive Christian worldview intentionally. Furthermore, it will need to critique the PCWV. I offer my following critique as a beginning to the second part of that curriculum: naming the idols of our day.

Here is my second qualifier. When the CWV had a status of being shared and assumed, if someone attacked it, Christians felt compelled to defend it. Apologetics defended the existing assumptions then built upon them by encouraging people to believe in and move towards God.

In the PCWV, shared assumptions about God between Christians and non-Christians no longer exist. No longer can Christians assume everyone believes in a knowable God who defines right and wrong, reveals himself, and is a loving and just judge. In short, we have lost the plausible home ground advantage. We will feel attacked and, given 1600 years of habitual defending, our inclination is to defend the faith against attack and do apologetics in ways that are similar to how we did it in a more Christian era.

In debating terms, this is called accepting the burden of proof. We quickly find ourselves defending the claims that God knows better than humans do, that we are sinners in need of forgiveness, that church is more than a power-hungry, abusive institution.

My contention is this. As we disciple young Christians, part of what we need to do includes deconstructing the PCWV by showing where its flaws are and why it is not a progression of thinking, but a regression in many of its core assumptions. In debating terms, we do not just accept that in a religious discussion our task is to defend belief in only one God. Instead, at times, we need to present arguments that challenge the new consensus. The PCWV does not know better. We need to ask Average Joe to accept the burden of proof and defend his assumptions.

In this spirit, here is my brief attempt to begin a deconstruction of the PCWV.

Deconstructing the PCWV

At the center of the PCWV is individualism. Is a person best understood as an individual entity, free from the influence of others, capable of making autonomous choices? Let us try some thought experiments.

Imagine you wake up tomorrow morning and you are the only person in the world. Everyone else has not only died, but they have also disappeared. There is no trace of anyone. You could now live anywhere you wished, just move in. After all, no one can stop you. You could drive any car you desired. If you lived in Australia, would you move into Kirribilli House, the prime minister's residence in Sydney, under the Harbour Bridge? If you lived in England, would you move into Buckingham Palace? Would you choose to drive a Ferrari?

The answer is likely no. Humans expend much energy trying to own a more impressive house and drive a more prestigious car. They are not just modes of transport or residences; they are status symbols. Yet if there was

no one to impress, we would not choose them. Conclusion: we are not autonomous, free from the influence of others. Instead we are social animals.
Our actions are shaped by what we think others think of us.

Here's another thought experiment. Imagine your spouse, partner, or
some significant other you know well has a windfall and receives a payout.
Imagine they already have excessive income, or insufficient income. Could
you trust them to make the wisest financial decisions? Would they buy something that they didn't need, such as a new pair of shoes, when they already
have fifteen pairs? Would they maintain a habit or an expense that was simply no longer warranted, like buying an expresso hit most days?

As I think about the people I know the best in my life, I can see in
each of them orientations, fixations, weaknesses, and inclinations that are
unnecessary and excessive, at times even counter-productive. I do not
think they always know what is best for themselves. They see themselves
from a bias. They are not the best judge of themselves. Why would I imagine I am any different from them?

Is empowering others so that they can make the right choice for
themselves, so long as it does not hurt anyone else, a good way to make
ethical decisions? Imagine if I won the lotto and suddenly have access to
serious funds that I did not previously. Can I decide to use those funds to
take up gambling as a hobby? Imagine if I lost all recent windfall funds,
then I stopped gambling. It's my choice. No one was hurt or worse off than
before. How could that be wrong?

How do we define "good," if the quest of existence is about living the
good life? Are people best positioned to decide for themselves? Is their personal sense of pleasure and fulfillment a good measure? Mark Manson's *The
Subtle Art of Not Giving a F**** made number one on the *New York Times
Bestseller* list in 2017. He writes,

> Pleasure is a false god. Research shows that people who focus
> their energy on superficial pleasures end up more anxious, more
> emotionally unstable, and more depressed. Pleasure is the most
> superficial form of life satisfaction and therefore the easiest to
> obtain and the easiest to lose . . . . Pleasure is not the cause of
> happiness; rather, it is the effect.[4]

Are self-esteem and self-actualization the best paths to personal fulfilment? With Manson, I can't see that. Statistically speaking, most people will
not be able to chase their dreams and be a world-beater at their chosen
thing. Most people will, statistically, and by definition, be ordinary. The high

4. Manson, *Subtle Art*, 82.

achievers I know tend to be high achievers in one part of their life at the cost of being less functional in other parts of their lives.

When I went to my daughter's debutante ball (an end-of-high-school becoming-an-adult dinner), the most common goal of her fellow students was to be professional sportsmen and women. As far as I know, none of them succeeded. Even if one or two did, current and retired sporting professionals are more vulnerable to mental health concerns. The most likely outcome of chasing your dreams is disappointment, non-achievement, and possible mental health and addiction struggles if you do make it. Are we not asking the next generation to satisfy their souls and quench their thirst by drinking from a poisoned chalice?

As our culture has outlined healthy (by which it means assured and optimistic) self-esteem and expressing your identity as the path to flourishing, sexuality has taken on the mantle of being the most core and ultimate expression of your identity. Can it bear that weight? Are more sexually expressive and active people happier? It does not appear to be the case. Self-restraint used to be a virtue. Freud reframed sexual self-restraint as repression. Is there no insight behind the Buddhist monk, or the life of an ascetic in antiquity, as a higher mode of being?

Why is sexuality now the essence of being? Surely I am more than my sexuality? If, as an older male, I suffer from prostate cancer, have an operation, and can no longer achieve erection, am I less of a person? Am I less of a husband? Is my marriage worth less? Is my wife's life now less meaningful? To suggest that because part of my body does not function as it ought, I am less, is surely a form of discrimination.

I once met a couple who had been faithfully married to each other for about fifty years. They had children. Some time ago, the male husband undertook gender reassignment surgery. I asked the wife, "Are you married to a man or a woman?" Answer: "A woman." Next question: "Are you now a lesbian?" Answer (with some disgust): "No." So, is our identity defined by our relationships, or just by our view of ourselves?

While we are on that topic, the progressive, enlightened ones now tell us that human sexuality is a fluid continuum, that I am neither male nor female. Gender is not determined. Gender essentialism is now debunked. If that is true, then surely it follows that being homosexual (or other LGBTI+ expressions) is not fixed either. All sexuality is fluid. You may feel gay today, but straight tomorrow. What I am today is fluid, not fixed. Yet what we hear from the gay community is, "I was born this way, I did not choose this." How can both be true?

The PCWV values the freedom to choose with our finances. What choices are we making? Are they good choices? In the past sixty years, the size of Australian houses has more than doubled, yet the number of people living in houses has dropped by thirty percent.[5] Since the year 2000, luxury car ownership has almost doubled.[6] Philanthropic giving is in decline.[7]

It appears giving people more resources and more freedom to choose leads to people making more selfish choices. This is contrary to what the PCWV would have us believe. The belief that a flourishing person will somehow be a blessing to others seems naïve. Surely the former practice of religion as a prompt that nudges people to do right, rather than leaving it up to their good nature, was preferable?

Owning a bigger house is not neutral. It uses more energy and is bad for the environment. It requires more personal debt to finance. Viewing goods as neutral and selfish motives as the engine that drives our economy is flawed. Adam Smith initially balanced his notion of self-love with proactive mutual empathy. Our culture has fed steroids to the former, but then watered down the latter by making mutual empathy an optional choice.

Some will wish to push back on me. Is not our culture so much more inclusive, accepting, and tolerant? If by accepting you mean that a person can make whatever choices they think are good for themselves, and you must let me do the same, then yes, our culture is more accepting. But when someone says it is unwise to choose an addictive lifestyle, or it is wrong to end your own life, or be unfaithful to your life partner, to choose a partner of the same sex, they are excluded. It is an inclusion built on excluding some. How is that position sustainable?

The PCWV has a vague divinity who is knowable either by intuition or in a second-hand kind of way. If God is God, why can't he speak? Even if there is a gap between heaven and earth, between the noumenal and the phenomenal, why can't God speak across the gap? Put another way, who says the Western gap between the physical material world and the spiritual other world is the best way to understand the cosmos? That sounds like Western neo-imperialism.

If Nietzsche was right, as scientific knowledge grows, religious beliefs should decline. While affiliation to religious institutions is shrinking in most Western European countries, spirituality is not. Furthermore, at a global level, faith in God is growing.[8] How can this be so? High levels of correlation exist between being a Christian and education.[9] The more

5. Stephan and Crawford, "Size Does Matter," paras. 4 and 5.

6. Chesterton, "Australian Car Market," para. 9.

7. Sedauskas, "Percentage of Aussie Taxpayers," para. 1.

8. Barrett and Johnson, *World Christian Trends AD 30–AD 2200,* 321.

9. Pepper and Jacka, "Highly Educated Churchgoers," paras. 1 and 2; Burge, "Does

educated a person is, the more likely they are to be religious. How does Nietzsche explain that?

Regarding the use of power, on what basis has it been concluded that groups of people use power for ill and individuals do not? As Stark and others highlight, the church has consistently used its power for the greater good. Western civilizations have been fruitful on the back of this. Conversely, individuals often make poor choices for themselves and others. Consider our diet choices, lack of exercise, excessive consumption, credit card debt, and rising levels of waste disposal.

I think this rant will suffice. For accessibility, I will restate the essence of this list in a series of one-line questions.

- Are individuals really free from the influence of others?
- Does a person know what is best for themselves?
- Is freedom of choice a capacity that individuals will use wisely?
- Is living for my pleasure a fulfilling life?
- With all this focus on self-esteem, why is mental wellbeing not on the rise?
- If we don't nudge persons towards good, will they get there by themselves?
- Should not virtue best be a force for good, rather than just do no harm?
- Why is sexuality now the core of identity?
- If my marriage partner changes their identity, does that not change mine too?
- How can an inclusive culture be so exclusive?
- Why do we imagine power is only used by the collective for bad?
- Are not individuals also inclined to evil, and the collective to good?
- Is it not naïve to think that our possessions have no hold on us?
- Why is belief in God and spirituality on the rise?
- If God is God, could he not make himself known, and knowable?

Education 'Cure' People?," para. 4.

A Concluding Metaphor

I shall close out this chapter with a metaphor. The CWV was a coherent, functioning, constructive mindset. It delivered most of the time, for most of its citizens. You might want to think about a worldview as being like a diet.

My grandparents ate a very stable diet. Cereal and fruit for breakfast, salad and savoury sandwiches for lunch, and meat and three veg for dinner, six days a week. Sunday was a roast lunch, and then toast or pancakes for dinner.

Now, you could change the meat, choosing to buy what was on sale. (My grandparents lived in occupied Holland throughout World War II. Buying things on sale and saving for the future was deeply ingrained.) You could change out two vegetables, depending on what was in season, but potatoes were a given, a staple. You could have a treat for dessert sometimes. Occasionally you could have pasta, or curry, or go out to eat, but these were exceptions. In short, food preparation took place within certain fixed guidelines.

What this meant in practice was that my grandmother usually prepared a tasty, nourishing, and healthy dinner. I doubt she was taught the food pyramid at primary school. I never heard her talk about the need for protein, carbohydrates, iron, or vitamin B. Nor did she ever serve up something that tasted bad.

Though she may not have been able to articulate them, she knew certain rules or principles to cooking. Some things complement each other. Bacon and eggs go together, as do pancakes and syrup, pasta and cheese, and potatoes and gravy. Other foods do not mix well. You don't put custard on your meat, you don't serve a banana as one of the three vegetables, and lemon causes milk and yogurt to curdle.

Life, like cooking, has rules. When one lives within a time-honored and proven worldview, it works. If you follow the basic rules such as life includes components of work, play, time with family and friends, and rest, you will likely live a balanced life. Certain things are good for you, and others are not. Some things are okay in moderation, and others need to be a staple in your life.

If you follow this recipe, even if you don't understand all the science behind it, chances are you will serve up a nourishing, fulfilling life. The recipe gives you some choices. You can choose which job, or how many children to have, or in which suburb to live. The general principles and equilibriums that sit behind the rules mean that, whatever choices you make, your chances of living a successful life are maximized.

The PCWV wants to deconstruct all of that. It wants to say why restrict yourself to the Western diet. Your palate is unique. You are missing out on Asian and Middle Eastern cuisines, and other food sensations. There are other ingredients, other ways of preparing a meal. Thai cooking follows different principles, why not include some of those in your cuisine?

You could. Asian-Western fusion cooking can deliver some fantastic dishes but the chefs who manage to prepare those amazing dishes are experts in the principles of multiple cooking styles and food preparation. In a post-deconstructionist kitchen with an average home cook, what is far more likely to occur is a fiasco. The chances of success are reduced. But the PCWV goes further. Not only does it deconstruct the Western practices of cooking, telling us there are no universal principles to food preparation, it then invites us to make up a new and unique set of rules just right for ourselves. We also have to use our subjective judgement to decide if the diets we come up with are tasty in the short term and healthy and nutritious in the long term. The kicker is that we won't know until we have fed on a made-up diet for years, if not decades.

Giving a cook freedom, choice, more ingredients, and fewer guidelines will not necessarily lead to a better diet. Freedom and choice alone do not guarantee success. Instead they are more likely to lead to flops, to meals that mix clashing ingredients, or lack protein, or have too many fats and carbohydrates, not to mention the planning involved if you have to plan every meal where there are literally millions of possibilities.

Likewise, deconstructing the patterns of our culture and giving people freedom and choice to change the elements and ratios of life is risky. People will likely make short term and ego-referenced decisions. As politically incorrect as it sounds, life is too complex and precious to leave it up to the individual to decide how it is best lived. We are too close to the action. We lack the wisdom of hindsight. Making it up as we go is unlikely to result in a good life.

Life works better when you do it by the book.

Simplicity on the Other Side of Complexity

Part 1 of this book described where we are. Part 2 of this attempts to explain how we got here.

1. Descartes's *cogito ergo sum* introduced a major shift. The discourse moves from a search for truth as revealed by God to certainty as it can be known in the mind of the individual.

2. Rousseau identified society as having negative impacts on individuals. We become comparative, competitive, and greedy. The answer is to return to our childlike, innocent, and uncontaminated self. This self has a healthy self-love and empathy for others.

3. The Romantic poets Wordsworth, Blake, Shelley and Keats popularized these ideas in the English-speaking world. The division lines between the haves and have nots are emphasized.

4. Karl Marx read history as the working class and ruling class in a never-ending struggle for resources. Derrida and Foucault reframed the battle as being around power. Power is something abused by institutions. For the good of all, institutions ought to have their power diminished.

5. Freud and Jung reframed our search for meaning. Instead of searching for a God out there who reveals morality and the good life, we ought to look inwards to our childhood experiences, our drives and desires (Freud), or our collective subconscious (Jung).

6. Freud believed that our sexual urges drive much of our identity. While some sexual oppression is unhealthy, other parts of self-denial are appropriate. To become a functioning member of society, some urges must be curbed.

7. In the popular mind, post-Freud, the self is sexual, and any form of repression is unhealthy.

8. Developmental psychology tells us humanity develops through a series of stages. Investing in our children or ourselves to achieve our greatest potential is to follow natural patterns.

9. Economist Adam Smith told us that selfish motives bring good outcomes in a free market. The free market produces more goods and choices, and my consuming those leads to personal happiness and has positive side effects for others.

10. Globalism helps us all appreciate that our traditional ways of seeing and doing things seem right to us only because of our cultural bias. The internet gives us access to other equally valid perspectives. Our choices are endless and overwhelming.

11. The PCWV has deconstructed and abandoned some of the previously shared CWV assumptions. Having said this, much of PCWV is precisely that: post-Christian. Many of its features, such as individualism, freedom and autonomy, progress, and reason, are the former CWV's remnants.

12. These continuing or carried-over virtues are now somewhat detached and disconnected from a coherent framework that sustains them.

13. It is possible to deconstruct the deconstruction. The PCWV has some serious flaws and inconsistencies. Being and remaining a Christian in a PCWV necessitates becoming conversant with the flaws of the PCWV. Missional conversations will also be aided by such knowledge.

6

Other Ways to Approach Life

At present, it's fashionable to see things as unique. People are unique; cultures are unique; everything is unique. We should simply appreciate them for what they are. Any attempt to categorize things somehow fails to appreciate their beauty. Categories are imposed social constructs. They are not real and are perhaps remnants of controlling narratives. As such, they are best avoided.

The above argument is widely held and rarely questioned, but it obstructs learning and wisdom. Without categories, we have information, but not knowledge. We need to understand patterns, groupings, and types to meaningfully interact with the world. To what extent those categories are real or collective constructs, or both, is tangential to our concern.

Allow me to illustrate. It is presently unacceptable to group people into categories. There are no longer just males and females; we are now post-binary. Individuals are no longer reducible to their skin color; they are not blacks or whites or browns. Skin color is peripheral, almost accidental, as is their nationality or their occupation. A person is too exceptional, too distinctive to be characterized by reference to one or two of their attributes.

Imagine if we took this approach to animals—let's choose dogs. Imagine you could not use the categories like labrador, poodle, big, puppy, or farm/work dog. How could you hold a conversation with someone and describe the type of dog you were looking for? What if you went a step further and chose to suggest that dog versus cat was too binary? Imagine trying to teach a cat to become a working farm dog. Without categories like dog, cat, and border collie, you cannot understand, organize, or seek to manage the world.

Categories give us a handle on things so that we can understand them, then work with them. One way to understand our culture is to distinguish it from other types of cultures. Anthropologists suggest that cultures can be divided into three groupings. There are honor-shame cultures, guilt-innocence cultures, and power-fear cultures.

Honour-Shame, Guilt-Innocence, and Power-Fear

Let us begin with the known. The West is populated with guilt-innocence cultures. Here, individuals are taught to listen to their conscience. If Average Joe feels guilty, this indicates he has done something wrong, unjust, or unfair. It is up to him put it right. Joe is independently responsible for his actions, and is capable of acting outside of the influence of others. He must make decisions by himself, to do what is right. If Joe is feeling innocent, this is an indication he has done the right, just, and fair thing. He has nothing to fear when he has done what is proper; his world is in order.

Honor-shame cultures see the world differently. Asian and Middle Eastern countries function this way. In this approach, Saanvi is taught to be sensitive to what others think of her. Her actions will have consequences for the reputation of her family. The role of the individual is to bring honor, and not shame to their family, tribe, or group. Maintaining good relationships determines how you ought to behave. This is more important than your own personal feelings or following your conscience. Saanvi's world is in order when she brings honor to her extended family. In turn, the family confers its status back to her, and protects her as one of its own.

Power-fear cultures see the world differently yet again. Classically, much of Africa operates this way, but so do parts of Asia and the Pacific. Power-fear cultures often correlate with animistic spirit worship, that is, a belief that spirits animate the river, or the local tree, or animals. Uma is taught to follow the rules and folklores of her forefathers and not upset the spirits. Rituals and sacrifices may appease the gods. Powerful people can even harness the force of the spirits, and use it against others. Uma fears upsetting the spirits or powerful, spiritual, connected people. The more she is aligned under the most powerful people and spirits, the more her world is in order.

My point is this. Australia is an example of a type of culture. This culture has principles or patterns to it. It's not just random. There are other types of cultures out there that have a different set of principles and patterns. A culture is not just some random, historically accidental mix of beliefs and values. What we experience in the West is one tried and tested way to approach the world. There are other long-term, successful, stable "recipes" out there. We could have followed those recipes, but we did not.

Table 1: Three different cultures

	Honor-Shame	Guilt-Innocence	Power-Fear
Identity	In one's family or tribe	Individual's attributes	In family or tribe, subservient to spirits
Purpose	Bring honor to family	Act morally and have a clear conscience	Avoid fear by aligning with the powerful
Benefit	Family honor conferred onto you, family support	No guilt, high self-esteem, virtue is its own reward	Trouble-free life, may use power against your foes
The great "Sin"	Shame family, individual actions reflect on others	Wrong choice leading to personal guilt	Upset the powerful, be they spirits or people
The risk	Family disowns you, loss of status/support, isolation	Carry the burden of guilt, risk punishment	The powerful will curse you, complicate life
Solution	A season of shame, maybe slow reintegration, moment of readmission	Individual must show remorse, somehow pay, the offended may forgive	Appease spirits by sacrifice and compliance, or align with other more powerful beings
Harmony exists when	Individual is integrated into family, playing their part bringing honor	Individual is virtuous, in good standing with others, free from guilt	Powers-that-be are ruling, subjects are compliant, everyone in their place

This brief introduction to some other world views grants us different lenses to see the dilemmas our culture seeks to respond to. To return to the image of Neurath's boat, it gives other vantage points from which to look back at our location and make an assessment from the perspective of that alternate vantage point.

Using these lenses, let us consider the pressing concern of our present culture, which is to empower individuals so they can choose their best path to flourishing. The West says, certain groups have experienced sustained discrimination and are not flourishing. This has occurred because the previously powerful church and Christians have been judgemental. There is a shared belief we ought to have a season of bias and affirmation towards the previously discriminated against so that they can catch up.

If we look at all this through honor-shame lenses, or from the Neurath's boat perspective, we will see that another analysis and solution is conceivable. From the honor-shame perspective, people fail to thrive or flourish when isolated from their family or tribe. When one's aim is personal advancement, this will ultimately lead to disconnection and floundering. Our nature and identity are found in relationships, not primarily in ourselves. Seeking the best for our family or tribe is our highest calling. This is the most natural and true expression of personhood. Individuals flourish as a subset of a family that flourishes. Joy and growth are experiences that are shared.

Our diagnosis (or misdiagnosis?) of the problem and solution flows from the assumption that society's basic building block is the autonomous individual. The West sees the family as a joining together of individuals. In contrast, honor-shame cultures perceive the family or the collective as the basic building block. Individuals exist within families. An individual cannot be born, grow, learn, belong, or thrive without a family. Individuals are components or subsets of the family. Just as a tire is a subset of a bicycle and fulfills its potential only when it is part of something more significant than itself, so too individuals can only ever fulfill their potential as part of a family.

The problem then, when explored from an honor-shame perspective, is not disempowered individuals but disconnected individuals. The solution is not to empower individuals. This will most likely further accentuate the problem. The answer is to reconnect individuals, because it is in the web or networks and relationships that individuals find the mutual support, reference points, and sanctuary required to flourish.

Honor-shame advocates believe they have evidence to support their insights. The growth of social isolation and loneliness induces anxiety. There is something hollow and unfulfilling when persons seek to live for themselves. Meaning is not something one can create alone. What individualistic Westerners label as FOMO, but have in mind missing out on experiences— an honor-shame perspective would reframe as a fear of missing out on being with others. It all sounds plausible, even persuasive, does it not?

Let us change lenses again. What will a person reared in a power-fear culture see? They share a collectivist understanding of personhood. The head of the family or tribe is a patriarch or matriarch, who themselves sits under another authority: one that is in solidarity with the spiritual realm. Everyone belongs somewhere in a pyramid-shaped hierarchy and when everyone is in their proper place, there is an equilibrium within the system that means everyone feels at ease.

Recall the opening scene of the movie, *The Lion King*. Mufasa the king sits on the throne, with Sarabi, his counter-balancing queen, Rafiki, his shaman, and Zazu, his all-seeing eyes at his side. When all the animals come and assemble before him, the world is as it should be. All are at peace, secure. As long as proper order remains, serenity reigns. When the wrong person inhabits the wrong place, the equilibrium is upset, people become unsettled, and chaos becomes almost inevitable.

In this sense, the power-fear view of the world is incorporated within the theories of Jung. The key archetypal figures must occupy their place within the archetypal motifs or shared narratives. When they do, our collective subconscious is at ease. When they do not, we are, individually and collectively, anxious.

The present orientation of the West is that we need to empower every individual to have the capacity to make choices, particularly those individuals who have experienced sustained discrimination. The power-fear perspective sees this diagnosis and treatment as flawed. Not everyone can be empowered. We were not all born to reign, even over ourselves. When all are the kings of their domain, no one exists within the hierarchy. To promote people who may have held lesser standings, simply because it is fair or equal, is to mess with the natural order of things.

If this is the first time you have encountered the power-fear worldview, intuitively, it will not sound winsome or compelling. On the contrary, it will sound archaic and hierarchical, especially to egalitarian Australians with a convict history. Allow me a paragraph or three to attempt to persuade you of the insight in this perspective.

My family has a pet dog. Dogs, like humans, are social animals. They live in packs. My dog understands herself to be a part of our family. We are her pack, and she knows where she belongs and where she fits in. Then she is content, or happy. If my dog believes she is at the top of our family pack, and we all go out for the day without her, she will be anxious. She did not permit us to go. She does not know where we are, and she cannot protect us.

However, she is not at the top of the pack; she is nearer the bottom. She does not need to worry if we come and go. That's not her job in our pack. If she worries about things she cannot control, she will be forever anxious. It is appropriate for her to only worry about things the system asks her to be responsible for. She needs to be happy when we come home, bark when something is wrong, and not much else. She can do all that. She is happy, and we are happy.

If my daughter lets the dog sleep on her bed at night, the dog is happy. If the children put the dog on my bed at night, she is anxious. She knows she is out of her place. Being in a system, and in her place in that system, brings perspective, peace, and happiness. Others within the system have more responsibility and more capacity than her, and that is fine. If she fulfills her role and I perform mine, we are a content pack.

So it is in a power-fear culture. As Westerners, we suspect everyone is clamoring for power, bitter about what they don't have. If everyone leads a tribe of one, we have no packs. A simple inner peace comes when others who have more responsibility and more capacity than you have your back. That is their job. You don't need to worry about that; you can find fulfillment in doing what your role or contribution is.

Remember, this chapter aims to broaden our minds to possible ways to understand the contours and solutions possible to the dilemma our culture is focusing its attention on. I say this because, in my observation, the debate so quickly degenerates into a binary of old versus new, faith versus reason, conservative versus progressive. The CWV is dismissed because it has been tried and failed. It is viewed as part of the problem, not the solution. Having fashioned a CWV straw-man, and then dismissed him, there is only one other option on the table: to subscribe to a PCWV. If I am not Christian, then I must be post-Christian in my mindset.

Beyond that simplistic binary, the two alternate frameworks of honor-shame and power-fear show that there are other ways to diagnose the problem and the solution. Let's play this out, again in relation to Israel Falou. Falou's posts elicited a response from former professional Rugby League player, Ian Roberts. Roberts was the first high-profile footballer to come out in Australia. Roberts criticized Falou's post as contributing to the high rates of suicide. "These types of remarks can and do push people over the edge. . . . There are literally kids in the suburbs killing themselves."[1]

Roberts' logic fits within the PCWV. Gays have long been judged and discriminated against. Experiencing judgement causes angst, lowers self-esteem, and may lead to suicide. LGBTI+ people have poorer mental health and higher rates of suicide. Hate speech like Falou's contributes to higher suicide rates. Therefore it is wrong. It cannot be tolerated. Roberts claims evidence for his position. If you ask LGBTI+ people about their mental health challenges, they will likely self-report fearing judgement and hate speech as a causal factor.

But a different pair of lenses reveals a different analysis. Sex is not just about personal pleasure. Procreation is about the next phase of continuously binding yourself into your family. One becomes an adult who then marries and parents the next generation. They are not just your children; they are simultaneously grandchildren, cousins, nephews, or nieces. Becoming a parent reinforces your role as a son, daughter, aunt, or uncle. Removing sexual activity from its natural order and using it to define your identity induces anxiety. It leaves a person prone to isolation, chasing that which

1. ABC News, "Gay Former Rugby League Star," para. 9.

is hollow, and seeking meaning where it cannot be found. Viewed from a different lens, LGBTI+ people having poorer states of wellbeing is evidence of the breakdown of family and withdrawing from the family order, not of hate speech resulting in low self-esteem.

Whether or not this argument sounds initially plausible to you is not the point. It works. It's consistent and coherent. It is a logical explanation, but one made from another vantage point. Likely, it will intuitively seem right to traditional Pacific Islanders. The fact that it might not make sense to a Westerner tells you more about Westerners and their assumptions than it does about the value of the insight.

A Neo-Buddhist Perspective

This chapter could have a thousand variations on a theme. What do teenage Inuit (native Alaskans) think of the PCWV? As enthralling as that paragraph sounds, I shall refrain from writing it. My aims are more modest: first, to show alternate ways to diagnose the problems and solutions the West is conscious it faces; and second, to highlight some assumptions within the Western echo chamber, by looking at ourselves from other perspectives.

I shall indulge twice more. First, by outlining a neo-Buddhist perspective on the West. I shall do so because the Buddhist critique of us is telling. It speaks to a core assumption in the PCWV. Second, by outlining approaches to ethical dilemmas.

I have already alluded to Mark Manson's book, *The Subtle Art of Not Giving a F****. Manson approaches life from a Buddhist, and to a lesser extent, a Stoic perspective. He begins by noting that conventional self-help books invite you to get in touch with your passions, visualize where you would like to be, and then choose and walk that path—all classic PCWV ideas.

But Manson says this approach is flawed, even counter-productive. Imagining, then focusing on what you are NOT, will only reinforce your sense of disappointment. It will reaffirm your desire for things not currently in your reach. And perhaps they never will be. Going back into this headspace creates a "feedback loop from hell." Here Manson is very Buddhist; desire is at the root of suffering.

The solution is not to care, not to give a proverbial, hence the title of the book. If you don't desire, you won't be disappointed, and you won't suffer. Life will inevitably throw many challenges your way. If you expect all pleasure and progress, you are deluded and will become even more disillusioned. Accept that some pain and loss is inevitable. Again, very Buddhist and Stoic.

At this point, Manson risks falling into nihilism. Don't care about anything—nothing matters. But he avoids this. The (subtle) art is not to care about nothing. The art is in being conscious of the things you notice, then choosing to care more about the select things you can change, and less about the ones you cannot.

Furthermore, accept that caring will bring focus and desire back to the table, a desire to change. Be prepared to accept that caring will lead to disappointment, suffering, pain, and problems. You must care enough to face up to these inevitabilities and to toil through them.

Happiness then is not about avoiding or fixing problems. It is about the joy of overcoming the current incarnation of them—only to be faced with the following problem. Life is a continuous, uphill slog. Simple pleasures do not fulfill. Like candy, they are fleeting and leave us wanting. It is a love of the journey of constant growth and overcoming in the focused arena where you can make a difference; embracing the pain of that journey, and accepting all other pains you cannot change. That is the art of living well, according to Manson.

What makes Manson so pertinent to our concerns is that he is in a parallel business to us. He is also critiquing the PCWV, but from another perspective, or another boat. He also finds the PCWV lacking. It pursues desires it cannot attain, and do not fulfill. The intuition of a person to seek pleasure and avoid pain at this moment is short-sighted. Some pain is inevitable. For Manson, personal growth is possible only on limited fronts and it requires embracing suffering.

To reframe Manson in ways that align with our journey, the Western focus on empowering the individual to make choices is unsound. The problem is not that institutions have disempowered some, such that they cannot choose and flourish. The problem is that people make selfish, short-sighted choices they believe will lead to happiness but instead lead to insatiability, instability, and anxiety. The problem is that people think they have a right to avoid suffering, that they can achieve their potential without suffering. For Manson, the missing part of the solution is that people need to learn to be "happy" when things are not all positive and pleasurable; people need to re-learn that suffering is an inevitable part of life, which must be embraced if we hope to grow. The West must re-value resilience. Manson presents a timely, persuasive, and compelling argument that the PCWV cannot deliver all its promises.

We have now viewed the PCWV from an honor-shame perspective, a power-fear perspective, and a neo-Buddhist perspective. For good measure, let's try one more vantage point. What does the history of ethical thought make of the PCWV?

Approaches to Ethics

I have breached the topic of ethics already. I noted a drift towards consequentialist ethics. As its name suggests, an action is good if its consequences
are good. Utilitarianism is the best-known version of consequentialist ethics.
Ethics is about delivering the greatest good for the greatest number. I have
also noted a shift away from ethics as a positive obligation to intentionally
do good for the greatest number, retreating towards a do-no-harm ethic, and
empower others to have the capacity to make choices for themselves.

Consequentialist approaches to ethics are but one approach, and are
not without their problems. The most significant dilemma with consequentialist ethics is which consequences are we assessing. Let's imagine I have
a challenging work colleague, and there is unease between us. I decide to
speak to them about it. I anticipate that the consequences will be a return
to collegial relationships. Instead, the actual outcomes are different. I am
misunderstood and accused of bullying. Is the morality of my actions to
be weighed against my intentions or the actual outcomes? If we answer the
latter, what if my intentions were good, but my execution was poor? Was I
oafish, or were they hyper-sensitive?

Part of the present appeal of consequentialist ethics is that it fits well
with autonomous individualism. Actors are granted freedom to choose the
actions they believe will bring about the most desired outcome.

If you listen to any ethical debates in the public domain, my observation is that a consequentialist framework for discussing ethics is assumed.
Debates revolve around which outcomes are the best, for whom, and who
gets to decide. Taking a step back, this is a shallow and simplistic way to do
ethics. There are other, and I suggest better, ways.

Virtue ethics is one alternative I have already mentioned. Virtue ethics encourage people to practice noble behaviors and integrate them into
one's character. For example: pursue virtues such as honesty, which is the
best policy; it is better to forgive than to be bitter; see the best in others,
not the worst. A virtuous person then tells the truth, is forgiving, and is
gracious in assessing others. We may also consider generosity, justice, or
even-temperedness as other desirable personality traits.

Virtue ethics move us away from choice, particulars, and an obsession with the best decision. Instead, there is continuity and stability in trying to be a type of person who behaves reasonably, graciously, or honestly
in all situations.

Yet another approach to ethics is teleological ethics. The word "teleological" comes from the Greek word *telos*, meaning "end, or goal, or purpose."

In teleological ethics, things have a purpose. The goal of business is to make a profit, or the goal of producing food is that someone eats it.

Teleological ethics facilitate a more nuanced or sophisticated debate than just me getting to decide my goals and then chasing them. Let's take business as an example. The goal of a business might be to make a profit. While accumulating profits might be my goal, accrued personal wealth might not be considered a worthy end in itself. It might be better understood as the means to something else. It could be argued that the best end or *telos* of excess production is sharing with others.

In other words, wealth itself has an end. This is how Aristotle argued. Things have a *telos*. Bricks exist to make houses. Food exists to be eaten. An action is moral when it uses or moves a thing towards its highest end. It is wrong to waste food, especially when others go hungry. The CWV overlays a purposeful divine mind. Whereas for Aristotle, things have a *telos* in themselves, in monotheistic religions, God has designed things with an innate purpose.

Teleological ethics also steer ethics away from personal choices about the best consequences towards acting in ways that align with the purposes of things as they exist. If food is made to eat, or wealth to share, then it is wrong to hoard or waste. It does not matter who chooses or has the right or the freedom to choose.

Lastly, there are deontological approaches to ethics. In this approach, things are wrong in and of themselves. Murder is always wrong, as are lying, stealing, and cheating. There is an order behind rules, and persons are duty-bound to obey them, no matter the consequences. The most notable versions of this approach look for universal principles. Jesus' "do unto others as you would have them do unto you" (Matt 7:12) is the best-known example of this. It is my responsibility as a human being to treat others as I would wish to be treated. If we all acted this way, the world would be a better place. While deontological approaches are clearly out of vogue, we do still hear echoes of this reasoning. For instance, domestic violence is always wrong, as is abuse.

It is not our task to decide which ethical theory is the best. My point is this: we have inherited a rich and sophisticated history of ethical reflections. This heritage is being ignored. We no longer consider which ethical theory might best fit this scenario. In the PCWV, we assume a consequentialist framework, perhaps we debate the merits of various choices, but mostly reaffirm that the individual gets to decide for themselves. Such moral debates appear selfish and shallow in the light of our rich traditions.

Two Stark Observations

Now that we have three or four vantage points from which to consider the PCWV, two observations are shouting out at us. The first is that no other worldview makes personal happiness its goal.[2] Manson, Buddhism, and Stoicism all tell us that life will have more than its fair share of hardships. To imagine that human existence is typically pleasurable is naïve. To imagine that we have sufficient control over our circumstances such that we can manufacture bliss is foolish. Living for pleasure is a goal that fills our minds and hearts with desire. Desire increases the inevitable disappointment. In any case, pleasure is a superficial goal that delivers short-term hits but more long-term anxiety and distress.

The honor-shame approach tells us that the goal of life is belonging to the family, then bringing honor to it. As your family is honored, you are embraced, you belong, and some of that honor is reflected back on to you. In a power-fear context, the goal of life is to live in harmony or at peace with others, to live well within the equilibrium. The Western Christian (guilt-innocence worldview) goal is to love and honor God and love and serve your neighbor, which delivers a clear conscience and inner peace.

Most ethical perspectives do not make personal happiness a valid goal either. Many choices that bring me short-term pleasure, such as the accumulation of wealth, or excessive consumption and hoarding, may have ethically questionable outcomes for others.

In each of the above-surveyed approaches, personal happiness is never the goal. Further, you cannot find happiness by making it your goal. Happiness is a by-product of being focused on others.

A core notion of the PCWV is that if you seek experiences and make choices that bring personal happiness, it will make you feel good, increase self-worth, help you flourish, and this is good. This idea is novel. The accumulated wisdom of human experience and folklore tells us that seeking pleasure as its own end is like chasing after the wind. We exist for a higher calling than a string of momentary happy experiences.

The second observation that shouts out to us as novel is to consider a human being as an isolated individual. Autonomous individualism is another core notion in the PCWV. The honor-shame, power-fear cultures do not understand persons as individuals. Nor does Buddhism. In classic

---

2. Aristotle defines the purpose of life as happiness but does not have pleasure-focused hedonism in mind. For Aristotle, happiness is intellectual contemplation. Given that what distinguishes humans from animals is the capacity to reason, the highest end of humanity is contemplation. When we are thinking, when we are achieving our highest end, then we experience happiness.

Buddhism, there is no "self." The concept of the self soon evolves into self-satisfaction and self-advancement. The idea of "self" facilitates desire. Only when one comes to realize there is no self can one escape the endless cycle of reincarnation.

Even classic Christianity has strong elements of collectivism. In the Old Testament, God saves a people. In the New Testament, Jesus calls twelve disciples, and in so doing, constructs a new people. Jesus practices his ministry in community. Paul talks of the gathered local church as family, or as one body with many parts.

It was from within the Protestant Reformation, emphasizing the individual believer, and away from the Catholic (aka worldwide) Church, where modern individualism began. Luther's dictum, "Here I stand, I can do no other," sets a precedent. Descartes provided the philosophical underpinnings for Western individualism, with his *Cogito ergo sum*, "I think therefore I am." Descartes refocused the philosophy of how we know things (epistemology) away from truth towards certainty. Truth was previously focused around what God has ordained and revealed. Certainty is now about what individual humans can know and be certain of.

Fast forward almost 500 years, and the PCWV is abandoning the last vestiges of the collectivist dimension of the CWV. Christianity understands humanity as individuals who exist in relationships. This is why we find ourselves in loving God and others. The PCWV is going one step further, and now understands people as individuals in isolation or as individuals who are defined with reference primarily to their inner selves.

Western civilizations were already at one extreme of the collectivist-versus-individual continuum. The shift from the CWV to the PCWV is a shift from individualism towards extreme individualism. It is a step away from the fringe of the pack, towards a more radical outlying position. Is this is the next logical step? Or is this a step too far?

Extreme individualism pairs well with the belief that choices that make you feel good increase self-worth and lead to flourishing. That is a potent concoction that appeals to the ego. As enticing as that concoction smells, history and consensus would suggest it is unbalanced and back-to-front.

Isn't Selfishness Simply Sin? Why Not Call a Spade a Spade?

If you are a Christian who reads Christian books and listens to sermons and Christian social commentators on podcasts, you may be increasingly impatient with me. You may be thinking something like: "I am getting paralysis by social analysis! Turning from God to self and selfishness is the great sin. Let's just name up sin for what it is. You are over-complicating things!"

Naming individualism as selfishness and as the great sin attempts to explain a social phenomenon through a theological argument, as if somehow theology trumps sociology or any other -ology. This approach is flawed. It imagines God intervenes in human history for theological reasons, not social reasons, or that a theological and a sociological explanation are competing and mutually exclusive accounts.

Again, a thought experiment will help ground my point. Some Christian authors and commentators mount a case that goes something like this. In the Reformation, Christians believed that God was the author of truth and morality; they trusted and obeyed his words, made decisions about how to shape culture accordingly, and what we had was better marriages, families, less mental illness, etc. What went wrong was we started to trust ourselves. With the growth of (scientific) knowledge and technology, humans started to imagine they were in control. We began to believe man was at the center of his universe, and not God. We now make decisions about life, culture, and morality based on how we wish to express ourselves. Now, what we have in the West are rising rates of depression, anxiety, suicide, and relationship breakdown. The answer is to go back to the Reformation principle of God as the source of truth.

Underneath this argument sits a certain logic. You can either trust God or you can trust self. Trusting God draws us beyond ourselves to put the needs of others first and builds loving nurturing communities. Trusting self results in excessive introspection, pride, greed, mental illness, and the breakdown of society.

There is some truth in this view but it is a Western-centric way to view history, and then makes a universal application on the back of Western experience. Consider the following anomalies.

What if we call to mind African history? In the twentieth century alone, African Christianity exploded from about eight or nine million in 1900 (8–9 percent of the population of Africa) to some 335 million in 2000 (45 percent).[3] This represents a significant movement towards God, not away from him. Is Africa becoming less individualistic? No. Depression, one of the symptoms of Western individualism, has grown in Africa by a third since 1990, suggesting individualism is on the rise at the same time Christianity has exploded.[4]

3. Barrett, as cited by Christianity.com, "Explosion of Christianity in Africa," para. 1.

4. Dewey, "Stunning Map of Depression Rates," paras. 1 and 4.

In Russia, religious affiliation grew from 31 percent to 72 percent of the population between 1991 and 2008. In the same period, those professing no religious affiliation fell from 61 percent to 18 percent.[5] Has Russia moved away from a me-centered view of the world towards a God-centered view of the world? It appears not. Russia has rising rates of depression and schizophrenia: up 50 percent in adults, and 100 percent among teenagers and younger children (1990–2000).[6] Russia also has persistent drug and alcohol problems.[7]

The #MeToo movement has brought a timely awareness to domestic violence. It appears that rates of reported abuse are on the rise. Some might envisage rising rates of domestic violence correlating with a culture-wide movement away from biblical values. One of the countries where intimate partner violence is most prevalent is the Solomon Islands. Sixty-four percent of women there report physical or sexual partner violence.[8] Domestic violence is rampant across the Pacific nations.[9] And yet, the Solomon Islands is now one of the most Christianized countries globally, with 90 percent of the population now professing religious affiliation and about 70 percent regularly attending church. Other Pacific nations are similar. If domestic violence is a sin related to the abuse of power, why has it not fallen as a nation becomes more Christian?

To add to that, here is another statistic that will confound Western readers. Despite high rates of domestic violence, the Solomon Islands have the lowest rates of depression in the world, followed by another six Pacific Island nations after it.[10] It appears that the link between domestic violence and depression is not universal, or necessary.

Africa, Russia, and the Pacific Islands are not cultures that have drifted away from God towards extreme individualism. In all three, religious affiliation has grown. Yet, in all three, there is evidence of high or increasing rates of social problems. It seems there is something cultural about Russians and vodka, about Pacific Islanders and domestic violence, that is not reducible to "sin is trusting self instead of God" as an explanation.

The simplistic explanation that we can trust either God or self, and to trust self is selfishness, which equals individualism, which is evil, fits our

5. Pew Research Center, "Return to Religion," para. 1.

6. Stolyarova, "Russia: Mental Illness," para. 3.

7. Lobodov, "Alcohol and Illicit Drug in Russia," para. 1.

8. Secretariat of the Pacific Community for Ministry of Women, "Solomon Islands," 17.

9. Asian Pacific Institute on Gender-Based Violence, "Pacific Islanders," 2-5.

10. World Health Organization, *Depression and Other Common Mental Disorders*.

Western intuition. Such one-dimensional explanations fail to capture the complexity of what is happening. It is naïve to crudely announce that in trusting self, and becoming individualistic, we have turned from God and this is the sum of what has gone wrong.

Individualism is dangerous, as is collectivism. The belief in a personal relationship with Jesus is a core Western Protestant conviction. In section 3 we shall consider what has gone wrong, and it will include the rise of the individual self, but more than just that one point must be made.

Conclusion

If you have read these two chapters and not skipped the history bit, well done. We Westerners are poor students of history. We risk not learning from the mistakes of others, and repeating them in our own time. As I said in the introduction, our culture has this perversive "we-now-know-better" arrogance. The flip side of this arrogance is ignorance.

Was the CWV in a crisis at the end of the twentieth century? Probably not, but social change is inevitable and irreversible. We can't rewind the clock. My aim in chapter 5 was to survey the key thinkers and shifts that framed the West's analysis of the end of CWV, and the birthing of the PCWV. The reasoning behind this deconstruction is not lightweight. It is no small thing to take apart a 1600-year-long legacy.

In this chapter, I have attempted to analyze the assumptions of the PCWV from the vantage point of four other "boats." Honor-shame cultures, power-fear cultures, Buddhism, and the history of ethical debates are not merely four random perspectives from a few odd, quirky individuals. These are heavyweight stayers, worldviews, and philosophies that have passed the test of time.

The analysis reveals two things. The PCWV might be good at poking holes in other worldviews, but it has some severe leaks itself. Two of the novel and central planks of the PCWV, namely that seeking personal happiness is a path to flourishing, and that the individual is best understood with reference to their inner self, are radically experimental. Other worldviews have found such assumptions wanting.

Second, as the PCWV has responded to what was perceived to be presenting dilemmas at the end of 1600 years of the CWV, the responses it made were not obvious, nor the only option. There were alternate paths not chosen that would have led to different and arguably healthier conclusions.

I trust you now understand the present spirit of this age (a.k.a. the *zeitgeist*) more insightfully. Having said that, the PCWV is what it is. It is becoming more established after having displaced the previous CWV. It is not my aim to attack or destroy it. Instead, my aim is to help you understand it and consider how to live as a follower of Jesus inside it. In the next chapter, we shall consider how the church has responded to the shifting goalposts.

Clarity on the Other Side of Complexity

1. At present, it is in vogue to view all things as unique. This leaves us without categories, and ultimately, without knowledge. Identifying patterns and groupings is part of knowing.

2. Cultures, however, can be meaningfully understood as falling within one of three more established set of patterns and principles. Likewise, established religions and philosophies offer a time-tested coherency, providing a sound vantage point from which to understand our present take on things.

3. Western cultures are guilt-innocence driven cultures. This means a person acts and understands themselves as an individual. Acting in line with one's conscience brings a guilt-free state of inner peace. The PCWV has spring-boarded from this launching pad.

4. The honor-shame and power-fear lenses suggest that identity is found in kinship networks, not the self. Focusing on the self as autonomous from relationship networks risks leaving individuals socially isolated, lonely, vulnerable, and without connection to substantial reference points.

5. A Buddhist lens suggests that chasing pleasure is a sure-fire path to increasing your desires and expectations, which will amplify life's inevitable suffering. Instead, we ought to focus on what we can change, accept what we cannot, and enjoy the growing inner peace that swells as we face many challenges, overcoming some, and not being overcome by others.

6. The history of ethics would suggest that our current moral deliberations take place on a very narrow bandwidth. Ethics are much richer than simply who gets to decide and who benefits.

7. Our present preoccupation with personal happiness and our right to choose is back-to-front when compared with other worldviews. The consensus of human thought over history is that one does not find personal happiness or one's self by seeking it directly. Instead, they are found as a side-effect of serving others and seeking their wellbeing.

8. The simplistic view that individualism causes selfishness which is sin
   and leads culture away from God fails to explain what is happening outside the West, let alone capture the nuance and complexity of
   what is happening inside the West.

7

How the Church Has Responded
to Shifting Goalposts

THE DEMISE OF THE CWV, its deconstruction, and its replacement with something else is not a trend that began last month. Various scholars will highlight the seeds of change as far back as the fifteenth or sixteenth century. It is common, for instance, to note the rise of the scientific revolution and the Enlightenment as gaining momentum not long after the Reformation. These phases of human development reframed events as the consequence, not of divine providence, but rather of natural laws. I do not disagree; the present critique of the CWV has its origins centuries ago.

My observations are as follows. Even after the Enlightenment (seventeenth and eighteenth centuries), the CWV assumption that God exists as the divine cause for existence, morality, and reason remained common. Belief in a supreme being was still a core part of the fabric of civil society.

This shared belief played itself out in very concrete ways. The growth of the local suburban church in Commonwealth countries after World War II is a clear example of this. New suburbs needed local churches because the church was still valued as an integral part of a strong community. The church looked alive and well in the 1950s.

However, decline in local church attendance from the 1960s onwards is evidence that all was not well in the house of God. Most Christians have not been able to articulate all the reasons why attendance and influence began to fall. While the explanations might be vague and fuzzy, the awareness of it is palpable.

There are competing narratives about where we are, and what has gone wrong. Christianity is very tribal at present. These competing explanations give reasons for what has gone wrong, and what the solution could have been, or might yet be. These narratives are, I suggest, partial. They are re-hearsed by people standing on a leaking boat, trying to diagnose and fix it while still at sea. Most of them offer some insight, but none of them provide the whole picture from an objective point of view.

In this chapter, I shall map the range of responses to the passing of the CWV and consider the assumptions and dilemmas within each answer. I will do this from a sociological perspective, asking the questions, "what social phenomena are various Christian tribes responding to?" and "how does their response disclose their assumptions?"

I will not be undertaking a theological analysis of each tribe. This is not because I think it is unimportant or too complex. I firmly hold to my bibli-cal and theological beliefs. In my local church from the pulpit, I aspire to contend for my beliefs with passion and clarity. There are many good books already in print that attempt to do the same. This is not one of those books. This is an inter-disciplinary, social-sciences perspective on the changing of Western culture and the place of Christians and the church therein. What follows then is a survey of competing explanations of where we are and what has gone wrong such that we are here.

Liberals or Progressives

Liberalism is an ambiguous term that can have an economic, political, so-cial, and theological meaning. Theologically speaking, liberalism is a move-ment with roots in responding to the rationalist Enlightenment. In line with the Enlightenment, liberalism values human reason and contemporary thought. For liberals, current best thinking has the authority to re-interpret the scriptures and theological traditions, rendering modern-day Christian-ity more up-to-date, more engaged, and less offensive.

Valuing human reason and its present insights means acknowledging, if not agreeing with, the philosophers of the day. David Hume (1711–1776), for instance, argued that if someone told you a miracle had occurred, it would be more reasonable to assume that the person is lying or misguided than to believe a miracle had occurred. Liberalism agrees with Hume, and reinterprets biblical miracles as myth, not fact.

The feeding of the five thousand is a moment of unbelievable shar-ing, inspired by the generosity of a boy. Reports of Jesus' resurrection are best understood as spiritual metaphors rather than literal accounts. The life-affirming spirit of Jesus rises with his people as the disciples remember and revive the central motifs that good overcomes evil, that love overcomes hate and fear. Any talk of the Second Coming is more correctly interpreted as consciousness that Jesus is eternally imminent. He is always coming, and we should be ready to meet him at all times.

Theological liberalism is not a new phenomenon. Our question is this: how are liberal theologians intersecting with the insights and assumptions of PCWV? The answer is: by adopting them as is their wont because current thinking supersedes the old.

A long-standing motif of liberals (or social progressives, as they might prefer to call themselves) focuses on Jesus' message of love and hope. They major on the positive, more so than on Jesus' call to righteousness and avoiding future judgement. Liberals are presently reframing Jesus' love such that it is defined as acceptance, tolerance, being non-judgemental, for the marginalized and the empowerment of others. Jesus' love was an all-inclusive love, with the noted exception of those who practiced exclusion and abused power in their day, that is, the religious leaders.

For liberals, biblical justice and social justice are almost synonymous. Bringing the kingdom of heaven, as Jesus did, is about caring for the poor, standing up for the down-trodden, reaching out to the last, the least, and the lost. This is the core mission of the church. Evangelism is frowned upon because it comes with patronising or colonial assumptions. Evangelism as proselytizing is a classic example of knowledge used as power to enlist adherence to my way of seeing things.

Like the PCWV, for liberals, sexuality has become a symbolic issue. Given that God is a God of love, and that Jesus tells us not judge but rather to accept and include, for many liberals being pro same-sex marriage is the logical next step in caring for the marginalized. By contrast, the liberals' commentary on pre-marital sex, or dissuading Christians from marrying non-Christians, is absent. Their silence on some of the broader issues of sexuality and relationships is deafening.

Liberals have adjusted and evolved alongside the post-Enlightenment shift away from rationalism and towards a more intuitive and subjective form of knowing. Liberals would view evangelicals and fundamentalists as dry rationalists. In contrast, they would see their own form of reasoning as more holistic, more relational, and more aligned with the wisdom and spirit of today.

Herein lies the rationale of the liberal position. The church ought to respond to the shifting sands of culture in two ways. First, by evolving with it. For liberals, truth is progressive. The church is incarnated within a host culture and is in dialogue with that culture. The church must evolve with its host culture and interpret its sacred texts and symbols in ways that speak to and inspire the best in the present.

Second, the church must remain relevant and accessible. Some concerns that are now outdated and offensive must be pruned back to remove obstacles to people joining a faith community and sharing that journey with others. Having said this, other concerns are perceived to be prophetic. The church still has a role of speaking truth to power. There will evolve a nucleus of core life-affirming concerns as the causes of the day around which the people of God will rally. This is perceived to be bringing in the kingdom, replicating the essence of what Jesus did.

This is liberalism's greatest strength or contribution. The liberal church sees itself as holding a prophetic mantle. It tends to position itself as semi-aligned with culture, yet remaining critical of selective elements of it. In the present, this looks like being for same-sex marriage and the indigenous, and against racism, domestic violence, and other forms of abuse while being critical of our politics regarding our lack of public housing, or embracing gaming and gambling multi-nationals. That is, critical of a type of capitalism that is selfish and greedy. There is something shrewd about this strategy, about picking your battles and not defending the indefensible.

The problem for liberals is that it just is not working anymore. Of all the denominations and tribes that are in decline, attendance rates among liberals are in the sharpest of falls. Why is this the case, from a sociological perspective? Their strategy has a certain logic. Hasn't liberalism been a force to be reckoned with within Christianity for two hundred years or so? Why is it imploding now?

A quick digression is warranted here. Note I have asked the question why is it imploding "now?" If I had simply asked the question "why does liberalism fail?," many would have answered with a theological answer. Liberalism fails because it compromises on the truth. It is clear that liberals take a stand on certain matters, but may remain silent on other politically incorrect biblical truths. So the standard answer to why liberalism fails is because it does not stand up for the gospel.

However, this answer is unsatisfactory. As observers of social trends, we must ask ourselves, how did liberalism thrive in the early to middle stages of the twentieth century or even from the mid-nineteenth century onwards? Liberalism was progressive, selective, and compromising then. And yet it grew.[1] So, the astute question we must ask is, why is it imploding now? Theological lenses alone are insufficient to answer such questions. There are insights to be gained from the social sciences we need to hear.

1. See Gaustad and Barlow, *New Historical Atlas of Religion*, 96–109. Here the growth of denominations such as Congregationalists, Episcopalians, and Lutherans is documented. All grew significantly from 1850 onwards, and growth rates increased from 1930 to about the 1960s, after which they declined.

Back to our question. Why is liberalism imploding at the moment, when the strategy of remaining relevant, semi-aligned, and selectively prophetic has been somewhat successful in the past? I will use a sporting analogy to answer.

I have lived a good part of my life in the city of Melbourne, Australia. Melbourne considers itself one of the sporting capitals of the globe. We have a sporting precinct near the CBD, and the jewel in the crown is the MCG, the Melbourne Cricket Ground. Apparently, the MCG still holds the record for being the most attended single venue ever in the history of the Olympics. It also has the records for the largest crowd at a one-day cricket game, an international cricket test, and a domestic game.

While the ground is named the cricket ground, it is considered by most to be the spiritual home of Australian Rules Football. In Melbourne, the first question you ask a person is, what is your name? The second question is, what footy team do you barrack for? You have to love footy to be welcomed in Melbourne. To not barrack for a team makes you a social outcast.

As in every sporting code, there is the pretentious team everyone loves to hate (Collingwood, or Manchester United in the EPL). There are the teams that are perennial under-achievers (Melbourne, though they have just won the flag, or Newcastle in EPL), and only the most loyal die-hard supporters follow those teams. Then there are the teams that are easy to support. They are popular, always competitive, have a great marketing strategy, and no one hates you if you follow them (Tottenham Hotspurs in EPL). The Melbourne version of a team that is always there, or thereabouts, would be Hawthorn.

So, if you live in a city where everyone follows footy and you must support a team, then teams like this are a logical choice. Friends of mine who recently immigrated from overseas chose Hawthorn as their team. That's because they were on top at the time.

Now imagine footy goes out of vogue. Imagine it becomes a marginal sport, as rugby union is (outside of New Zealand, the Pacific, and South Africa). Imagine footy becomes a niche sport of yesteryear, and another code like soccer becomes the dominant sporting code. What will happen to our footy team's supporter base?

For the underachieving team, with loyal die-hard supporters, probably not much. Their supporters have always coped with adversity. Success or popularity never drove allegiance. For the team everyone loves to hate, they too will likely do okay. They are used to criticism and detractors. But the easy-to-join, inclusive, always-competitive team is prone to struggle. Their supporters are what is called fair-weather supporters. Easy come, easy go. These type of supporters will switch codes and support teams like Manchester City or Barcelona.

Liberal churches have this problem. Within a CWV, most people believe in God, in Jesus as an example of a good life and a teacher we should follow, and in a judgement and an afterlife. If you need a team to belong to, a place to get your kids baptized or christened, a wedding venue and celebrant, a children's playgroup to be part of, or somewhere to go at Christmas and Easter, the liberal church is an easy and accessible option. Or suppose you have grown up in a Christian family attending a more conservative or even fundamentalist church, and you don't wish to be as full on as your parents, but nor do you desire to abandon your Christian values altogether. In that case, the liberal church is a viable option for you.

But we are no longer in that world; we are now in the PCWV. All churches are on the nose. They are an optional accessory, chosen only by those who still need a crutch. In this world, people have abandoned Christianity as a religion of the past. In this world, given that religious liberalism is so similar to social liberalism, religious liberals look as if they stand for nothing unique. There is no reason to join. Your motivation for social justice can come from within, and social media can provide you with a network of like-minded "friends." You can believe in and be passionate about the same causes without having to put up with the messiness of church, church goers, and institutions. Church is redundant and unnecessary.

Apart from this, liberalism has one other major dilemma I must mention. If central parts of your message are open to reinterpretation, how do you decide which parts can be reframed without undermining your core beliefs? Liberals focus on Jesus' message of love as primary. Presently that looks like focusing on Jesus' teachings about being non-judgemental, caring for the poor, proclaiming freedom for prisoners, freeing the oppressed, and proclaiming the year of the Lord's favor (Matt 7:1–2; Luke 4:18–19). The focus is on a sub-set of Jesus' teachings and life.

Put another way, for liberals, Jesus teaches about and then lives a life of generous love. Liberals, therefore, focus on the incarnation of Jesus. His earthy life, in the flesh, is an example, whereas classic Christianity emphasizes Jesus' willing and substitutionary death for our sins as the highest expression of his love. Liberalism has moved on from talk of blood sacrifice as atonement. Death as payment for sins is primitive. I suggest that to reframe away from Jesus being the Lamb of God who takes away the sins of the world (John 1:39) is to uncouple yourself from a core element of your tradition. And uncoupling from your core does not end well.

The Mainstream Church

The second tribe of Christianity I shall refer to as "mainstream." It's a term that has currency in the USA, if not elsewhere. It is a helpful category, and I shall use the term to demarcate a particular cluster of churches. By mainstream, I do not mean either liberals or evangelicals. That is to say, mainstream churches are not liberals who downplay and reinterpret scripture. Nor are they evangelicals who have a very high view of scripture, and preach their way through books of the Bible. Rather, they sit somewhere in the middle.

Mainstream churches are more likely to have topical sermon series than exegetical ones. They will heavily invest in contemporary worship ministries because they are concerned with not just good teaching, but also with religious affections. Church (by which the mainstream means the church service) should be a shot in the arm. You ought to leave feeling encouraged and inspired. Church is an experience.

The mega-churches of the 1990s and their leaders have profoundly influenced mainstream churches. Willow Creek and Saddleback are the best-known examples, but there were others before that, for example, Robert Schuller (1926–2015) at the Crystal Cathedral in Los Angeles, and perhaps even Harry Fosdick (1878–1969) at Riverside in New York before him. The common theme among these leaders is that church needs to be relevant to everyday life. A sermon series on the Ten Commandments might be framed as a topical series called "ten guidelines for healthy families."

Again, the question pertinent to our concern is how mainstream churches respond to the present changing times. I would describe their strategy, for the most part, as accommodating. That is to say, they are adjusting their messaging and ministry to include or accommodate the changing focus of culture. Let me outline three examples.

In the PCWV, there is a shift away from truth as objective and external, towards internal intuitions and passions. Conceptual statements may well be accurate, but the truth is real; it moves you. It does so because its essence aligns with your gut intuitions. Like an open string starts to resonate when it hears its tone being played elsewhere, so culture now views truth as a message that resonates with the personal subconscious and compels us to respond. Truth is authentic.

You might anticipate that a non-objective, non-external measure of truth was problematic for Christianity. After all, the Bible is an objective book. It is God's word. He has spoken it, external to me and before I heard it. Anyone can read it, and Christians have been refining their understanding of it for centuries. There is a shared consensus that the Bible teaches that we are saved by grace, that God is triune, that Jesus is both God and man. There are time-honored interpretations called creeds and confessions. An individual is not at liberty to arrive at a different interpretation. This is to step outside what is termed "orthodoxy" (Latin: literally "right teaching") into heresy.

Mainstream churches have not abandoned any of the core orthodox Christian tenets as captured in the creeds. They just don't talk about them often. They are considered dry doctrines. Instead, there is a far greater emphasis on topics of personal relevance. How is God speaking to me about my struggle with mental wellbeing, relationships, or health concerns? How will God lead the unique me on my path into blessing and prosperity?

Mainstream Christians quote the Bible less and less. They do not teach memory verses. Instead, people say, "God said to me . . . " The focus on the Holy Spirit has shifted away from the Spirit prompting Holy-ness, that is, on justification and sanctification. Increasingly, the Spirit is the inner voice of personal guidance. Sociologically speaking, it's hard not to notice a correlation between how our culture increasingly talks about listening to your intuition, and mainstream Christians increasingly talking about listening to the Spirit.

The second example of accommodating culture is the shift towards positive feelings rather than affirming time-honored truths. In the past, church services tended to include reciting a creed, at least one Bible reading, prayers that covered a diverse range of topics, and a stand-alone confession. In mainstream churches, most if not all of these elements have gone.

In their place is worship, usually in darkened auditoriums with lit stages. Songs are well-rehearsed, up-beat, longer, and cycle through moods. They begin in an understated cut-back tone, rise and fall, and climax with an often repeated anthem-like crescendo. When done well, it is all very moving. In Pentecostal speak, if worship goes off, then "the Holy Spirit showed up!"

Such worship leads into a sermon that is more than just informative. It must also be passionate and persuasive. Stories and testimonies are great tools used to capture people's hearts and to inspire. I do not wish to comment on the relative strengths or weaknesses of this shift. I simply note these practices align with broader changes in our culture, away from time-honored truths and traditions towards being and feeling in the moment.

The last, and most profound example of accommodation, is the embracing of individualism. Mainstream churches are less about "us" and more about "me." Of course we see this trend in the lyrics of contemporary worship songs. At a more profound level, mainstream Christianity has shifted from "I live for God and others," to "God is for me. God exists to bless me, heal me, forgive me, and prosper me." Jeremiah 29:11: "'For I know the plans I have for you,' declares the Lord, 'plans to prosper you and not to harm you, plans to give you hope and a future' " is now the most searched for and quoted Bible verse.

This transition is played out very clearly in contemporary funerals. Funerals used to be about God, and his sovereignty over this life and the next. They used to be about God's love, justice, and that he holds us all to account. Comfort to the grieving came because our loved ones are now at peace with God. Scriptures and sermons about hope after death were at the center of the funeral service. They have been displaced by eulogies about the deceased. A funeral is now primarily a celebration of an individual life well lived, and not entrusting our loved ones to God.

These three examples highlight how mainstream churches accommodate or adopt PCWV themes. This tactic is sometimes called syncretism: the amalgamation or blending of different schools of thought. Behind this approach sits an assumption that there is good in the PCWV, that the church can pick the bits of the PCWV that align with Christianity, that we can take those ideas and incorporate them into our present mindset.

To be fair, I am not sure syncretism is a useful term in this instance. It is a loaded or pejorative term and it carries within it an implied criticism. To label the present mainstream church as guilty of syncretism is short-sighted. It may be the case, for instance, that the Christianity of the 1950s was too rational and cerebral. It may be that 1950s Christianity was itself a syncretism of biblical Christianity and Enlightenment rationalism. It may be that the mainstream church is returning to something closer to authentic Christianity by being more affective. Much of Christianity is open to the charge of syncretism at each stage of history.

There is another alternative. It is also possible that Christianity is a faith that morphs when embodied by people who inhabit a particular time and space. It adapts to its changing context. We might say the gospel incarnates itself in culture. To paraphrase Paul, the gospel is rational to the rationalist, and affective to the sentimental. Just because liberal or mainstream churches are too accommodating of contemporary thought, does not mean that all expressions of contextualization are invalid.

Depending on your view, you may perceive the accommodating mainstream church as constructive evolution, a perversion and dilution of the truth, or bits of both.

A second and related assumption in the mainstream church is the belief that the church must be relevant. This, too, is something that cuts both ways. On the one hand, we want to say that God, through his prophets and apostles, speaks directly to particular audiences. The letter to the Galatians is different from the letter to the Corinthians. The sermon preached by Paul at Antioch is different from the one at the Areopagus. Jesus' parables to rural Galileans are distinct from his parables to Jerusalem-dwelling Jews. Yet we also want to acknowledge that God is the same yesterday, today, and forever, and that his word abides forever.

For now, we shall leave this matter as a tension to manage rather than a problem to solve. The gospel is both timeless, and yet expressed in time-bound contexts. Churches are called to speak eternal themes into present circumstances. Speaking in a way that fails to engage is one error, and speaking in a hyper-relevant way, and unfaithful to its foundations, is another error.

Yet another assumption of the mainstream church, understood through its response to the changing culture, is that we need not be alarmed. Mainstream churches are in business-as-usual mode. There is no alarmist critique of the PCWV. They just keep doing what they did last year, but with improvements: preach another sermon series on what is topical, introduce another new song, launch a new program, and steady as she goes.

There is an evident strategy in mainstream churches to avoid un-necessary confrontation with culture. What happens though, when the culture chooses to clash with Christianity, when Christians are forced to vote yes or no regarding same-sex marriage, or when abortion or euthana-sia legislation enters the local parliament, or when religious freedoms are curtailed? What you tend to get in mainstream churches is an awkward silence. Or perhaps an understated "this is the senior pastor's position, but I appreciate not everyone will agree with me." Mainstream churches tend to avoid sermons on divorce, pre-marital sex and cohabitation, male head-ship, hell, and judgement. This maybe couched in terms like "We want to be known for what we stand for, not what we stand against."

Behind all this sits an even deeper tacit assumption. What is going on in the world is not all that different, so we don't need to change. My view is that mainstream churches are failing to grapple with the seismic shift that has taken place in culture. Present social shifts are much more significant than just the shops being open for Sunday trading. To argue that we coped with that, and we will cope with the next thing, and the next, is naïve. We are living through the end of an entire worldview, not just the removing of one more strand, but the dismantling of the entire fabric, and replacing it with another.

If this is the case, a failure to regularly re-affirm the historical core Christian tenets is a problem. Mainstream churches lack and fail to give their congregation members the frameworks and filters they need to respond to the new world we all inhabit. Christians need to appreciate what is essential and distinctive to the Christian way of thinking and what is flawed about the emerging PCWV. You don't get this from a series of topical sermons on healthy families, followed by one on how love overcomes.

Instead, the desire to become relevant develops into hyper-relevance, as topical sermons chase cultural themes. If hyper-relevance causes a church to drift from its core foundations, it risks becoming irrelevant. It is irrelevant in as much as it is no longer a church, faithfully following the teachings of Jesus, and being a light in an otherwise dark world.

Successful Church

I want to say something briefly about what I shall call "successful church." Successful churches are often mainstream, but not always so. They can also be conservative evangelical in their teaching, but very hip in their use of multi-media, the arts, and contemporary worship style (if not lyrics). They are entrepreneurial in their self-organization and ministry strategizing. Successful churches tend to be strong at marketing. They have impressive websites and other social media platforms. And, like the next season of "My Kitchen Rules," their next sermon series is going to be the best ever, so you better not miss it.

Here is what annoys me about successful churches (and I speak as someone who has worked for one or two of them). They believe their own press. They run conferences and tell everyone else that if you become just like them, you too can be successful. In other words, for successful churches, the problem is not that culture has shifted away from its Christian assumptions. The problem is that, according to them, other churches have not had the right leadership, teaching, worship, focus, or creativity. To risk using another pejorative term, successful churches are technique driven, and want to reproduce offspring in their own DNA. To be fair and give credit where it is due, sometimes it works.

The critical question we must understand about them as a phenomenon is why they have been successful. Is it because churches like Hillsong, Bethel, Holy Trinity Brompton, or Bethlehem Baptist Church (John Piper) have the right approach, worship, teaching, or technique? If more churches had mirrored Hillsong or Bethel, would they have been more successful too? Could the decline in church attendance have been halted or slowed?

Some non-church vocabulary will aid our conversation at this point. Church attendance has been in what business people would call a shrinking market. Successful churches have managed to capture a growing share of a shrinking market, a larger slice of a smaller pie. This is no small feat. Using this lens, we can now distinguish between two possible explanations of why successful churches have succeeded.

Is pie-shrinkage inevitable? Do the macro-social forces at play mean that church attendance was always going to shrink in the West? Are these factors a function of social trends that are outside of any one local church? In the grand scheme of things, it is irrelevant how the pie is divided. The pie was always going to diminish.

Or, is it the case that the pie did not have to shrink? Decline was not inevitable. Decline is a not a function of external macro social trends. Instead, it is a function of internal performance. Pie makers failed to shift with the market, and some other producers, let's say pizza makers, have now captured what was once part of the pie market. In other words, if more churches had been like Hillsong, or Bethel, or Holy Trinity Brompton, or (insert your tribe's favourite successful church) and less like boring traditional churches, could church decline have been avoided?

This is an impossible question to answer. It is what we call a non-empirical question. We cannot test what Australia would be like if Hillsong planted one hundred churches forty years ago and compare that with an Australia where Hillsong only had one campus. Many questions and indeed theories are non-empirical. Just because a hypothesis cannot be tested does not render it a meaningless question. Asking how successful churches grew in a shrinking market is still a powerful question that reveals unspoken assumptions.

Again, let me extend our analogy. Physical sales of newspapers have been in decline all over the world. Traditional print media is in what is called a disrupted market. Newspapers are closing down, merging; some are trying online subscriptions. Others remain free, trying to sell online advertising and asking for donations. Which is the best way forward for a struggling newspaper?

While hundreds of local newspapers are closing, merging, or cutting back on staff, the *New York Times* is doing fine. A revamped *Washington Post* is also reinvigorating itself. These newspapers continue to focus on quality journalism that people are prepared to pay a fee for. There is some innovation; both papers have online versions with video and audio content and both regularly update their online content, but they remain focused on quality journalism as their core business.

Could every paper in the USA have survived if it remained focused on in-depth journalism? Clearly not. Part of the success of the "successful" newspapers is that a subset of the diverse audience who used to purchase physical copies of regional broadsheets now subscribe to online editions of the *Times* or *Post* from remote locations.

It is my opinion that something like this has happened in the disrupted local church market. Others may disagree. I readily disclose that I have not mounted an argument, merely proposed an analogy but I think the analogy fits. Successful large churches are like the *New York Times* in that they focus on excellence. They function as regional churches and have captured part of the decline of the local suburban church.

If this is so, what is the appeal of a successful church? Is it because they do preaching, worship, youth and kids programs, ministry strategy, or marketing better? Or maybe even all of them better? Partially. But I suggest there is a deeper, more subconscious reason.

Western citizens are used to progress. The latest iPhone or Samsung Galaxy is more advanced than the last. My new car is safer, has more features and better fuel mileage. New drugs combat more diseases. The economy is supposed to grow every year by 2–3 percent. Science learns and discovers more. Progress is normal. We expect it. We even feel anxious when the market goes into decline or house prices drop and think something is wrong and our politicians and economists need to fix it.

Western Christians are also used to progress. The kingdom is constantly breaking in, more and more. Just like we imagine the stock market or the economy ought to grow, we have this unspoken assumption that the kingdom, too, ought to grow by 2–3 percent per year. Isn't this what Jesus teaches and promises he will be doing? Jesus is constantly building his church, isn't he? Satan and the gates of hell can't stop him. So when it's not growing, we—as in humanity—must be doing something wrong.

When the local church is not growing, local Christians feel anxious. We assume that someone, like the leadership, must be doing something wrong. So I had better move to another local church, or a regional church that is growing. They must be doing something right. Going to that church will be a positive feel-good experience (how the PCWV measures truth); and not an anxiety-inducing experience (and given suffering has no purpose, it is to be avoided at all costs).

This phenomenon is not only true of Western Anglo-Saxons. It is even more true of Asians and others from honor-shame cultures. For those wired in honor-shame thinking, the appeal of belonging to a successful growing tribe is even stronger. Some of that success is conferred onto the individual and the anxiety one feels when your tribe is not doing well is far more internalized. As a member of a failing family or tribe, you are tainted by that and are responsible to do something to reverse it. Successful churches are often very multi-cultural and this is no mere coincidence.

Successful churches have often done things well. Be it good preaching, or music, or other, their success is not unrelated to their practices. However, this does not lead to the conclusion that if we were all a bit more like the successful churches, attendance decline could have been avoided. It is my view that the church of the 1970s and 1980s had their failings. They could have adapted more quickly, for instance.

Were they worse than the church of the 1940s and 1950s, when church attendance was growing? I doubt it. Why did church attendance grow across all of Australia in the 1950s? Did we have better preachers? Better music? Better kids' programs? Better lecturers at our training colleges? Was the growth in the 1950s predominantly the function of the internal performance of the church? And was the decline from the 1960s onwards because our music, preaching, and kids' ministry deteriorated? I cannot see that.

What I see is macro social trends. There was a fit between 1950s church and Christianity and the questions of the culture of that day. Post-war boomers moved to the growing suburbs and wanted a social fabric with community, morality, a safe place for kids and youth, and positive values. The local suburban church offered what citizens were looking for, so it grew. That social fit began to come unstuck from the 1960s onwards.

In the twenty-first century, people are looking for autonomy, freedom from authority, the resources and capacity to realize their personal ambitions, and feel-good experiences. In that marketplace, the church does not offer those goods and services. Our core message is that Jesus knows you best, and you should become more like him. The church is a bad fit, and, consequently, it is in decline. Successful churches do not radically change this macro reality.

Evangelical Church

Returning to my former analogy about football clubs and their supporter base, evangelicals are the club that was never too popular, with most of its supporters being purists. I mean, rusted-on, long-term, fully signed-up, die-hard members. Sociology tells us that moderate religion declines in the face of secularization but intense faith remains strong. Thus evangelicals are doing very well at present, both in the West and globally. They are the success story of the day. We shall come to that in a minute.

First, definitions. Evangelicals are not the same as evangelists. An evangelist is someone who has a passion and gift to share the gospel. They are often uncanny in their style and have success that is difficult to explain outside of spiritual gifting. They are concerned to share about Jesus and his forgiveness to all they meet. An evangelical is someone who is concerned with biblical authority and truth. Evangelicals love the Bible. They affirm (what they believe are) the core themes of the Bible, in particular the cross as an atonement, the reality of sin, the need for individual repentance, and faith in Jesus Christ as the only means for forgiveness and becoming right (or justified) with God. An evangelical will likely use the "gospel" as a shorthand summary for the above.

Evangelicals tend to have a belief in the importance of evangelism. Actual levels of evangelistic effort can vary among evangelicals. You can be an evangelical but not evangelistic. Likewise, you can be evangelistic and not very evangelical in your theological convictions.

An evangelical church then is one where they preach and teach the Bible, in season and out of season. The sacraments (communion and baptism) are secondary to the ministry of the word. Some evangelicals will also argue that worship is subordinate to preaching whereas other evangelicals will see worship as a ministry of the word. Songs are important in that as we sing, we remind each other of biblical truths. For evangelicals, songs need lyrics with substance and singing is a corporate activity, not a concert led by want-to-be rock stars.

To be transparent, I would describe myself as an evangelical. You might be saying, "I guessed that. You were so critical of liberals, mainstream, and successful church." Just wait. I will be at least as critical of evangelicals mainly because sociology is a critical discipline. It describes cracks. If you throw in some history, and join current cracks to previous ones, they look more like chasms. Sociology equips you with tools to critique everything, the movements you are partial to as well as the movements you are not. Given that I think through sociological lenses and value my evangelical heritage, I regularly find myself reflecting on it, including its current weaknesses and strengths.

Why are evangelicals presently, and relatively speaking, more successful? Evangelicals will likely answer, "because we proclaim the truth; we preach the gospel." This theological answer has insights but is not sufficient to answer our question. If proclaiming the truth and preaching the gospel was an adequate explanation, then we would expect that evangelicals would have thrived at every point in history, but this is not the case.

Again, I will bracket out theological answers for a moment, and seek insights from the social sciences. Why would evangelicals be growing their segment of the shrinking pie at the moment? What is it about their expression of the Christian faith that people presently find appealing?

Evangelicalism is, historically speaking, a young branch of Christianity. It is a subset of Protestantism, where Martin Luther, John Calvin and others affirmed the notion of *sola scriptura* (by scripture alone) as one of the pillars of the true church. Most historians identify the revivals of the eighteenth century as the birthplace of evangelicalism.

Evangelicalism clarified its founding and defining features during the period of the Enlightenment, which emphasized reason and the natural sciences. Using these resources, humanity could secure progress with certainty. Reason and logic displaced tradition and hierarchy as the highest source of authority.

The Enlightenment provided a significant challenge to the traditional church. Established denominations, particularly those who held the status of being a state church (Catholics in Italy, Spain, and France; Lutherans in Germany; Church of England in the UK), had much of their authority centralized in bishops, church councils, a connection between church and state, and creeds. These pillars were now being undermined.

Theological liberals, as we have seen, responded to this shift by aligning themselves with the new authority of reason. If reason undermined miracle stories, liberals downplayed the account as historically accurate, and re-interpret the narrative as myth, conveying a deeper meaning.

Evangelicals faced the same challenge of the Enlightenment critique, but they responded in both similar and different ways. Like the liberals, evangelicals agreed that reason can bring insight and progress. Like the liberals, evangelicals rejected tradition as a substantial source of truth. Unlike the liberals, evangelicals were skeptical of the capacity of the fallen human mind to discover God's greatest truths. For evangelicals, God is a God of reason who has revealed certain truths in the Bible. One looks to scripture to find truth and certainty, not to human reason alone.

The scientific method was also clarified and distilled in the Enlightenment. Using the raw data of nature, when studied in the controlled environment of a laboratory, scientific experiments discerned universal principles. There is progress through human reason.

Evangelicals are drawn to the scientific method. Indeed, to take a step back in history, and contrary to popular myth, the "*entire* puritan movement was conspicuous in its cultivation of the sciences."[2] Livingstone demonstrated that Puritans saw harmony between natural and revealed truth. Nature and scripture are the two sources through which God has revealed truth. Science and the scientific method is the proper discipline through which one understands nature and the God who stands behind creation. Theology, called the queen of the sciences by Thomas Aquinas (1225–1274), is the proper discipline through which to understand scripture and the God who stands behind his word.

2. Charles Webster, as cited by Livingstone et al., *Evangelicals and Science*, 47.

The evangelicals of the eighteenth century are descendants of the Puritans (English Protestants of the sixteenth and seventeenth centuries). They lived in an era when the Puritan heritage combined with Enlightenment values to sharpen science as a discipline, which was now capable of delivering universal truths and principles. Evangelicals affirm the natural sciences as God's natural revelation and they take a parallel step within the queen of sciences, theology.

God's other source of revelation, scripture, must also be subjected to rigorous study. Commentary on scripture is not new. Jews and Christians have been doing it for centuries. What was new was that during the Enlightenment highly sophisticated linguistic tools emerged. They analyzed the source data (the original text in Hebrew and Greek). These techniques have names such as text criticism, philological criticism, source criticism, literary criticism, redaction criticism, etc.

For our purposes, you don't need to understand each of the techniques. I am suggesting that the various criticisms function like scientific methods. Theologians (like scientists) take the raw data of scripture, put it under the microscope of one or another form of textual criticism, disprove all false readings of the texts, and then announce the one true reading of the text as a triumph of reason and progress.

This metaphor allows us to distinguish the core features of three different Christian tribes. First, the liberals, who use an approach sometimes called higher criticism. They use their textual and theological acumen to arrive at new higher critical readings of scripture that are often at odds with the plain and traditional readings of the text. These new readings just happen to align with the politically correct thought of the day.

Fundamentalists, and I am trying here to use this word in its best sense, reject the higher criticism of academia. They take a straightforward and literal approach to interpreting the text. It says what it says, and it means what it means; no need to over-complicate it. If God said it, I believe it. It's the truth, popular or not, logical or not. However, such fundamentalism risks throwing the baby out with the bathwater. Any deviation from the literal reading of the text is viewed with suspicion. There is little appreciation or engagement with any scholarly reflection. Accepting the text with blind faith is seen as virtuous.

Evangelicals sit somewhere between the two. For them, the rigorous study of scripture is a worthy task. The biblical text is in some senses like all other texts. It was produced by people in specific cultures, and we must appreciate the linguistic, social, and theological context in which the text was constructed in order to interpret it correctly. Behind these layers sits a God who self-reveals and inspires by his Spirit, such that the Bible is a source of divine truth that is entirely trustworthy, and otherwise unknowable.

Put these three together: the raw data of the inspired word of God (that is absolute truth); in the hands (or the minds) of the properly trained person of God; and when they use the correct exegetical techniques, they can interpret scripture to deduce, pronounce, and apply eternal truths. Evangelicals believe they can know the mind of God with certainty.

This is the present appeal of evangelicalism. The PCWV is an age of uncertainty. It is an age of subjective internal true-for-you (a.k.a. opinion). It is an age where we have dismissed the wisdom of the past and we now know better. However, progress is coming so fast, who knows what we will discover next? The post-Christian world is fluid, ever-evolving, changeable, fast-paced, and for many, deeply unsettling.

Evangelicalism offers certainty about the objective truth built on continuity with the past, with firm foundations and principles such that you can construct a life of meaning and purpose with confidence. The best of evangelical foundations are rigorous and intellectually sophisticated. Though often not understood by Average Joe, evangelicalism cannot be dismissed as simple-minded fundamentalism. Evangelicals claim to know the mind of God with sophisticated certainty and certainty is a very, very appealing offer in unsettling times.

As I said earlier, this is the present appeal of evangelicalism. Before any evangelicals run a victory lap around the coffee table, you need to know you are in curious company. Others have recognized the insecurity of the masses because of the current *zeitgeist* of uncertainty. They, too, are offering certainty about the absolute truth.

Donald Trump responds to the uncertainty of white middle America, and his solution is to build a wall. Boris Johnson and others respond to the uncertainty of northern, aged, Anglo-Saxon English who fear EU migrants have taken their jobs. His response is Brexit. President Rodrigo Duterte of the Philippines responds to the uncertainty in his country due to crime and corruption by declaring war on drug dealers. In Australia, Pauline Hanson and her One Nation party exemplify a populist-nationalist right-wing response to fears around globalism, migration, multiculturalism, and social progressivism.

Trump, Johnson, Hanson and even Duterte are examples of what is now called right-wing populism. Populists offer a simple diagnosis and solution to current problems. Their position is often encased in one-line slogans like "make America great again" or "get Brexit done" or "no more dithering and delay."

Not all right-wing politicians that have been popular are populists. Ronald Reagan, Margaret Thatcher, and John Howard were all very successful politicians. All were socially conservative and economic liberals from the "right" but they were not populists. Likewise, we must acknowledge that the political left is not devoid of simplistic slogans from charismatic figures who desire to persuade the masses.

My point is this. In the past decade or so, there has been a rise in a particular type of simplistic right-wing populist politician, whose rhetoric usually revolves around migration, jobs, economic protectionism, and nationalism. Their vision is a type of "back to the future." Their stance is that we can recover stability, social cohesion, and certainty by returning to the core principles and practices of the good old days.

As a sociologist, I cannot help but notice that conservative, traditional, "right-wing" political positions that offer certainty in the face of complexity are presently popular. There are versions of conservative evangelicalism that bear remarkable similarities to populism: compelling and charismatic leaders with clear simple slogans that offer listeners certainty in uncertain times.

At the risk of being misunderstood, I am not saying all versions of evangelicalism are like this. Nor am I suggesting that evangelicals are misguided in their belief that God's word is truth and a source of divine guidance for life and doctrine. What I am making is a sociological observation. Evangelicalism's success or popularity is about more than just proclaiming the truth or preaching the gospel. It just so happens that certainty is a desired social commodity in short supply at the moment. Evangelicals have a product that happens to fit that need. Evangelicals are selling what some people are buying.

This new-found popularity is a double-edged sword. Compelling and charismatic leaders with clear slogans offering certainty are divisive. People either love or hate them. Trump, Johnston, and the like polarize. Furthermore, the back-to-the-future approach of reaffirming the core principles and practices of the good old days imagines that we can rewind the clock. If we could only return to the Australia or America of the 1960s, or the UK pre-European Union, things would be "great again."

History does not have a reverse gear. As we saw in chapter 3, our culture now values an intuition beyond mere cerebral reasoning, the subjective dimension to truth, the rights and freedoms of the autonomous individual, good as personal pleasure that does not harm others, and love as acceptance and non-judgementalism; all of which will empower a person to choose their own path to personal flourishing. Evangelicalism is traditionally critical of all of these.

In other words, evangelicalism is offering certainty in the face of in-security. Some people in the market are drawn to this but if the type of certainty that evangelicalism offers is the certainty of the 1960s, most will dismiss evangelicalism on the grounds that society has been-there-tried-that-moved-on. If the foundationalism that evangelicalism contends for is seen as being head but no heart and guts, as arrogant and not inclusive, as God knows best (and the church knows God the best so the church knows best), its appeal will increasingly be to a niche only.

I am still speaking sociologically. Of course, God is God, and he can save anyone from anywhere at any time he desires but a core contention of this book is this: God appears to limit or subject himself to engaging with humanity through their host cultures. In some cultures, at various points in their history, belief in God makes sense. In other cultures and in other times, belief in God makes little or no sense, so trust in God declines.

Evangelicalism faces a dilemma. Part of its present appeal is that it of-fers certainty and (some) people are looking for firm foundations. However, certainty is less valued; other qualities are displacing it. Does it make sense to frame our message in language that appeals to a shrinking and counter-cultural subset of the PCWV?

Which Approach Has the Most Explanatory Insights?

I have just surveyed four common responses to the reality that the world is changing and the church is struggling. One could suggest a fifth approach, and some churches represent a hybrid of two approaches. For the sake of clarity, I have named what I think are the big four.

Liberals, the mainstream church, popular churches, and evangelicals all have a narrative around where we are and how we got here. Each nar-rative focuses on a core explanation of what went wrong. Each narrative positions you or anticipates a different solution, a different way forward. Remedies include preaching the gospel, becoming even more relevant, aim-ing to give people an uplifting, inspiring experience, or living out our core convictions in a compelling, winsome way.

These competing readings and solutions sound, on the surface, poles apart. It would be your and my inclination to compare and contrast them against each other. That is a worthwhile exercise that others have under-taken. My perspective is that, while we tend to notice their differences, they have much in common. Behind these different approaches sit several shared assumptions because they are products of the same historical era. All these critiques are birthed from and make sense within the CWV. They share a cluster of unspoken assumptions that I wish to challenge in the next chapter. I suggest that the shift from the CWV to the PCWV means that more has gone wrong than just we stopped preaching the gospel, or being relevant, inspiring, or prophetic.

To close out this chapter, I shall use a table to summarize the insights and perspectives of each of the four narratives.

Simplicity on the Other Side of Complexity (in a table)

Group	Where are we?	How did we get here?	What went wrong?
Liberals or progressives	The church is struggling. There are pockets of life, often outside traditional Sunday services, but there is great need for hope everywhere.	Most churches got side-tracked in maintenance mode. Some fundamentalists died on the wrong hill, and gave us all a bad name.	We lost our core calling to be a radical, social, prophetic community. Our wider culture has become too self-focused and comfortable.
Mainstream church	The local church is doing okay. These are challenging times. Traditional and fundamental churches are in decline. Slow constant improvement is required.	Some adaptation has been necessary. Those with updated music, relevant preaching, a social media presence, and engaged multiculturalism are doing fine.	Some churches did not avoid the land mines. Some churches didn't evolve and became irrelevant. People are less committed to organizations.
Successful church	Some larger churches are doing great, but smaller and traditional churches are in decline. Success is repeatable for those that have the leadership to make it happen.	The growing healthy churches had a vision. They took risks, had a plan, were well led, and engaged culture in a real, authentic way with a positive meaningful message.	Smaller churches lacked entrepreneurial spirit and vision. Traditional churches follow existing formulas. If more churches evolved, we would be doing better.
Evangelicals	Churches that preach the gospel are doing okay; liberals who abandon the gospel are not. Popular churches may have some success, but lack substance.	God's Word does not return to him empty. Keep being faithful and God will bless you. At various places we see the truth is breaking through.	Some churches went soft, others went for what is popular. Our culture is increasingly spiritually blind, but God can break through that.

PART THREE

What Went Wrong?

SEEING THINGS DIFFERENTLY IS not a simple task. The apostle Peter said no to God's command to eat unclean meat three times. Imagine having a dream, hearing God, and then saying no three times. Peter did so because he was so wedded to his Jewish way of seeing the world. I am inviting you to see that the world has changed, and that we need to see how to posture in this new context somewhat differently. I offer this summary in the hope it will help you follow my argument, or analysis to date.

Summary of PART 1: Where Are We?

- Western societies lived through an era called Christendom that lasted almost 1600 years.

- In this era, citizens held to a shared consensus or worldview with deeply Christian assumptions.

- This CWV was founded upon shared beliefs in a personable God, who has created a world with a knowable moral fabric, and with beings who have a purpose. God sees our choices, and decides who deserves eternal life and who does not.

- The CWV also had shared values such as the dignity of all humanity, freedom of the individual, and rationality.

- Without being a practicing Christian, Average Joe held to these shared beliefs and values. They were the default position. Joe's behaviors included lifestyle choices that fit with the acceptable range of CWV practices.

- Society at large held to these values. Institutions like public hospitals, schools, and democracy are an outworking of our shared beliefs and values.

- Mission in this era was to people who believed in God, objective morality, and heaven and hell. We just needed to clarify with people that you get to heaven by faith in Jesus, not good works. (I will outline this in chapter 9.)

Summary of PART 2: How Did We Get Here?

- Recently, this has all shifted. Average Joe has transitioned away from a view of the world where God was the creator, designer, benefactor, and judge to a view of the world where the individual is at the center of their own universe.

- Spirituality is now an optional extra that I get to choose when and where to add into my story.

- The influences and reasons why we have made this shift are multiple but the consequences are real. Imagining that you are at the center of your own universe is a post-Christian way of seeing the world that now holds the default status. It is assumed and understood to be plausible.

- Christianity is now implausible. Society has been there, tried that, and moved on. The church is power-hungry, dangerous, and viewed with deep suspicion.

- The Western church has experienced major attendance decline since the 1960s.

- In response to this shift, Christians, in my opinion, have a short-range, one-dimensional analysis of the problem and its solutions. Four competing tribal answers dominate the discussion. Each blames the other for declines, and suggests it has the best way forward.

The shifts outlined above are complex and wide-sweeping. It is now time for a closer look at our third big framing question: what went wrong?

8

Is Our Intuition Correct?
Has Something Gone Wrong?

I WAS MEETING THE other day with an Anglican bishop who has led
churches in both Australia and the USA. We were discussing the health of
the Western church. His observation was that, intuitively, Western Christians have a sense that all is not well, that something has gone wrong. The
average person in the pews could not say exactly what has gone wrong or
why, but there is a shared unease that all is not right.

At the end of the last chapter, I suggested that within the narrative of
various Christian tribes, there are varied and competing explanations of what
has gone wrong. For liberals or progressives, we lost our core calling to be
a radical prophetic community that embodies hope and compassion. For
success-driven churches, many churches lacked entrepreneurial spirit and vision and could not evolve with a positive message encased within an inspiring
worship service. For the mainstream tribe, some churches did not find that
elusive balance between progress, taking most people with you, and remaining relevant and accessible to the local community. For evangelicals, churches
have moved away from their core convictions of believing in, proclaiming,
trusting, and obeying God as he speaks through his word.

Each approach has one big idea with variations on that theme. Each
approach has a nemesis that it fears. Each blames the other. Put another
way, each believes that if all churches were like ours, this would not have
happened. The solution is internal, therefore the problem must be within
us. In this sense, all the explanations have similar presuppositions, some of
which I now wish to challenge.

Here is the first: that local churches like St. James or New Hope
ought to be growing. We assume that church growth is natural and always

147

expected, that if local churches are not growing, something is wrong. Someone has made a mistake. Someone has not preached the gospel, or been relevant, or been inspiring, or prophetically compelling, or this or that. If the local church had done "that," whatever "that" might be, churches would be healthy and growing.

Why Do We Assume Growth Is Natural and Normal?

There are several layers of reasons why we as citizens in Western culture and members of the Western church assume that growth is expected. Let's begin with exploring why we think this way as Western Christians. Even if you have not read church history per se, chances are you hold a vague sense of a continually growing, ever-expanding movement. I sense the default take on church history, held by Christian Chris, goes something like this.

Acts 1:	120 disciples
Acts 2:	3,000 converts, plus the Lord added to their number daily
Acts 2–7:	The church grows in Jerusalem, and is then persecuted
Acts 8–9:	The church grows in Samaria
Acts 10–12:	The church grows in Gentile Antioch
Acts 13–28:	The church grows through Paul's missionary journeys
65–312 AD:	The church is persecuted, but continues to grow
312–325 AD:	Emperor Constantine is converted, convenes the Nicaean council, more growth
326–1516 AD:	Slow but continuous growth in Europe, then corruption sets in
1517–1700s:	The Reformation corrects churches abuses and bad theology
1800–1900s:	The modern missionary movement goes wherever the empire goes
1970–2000s:	Explosion of the church in China and Asia, but decay in the West.

If something like this is the common view of church history, two observations are apparent. First, growth is normal and continuous. Be it under persecution, under a Christian emperor, or through the British Empire and her missionaries to India or Africa, the church is forever growing. Second, decay and decline is rare, and is constrained to the West, and only recent.

As I shall demonstrate later, such assumptions are selective and misleading. The church has not always grown. The point I make now is this:

Western Christians have a shared belief that the church has continually grown. Therefore we assume it is meant to grow always. We believe church growth is natural, normal, and to be expected.

Furthermore, we usually add some biblical texts to bolster this assumption. Does not Jesus promise that he will build his church and the gates of hell will not overcome it (Matt 16:18)? God desires that none should perish (2 Pet 3:9). Jesus likens the kingdom to crops that produce more, or trees that grow bigger and bigger. The kingdom is always coming, constantly breaking in. We plant, we water, but God gives the growth (1 Cor 3:6).

Our potted knowledge of church history and selective referencing of scripture combine to give Western Christians the idea that church growth is expected. Given God's nature and promises, if it's not growing, there must be a problem with the way we are planting or watering. If it's not happening now, we must be doing something wrong.

The assumption that growth is normal is prevalent among Western Christians *and* Western thought in general. Growth parallels our Western value of progress. Let's return to economic theory for a moment. Western economics is built on the notion that the economy should grow by 2–3 percent every year. We all expect wages growth, for instance. We all anticipate property prices to appreciate. We all expect GDP to grow so that the government can build more roads, schools, and hospitals.

We also all expect that science and technology will continue to result in never-ending progress. My next phone will do more than my last one. My next car will be more fuel-efficient and have more features than the previous model. My next television will be bigger, my next laptop more powerful. Advances in computers and robotics will mean that the price of goods and services will also come down. So, for instance, the combination of more efficient airplanes and automated check-in will mean that international travel will become cheaper. Advances in science will mean more diseases will be curable and crop productions will increase.

When things are not progressing, something is wrong. If the economy is slowing, it's a result of corruption, inefficiencies, red tape, the lack of a free trade agreement, or a global financial crisis caused by greedy banks. When a pandemic strikes, it is the cause of increases in the cost of travel. When the economy slows, property prices fall. If reading and writing levels decline in our schools, we feel anxious and unsettled. It's not proper. Like on a graph, things are supposed to go up and to the right. Always.

As Western citizens, we bring these patterns of thinking to our contemplations regarding church. When church attendance and health are not going up and to the right, something is wrong. Someone has messed things up. As for the economy and technology, church growth and king-dom progress are natural and to be expected.

As I talk to my Christian friends, whether they are ministers or pas-tors employed by local churches or competent, educated, and committed congregation members concerned about the church, the assumptions are the same. Something is not right, and "leadership" is somehow to blame. We (or they) are making mistakes. Now I wish to get behind these ideas, and explore some of the deeper underlying hypotheses of Western Christian thought that lead us to these conclusions.

Why Do We Assume People Can Cause or Stop Church Growth?

I was talking with a businessman who had interests in a construction com-pany in Indonesia, a Muslim country. He said that it was hard to increase safety on Indonesian building sites. If something went wrong, it was the will of Allah. No one made a mistake. There was nothing to learn or improve. Fate, as dished out by a sovereign Allah, was outside human control.

Western assumptions are very different from this. We believe in a more or less "closed" universe. Whatever gods or spirits there may be in this world, they do not cause accidents on building sites. Following Im-manuel Kant, we suppose that if there are spiritual forces, they exist in an-other realm, another dimension. Our world is, in practice, a closed system of cause and effect. Natural laws cause the sun to rise and the rains to fall. We do not need a spiritual realm to explain natural events.

What this means for me as an individual is that I operate within a system of natural laws. If I control my diet and exercise, I will lose weight and become healthier. If I invest in my relationships, that will result in more harmony and connection. If I work hard, I will get ahead. If I invest astutely, my net worth will increase. If I practice good hygiene, I can avoid catching transmittable diseases. If I fail to do any of these, life could get messier for me.

Combine the idea that the gods do not interfere with naturals laws and that there is a high correlation between my actions and their conse-quences, and you conclude that we are in control of our destiny, that we sow what we reap.

As I write, it's the Australian summer of 2020. We are enduring the worst bushfires ever recorded in human history. So far, ten million hectares have burnt. That's almost the size of England! We have experienced a national sense of shock, then compassion, and now we are in a nationwide season of blame. Some people want to blame industry and climate skeptics for inaction that has led to global warming and longer dry spells. Others want to blame the "greenies" who protest against preventative controlled burns. Still others want to blame the government for mismanagement.

Our inclination to find blame displays an assumption that it's someone's fault, that it was preventable. To what extent it was preventable, I do not know. That we quickly assume, as Westerners, it was caused or was preventable by human actions, that is my point.

Back to my comment, we sow what we reap, biblical allusion intended. This is not just a Western thought; it is inherited from our CWV. When Western civilizations emphasize empowered individuals who act in accord with natural laws, they operate within (an Enlightenment version of) the CWV. This version includes patterns such as a rational God who has made an ordered world that follows natural laws, a God who created humanity in his image as rational beings, beings who are capable of wise and foolish choices who are responsible for their actions and will be rewarded accordingly, beginning in this life and then carried over into the next.

Christianity postulates rational, responsible humans, and it also supposes a God who is, habitually, somewhat "hands-off." As Paul says explicitly in Romans 1:24–27, God (at times) hands humanity over to experience the consequences of our choices. God lets our chosen paths play out. Put another way, the Christian view of God is that while he is sovereign and can choose to act when and where he chooses, he is not an ever-intervening God who stops all evil. Instead, he is a self-restrained Father who grants his creatures freedoms. At times, he intervenes, not to completely stop but rather to restrain evil.

The Australian bushfires appear to fit this pattern. God has allowed Western civilizations to use their God-given capacity for reason to evolve into patterns of unsustainable use of natural resources, especially the burning of fossil fuels. The consequences of these choices are variations in temperature and rainfall. Some Australian summers are hotter and drier than in the past. So it follows that our bushfires have become more intense. God grants us freedom and then allows us to experience the consequences of our choices.

This triad of assumptions, that our universe is (for the most part) closed, that it operates according to natural laws within a system of cause and effect, and that humans can control much of their destiny, is a potent combination. Add to that the assumptions that progress is normal, the church has continually grown, and God promises to grow his church, and you get a harmonious picture. You arrive at a compelling conclusion. The church should continue growing, and we ought to facilitate that, or at least not mess it up.

So, back to our third framing question. Has something gone wrong, as our intuition tells us? Have Western Christians, the Western church, or its leaders lost the plot? My suggestion: no. I don't think that conclusion best fits the social reality of where we find ourselves. I don't believe that explanation best aligns with the patterns of history. The explanation that it's primarily our fault is not the only explanation and I don't think it's the best one.

The Decline of the Church in the East

The church has not always grown. In certain places and periods, it has shrunk. No, I need to state that more strongly: on occasions, it has been decimated.

Recently I travelled to Turkey. My wife and I visited a place called Iznik. It's famous for its pottery. I am guessing you have never heard of Iznik, but you likely know it by its former name: Nicaea.

If you have been raised or worshipped in a more traditional or liturgical church, or even attended a church school, you would have recited the Nicene Creed. The original version of this creed was written at the first Church Council of 325 AD, held in Nicaea. About three hundred bishops and other Christian leaders from both the Eastern (Greek speaking) and Western (Latin speaking) Roman Empire gathered in Nicaea, in modern-day Turkey, under Emperor Constantine. The Nicene Creed articulates the shared fundamental beliefs of the Christian faith. It also countered the heresies of its day.

There were seven ecumenical church councils held between 325 and 787. The last of those was also held in Nicaea. Catholic Pope Adrian I, who resided in Rome, sent delegates to and affirmed the outcomes of this last council. Nicaea had its own resident Orthodox bishop who oversaw the local bishopric, or diocese. Nicaea was a destination on the early Christian map.

Iznik is now a Muslim township. If you visit the central mosque, which is called Hagia Sophia (but not the same one as in Istanbul), you will notice all the trappings of a mosque: domes; a prayer hall where you can't wear shoes; a fountain for ritual washing; a minaret tower that calls people to prayer; and a mihrab that faces east. For the very observant, in this mosque, the mihrab sits inside a half dome that was the former sanctuary. That is to say, the mihrab sits inside what was the front of a Byzantine Orthodox Church. This is the very building where the seventh council was held. There are the remains of a relief above one window where Jesus, speaking from the cross, asks John to look after his mother, Mary.

That is it! That is the strongest evidence you will find of the Christian heritage of Nicaea. As you marvel at these tiny remains of artwork, you cannot but help ask yourself, "what happened to Christianity in Nicaea? How did this place, once central in clarifying our core beliefs and a gathering point for the ancient church, lose its faith?"

Nicaea is not alone. It is not the only place where the Christian faith once thrived and is now absent. The same is true for all of modern-day Turkey and for all of the Middle East and Northwestern Africa as well. This territory was all a Christian stronghold and the center of the Eastern church.

Present day Istanbul was once called Constantinople, after Emperor Constantine. Constantinople was the center of the Eastern Orthodox Church. The Hagia Sophia, built in 537 AD, was the world's largest cathedral for almost a thousand years. From Constantinople, Christianity travelled east along the Silk Road into Asia and took hold in India and China. One of Genghis Kahn's (1162–1227) wives and one of his generals were Christian. Mongol armies are recorded in history as having destroyed mosques and protected churches.

The decline of the Eastern church is not so much about Christians losing their faith, but rather the rise of Islam. In the seventh and eighth centuries, Muslims conquered and controlled the Middle East. After that, Islam spread to the West to overtake North Africa and to the East to defeat Central Asia. From the ninth until the thirteenth century, Muslims subjugated but tolerated Christians. Levels of persecution waxed and waned.

Historian Philip Jenkins writes:

> Apart from its continuing strength in Muslim-ruled realms, Christianity still flourished as the dominant religion in those regions still under the control of the Byzantine Empire. Within the empire and beyond, Asian and African Christianity were still powerful forces in 1200, yet within at most two centuries that presence had crumbled. In this brief time, some of the most ancient Christian communities were all but annihilated.[1]

What happened in the early fourteenth century that caused Islam to become more militant? A common response is that it responded to the Western church's Crusades into the former Eastern Empire. Jenkins suggests that religious intolerance rose everywhere among everyone. English and then French Christian nations began expelling Jews. He identifies climate change as the primary causal factor. A warmer eleventh and twelfth

---

1. Jenkins, *Lost History of Christianity*, 114–15.

century brought a season of prosperity and tolerance. A thirteenth century Little Ice Age in Europe and the Middle East brought scarcity, nationalism, and persecution.[2]

Whatever the reasons, they are tangential to our concerns. My point is this: it's not that Christians or the church or bishops did something wrong. There is no evidence that the church suddenly stopped praying, or stopped caring for the poor, or became lukewarm and godless, or theologically lurched towards liberalism. Rather, another more powerful force, in this case Islam, itself responding to context and circumstance, destroyed the church.

All of this reminds me of Israel sojourning in Egypt. In Exodus chapters 1–2, Israel is a blessed nation, "exceedingly fruitful; they multiplied greatly, increased in numbers and became so numerous that the land was filled with them" (Exod 1:6). That is to say, they are fulfilling the divine mandate to "Be fruitful and increase in number; fill the earth and subdue it" (Gen 1:28). As a productive, peaceful nation, they are a blessing to Egypt, fulfilling the other great divine mandate: "all peoples on earth will be blessed through you" (Gen 12:3).

The only mention of Israel's spiritual health in the introductory two chapters is that Israel's midwives "feared God" (Exod 1:17). There is no mention of unfaithfulness, idolatry, or the like. The reason Israel is enslaved, according to Exodus, is a new king or pharaoh who has a hard heart and knows nothing of Jacob's saving works. Pharaoh sees the blessed nation of Israel, blessing Egypt, as a risk and a curse. That something has gone wrong is not always the fault of the People of God.

What about Church Attendance in the West?

The average Western Christian is unfamiliar with the history of the Eastern church. Beyond some vague consciousness that there are Greek and Russian Orthodox churches and Coptic churches in North Africa, we know little. We imagine its history and decline to be an anomaly and perhaps something to do with the fact that they were initially sectarian and heretics: Nestorians.

We sense that the Western church, centered historically in Rome, influential across Italy, France, Spain, Germany, and the United Kingdom, has always been dynamic and growing. Of course, it lost its way for a century or two and needed reforming, but from there onwards the church spread into the Americas, India, Africa, Asia, and the Pacific.

This is the church that we assume has constantly been growing slowly but steadily. These are the builders of the enormous cathedrals across Europe

2. Jenkins, *Lost History of Christianity*, 135.

that were once filled. This is the church Jesus said Satan would not over-come. This is the true church for whom growth has always been normal. This church is the very one we inherit and is declining on our watch, and we feel guilty and responsible for that. Are we right to feel that?

There is no doubt that Christianity and the church grew in the first four centuries. From the death of Jesus in 33 AD till the year 313 AD (Constantine's reign), Christianity was regularly, but not constantly, under persecution. Despite that, it also grew profoundly. Rodney Stark suggests that in 40 AD there were about 1,000 Christians,[3] equal to about 0.0017 of the Empire. By 300 AD, projected growth at 40 percent each decade gives 6,299,832 Christians, or 10.5 percent of the Empire. By 350 AD, the projected number had risen to 33,882,008, an impressive 56.5 percent of the Empire.[4]

If we fast forward about 1000 years to the late Middle Ages, or just before the Reformation, what is church attendance like in the West? Stark informs us that evidence from Florence, Tuscany, England, Germany, and Saxony is "in amazing agreement that the great majority of ordinary people seldom if ever went to church."[5] Statistics are not available for this era, but anecdotal laments from the clergy of vacant churches abound.

Historical Church Attendance in the United Kingdom

Let us narrow our focus to England. According to Scarisbrick, "Many Pre-Reformation English men and women probably did not go to church very regularly, and some hardly ever or not at all."[6] After the Reformation, measuring church attendance in England becomes complicated because it was made compulsory by law. The intention was to promote unity in the Church of England, and oppose Catholics, sectarian Protestants, and "practical atheists."[7]

The English were initially slow to comply, such that in 1563 the question was asked in Parliament why "the common people in the countrye universallie come so seldome to common prayer and devine service . . . ?"[8] A bill was debated requiring people to attend quarterly and to partake of

---

3. Stark does not trust the Acts 2 account of Pentecost and the three thousand converts. Whether there are one thousand or four thousand converts by 40 AD matters not. The projected growth rates remain astounding.

4. Stark, *Rise of Christianity*, 7.

5. Stark, *Triumph of Christianity*, 256.

6. Scarisbrick, *Reformation and the English People*, 163.

7. Field, "Shilling for Queen Elizabeth," 213–53.

8. Field, "Shilling for Queen Elizabeth," 215.

Holy Communion annually. Such laws, however, did not prevent up to half the people from being absent.

In 1650, laws mandating church attendance were repealed, the result being in 1655 that "not one in twenty in many towns go to any place of worship on the Lord's Day."[9] By 1657, fines were reintroduced but only sporadically enforced.

Now more than a century after the Reformation, matters had become more complex. By this time, some were dissenters or non-conformists. That is to say, they did not conform to the Church of England, perhaps being Baptists, Congregationalists, or later Methodists. Laws needed to allow dissenters the freedom to worship, fulfilling their legal obligation in a denomination other than Anglican. This created a loophole that many people used as a reason not to attend church at all. One person complained, "The very next Sunday after it was known [you were not required to attend a Church of England, and non-conformist churches did not keep a roll], the churches in many places were almost quite deserted."[10] Likewise, two bishops complained that many abused this loophole and attended no church at all.[11]

This state of affairs remained the case for the next 100 plus years. Legal loopholes and non-enforcement of requirements to attend worship persisted, such that in 1799 we again find the clergy bemoaning "the scandalous thinness of our congregations everywhere".[12] The prevalence of more women over men in church is also noted.[13]

As we come into the nineteenth century, statistics and record-keeping in some Church of England dioceses become more readily available. In 1836 the Vicar of Bowerchalke records that 92% of households have a bible, prayerbook, or both. Three out of four villagers were batptised.[14] So yes, nineteenth century UK was very Christian. On Census Sunday in 1851, however, only "20 per cent of people attended parish churches in England and 11 per cent in Wales."[15] Sermons and tracts remain rife with complaints of absenteeism. One Hampshire clergyman recorded in 1832 that 24 percent

---

9. The notebook of Rev. Thomas Jolly, as cited by Field, "Shilling for Queen Elizabeth," 219.

10. Leslie, as cited by Field, "Shilling for Queen Elizabeth," 220.

11. Field, "Shilling for Queen Elizabeth," 222.

12. Prince, as cited by Field, "Shilling for Queen Elizabeth," 224.

13. Field, "Shilling for Queen Elizabeth," 243.

14. Wood, "Spiritual Wilderness."

15. Field, "Counting Religion in England and Wales," 718.

of his congregation attended constantly, 20 percent generally, 37 percent occasionally and 19 percent never.[16]

Another factor affected church attendance in the nineteenth century:
revival. There was the Evangelical Revival in Britain in the mid-1700s, a
second revival in the early 1800s, and a third revival in the mid-1800s. A
French sociologist toured Britain and reported in 1828, "From the information I have gathered in both England and in Scotland, I am convinced
that religious observance has shown a marked increase among all classes
in the last ten years."[17]

Others concur with this observation. Field suggests that competition
between Church of England and Nonconformity churches resulted in increased evangelism, services, and church building. Ironically, during the
same period, the parliament began dismantling statutory churchgoing.[18]
Field also concludes that congregants represented about two-fifths of the
population according to the 1851 ecclesiastical census of England and
Wales. He believes this is the high point of church attendance.[19]

If this is the high point, what were the rates of attendance in prior
centuries? Likely lower, but how much lower is perhaps impossible to
quantify. Many historians view anything before the 1800s as "'a pre-sta-
tistical age' in religious terms."[20] Regarding rates of attendance after the
1851 census, Brierley Consultancy reported church attendance in Britain
in 1980 and again in 2015 as being 11.8 percent and 5.0 percent of the
population respectively.[21]

Why is it that we imagine historical church attendance to be so high?
Several factors are worth naming. First, as we understand the word in the
modern sense, atheism was almost non-existent in the past.[22] While pubs
may have been full on a Sunday with the irreligious, this did not mean patrons were atheists. Two-thirds of people were baptized in the nineteenth
century.[23] Britons remained adherents to what I am calling the CWV. The
nation held Christian beliefs and values.

Second, churches were full on occasion. Wood notes that services were
full on Queen Victoria's diamond anniversary in 1897, the "restoration of

16. Field, "Counting Religion in England and Wales," 712–18.

17. G. d'Eichthal, as cited by Fields, "Shilling for Queen Elizabeth," 245.

18. Field, "Shilling for Queen Elizabeth," 245.

19. Field, "Shilling for Queen Elizabeth," 247.

20. Currie, as cited by Field, "Counting Religion in England and Wales," 693.

21. Brierley, "Church Attendance in Britain," para. 7.

22. Field, "Counting Religion in England and Wales," 716.

23. Wood, "Spiritual Wilderness " 80.

peace in South Africa" in 1902, and the outbreak of World War I.[24] Historical photos suggest the annual Sunday School picnic was well attended. Yet, on regular Sundays, service and Sunday school registers reveal that on some occasions no one came to Sunday school, and service attendance was between 4 percent and 18 percent of the village.[25]

This is to say that in Victorian Britain and before, the church functioned as more than a provider of religious services for those who had a personal faith relationship with Jesus Christ. The church was also a social institution that gathered the masses to mark significant civic occasions. Average Joe villagers did not distinguish between belonging to a community that celebrates civic/religious occasions in the local church and being a practicing member of a congregation. People saw themselves as members of their local church. None of this meant that most people regularly came to ordinary Sunday services. Our corporate memories of full churches are fuelled by nostalgia, special services, and high participation rates in religious customs by irregular churchgoers.[26]

If the historic English local church was not as well attended as we assumed, what does this mean? Before we consider the repercussions of this question, we shall broaden our picture, briefly tracking historical church attendance in both America and Australia.

Historical Church Attendance in the United States

America is a unique place, so we imagine. Australia was founded by criminals who disembarked from convict ships, whereas America was founded by religious pilgrims fleeing persecution on board the *Mayflower*. Australia is a-religious and anti-authoritarian from the get-go, while America is pro-religion and pro-individual freedom. Does history support this view?

A full answer is beyond our brief but there is no doubt that the United States has much higher rates of church attendance presently than Australia does. We shall briefly now explore American rates of church attendance.

Respected sociologists of religion, Roger Finke and Rodney Stark, note that "America shifted from a nation in which most people took no part in organized religion to a nation in which nearly two-thirds of American adults do."[27]

---

24. Wood, "Spiritual Wilderness," 79.
25. Wood, "Spiritual Wilderness", 80.
26. Wood, "Spiritual Wilderness", 80.
27. Finke and Stark, *Churching of America*, 1.

Similar to the case of Britain, American statistics before 1890 are problematic. Broadly speaking, European history in America began in 1565, with the Spanish arrival in Florida. The English founded Jamestown in 1607 in Virginia, on the east coast. The pilgrims arrived in Plymouth (also east coast) in 1620. From here, the east coast was rapidly settled by the English, French, Dutch, and Spanish. By 1763, when the British defeated the French, the English controlled about one-third of America as we now know it, being the northeastern area, in thirteen colonies. In 1775, these colonies revolted against the English, and in 1776 they declared independence. Perhaps 2–2.5 million people were living in these colonies.

Finke and Stark conclude that 10–12 percent of the colonial population in 1776 was churched.[28] By "churched," they mean members who regularly attended. Regarding adherents, including the more irregular attenders who may define themselves as belonging to a church, they believe that figure to be 16 or 17 percent.[29] They claim their conclusions, while more rigorous and evidence-based, still fall within the consensus of previous estimates.[30]

From this low ebb, the American church grew to 62 percent participation in 1980.[31] The growth is not entirely continuous; they report a decline in national religious adherence from 1860 to 1870, but all other eras show consistent growth. Their final high figure is supported by other research. The Gallup Poll reports that in 1980, 71 percent of Americans were members of a church. Barna Group reports that in 1993, 45 percent of Americans reported attending church weekly, with a further 35 percent of Americans categorized as non-practicing Christians.[32] The trend from 10 percent to 62 percent is surprising. If Finke and Stark are correct, America became Christian; it was not birthed or colonized that way.

Their account does not suggest all American churches grew between 1776 and 1980. Herein lies the contribution of Finke and Stark. At any given point in time, there are some denominations that are growing, not just in terms of total attendance, but also in terms of the percentage of church attenders, or "market share." Some denominations are in decline. There are winners and losers. In simple terms, Congregationalists and Episcopalians tend to be in decline, while Baptists and Methodists grow.

28. Stark and Finke, "American Religion in 1776," 50–51.

29. Stark and Finke, "American Religion in 1776," 51; Finke and Stark, *Churching of America*, 23.

30. Stark and Finke, "American Religion in 1776," 39.

31. Stark and Finke, "American Religion in 1776," 55.

32. Finke and Stark, *Churching of America*, 23; Jones, "U.S. Church Membership," para. 1; Barna Research Group, "State of the Church 2020," paras. 9 and 10.

So the question becomes, "what causes a denomination to grow?" Finke and Stark answer: "to the degree that denominations rejected traditional doctrines and ceased to make serious demands of their followers, they ceased to prosper."[33] When a movement becomes too accommodating to its host culture and loses its "otherworldliness," it dilutes its appeal and ability to engender adherence.

At this point, it is helpful to distinguish between Finke and Stark's observations and their explanations. To highlight that some movements grow while others decline is an insightful observation. To explain that phenomenon as a movement towards theological liberalism is an interpretation, a conclusion others suggest is not borne out by the data.

It is true to suggest that (Southern) Baptists require an "otherworldliness" from their adherents, temperance, for instance. Yet part of the success of Southern Baptists in the south and west of America is that the denomination shares a frontier pioneering spirit with those moving west. The Baptists are a non-establishment movement; that is part of their appeal. It is more accurate to say that Baptists are part aligned, and part out of step with their culture.

Second, not all denominations that remain "otherworldly" prosper. Not all Baptist denominations grow. The Mormons win market share, yet the Jehovah's Witnesses do not.

Third, there is the issue of timing. Finke and Starke claim that decline follows a movement away from sectarian otherworldliness towards accommodating liberalism. However, as their data shows, Congregationalists and Episcopalians were losing market share, while Baptists and Methodists were exploding at the time of the Revolution (1776). Their decline was some 100 years before theological liberalism had a widespread influence.[34]

What conclusions can be drawn? Several. America grew to become a predominantly Christian nation. During this period of (mainly) sustained growth, some denominations exploded, increasing their market share dramatically. Others lost market share. It must also be noted that since 1980 the American church has plateaued and then declined, losing something in the order of one quarter of its members and one third of its attendees.[35]

The precise reasons why one denomination grows or declines are multi-factorial. Cultural accommodation and theological liberalism do correlate with decline but there is not a converse one-to-one correlation between sectarian otherworldliness and growth. To borrow a biblical

33. Finke and Stark, *Churching of America*, 1.

34. Weber, Review of *The Churching of America*, 138–40.

35. See Jones (of Gallup) and Barna articles cited above.

phrase, growing churches appear to be *in the world* or aligned with their host culture, yet calling people to be *not of this world*. The growing church speaks from within one part of the host culture, to an otherworldly spiritual longing that the host culture is not able to fulfill.

What are we to make of the American church after 2000, when it comes into widespread decline? Finke and Stark suggest that the secularization of one denomination leads to local decline, yet "*not to irreligion, but to revival.*"[36] In other words, decay in part of the church is the very context that gives rise to new birth in other parts. Does this thesis still hold into this century? The American church is in widespread decline, yet we do not see widespread revival. Or did this thesis hold in Christendom (in America), but no longer appears to be the case in the PCWV? These are the fundamental questions we are exploring.

Historical Church Attendance in Australia

The relationship between the church and the convict colony founded in 1788 is an often misunderstood one. For the most part, scholarship and popular opinion has assumed a negative role of religious movements. The church existed to validate and reinforce the moral standing and code of the British Empire. Church attendance was initially compulsory, resulting in the chapel being burned as a protest.[37] The colony's second chaplain, the so-called flogging parson Samuel Marsden, is also cited as evidence of this state-aligned moral chaplaincy view of the church.[38]

The 2018 publication by Piggin and Linder, *The Fountain of Public Prosperity: Evangelical Christians in Australian History 1740–1914*, rights this wrong. Recent historical research has revealed the caricature of Marsden as unfair. In fact, evangelical Christians have had an overwhelmingly positive impact on Australian values and livelihood.

As with the US and UK, quantifying church attendance and adherence in the eighteenth and nineteenth centuries is problematic and attempts are imprecise. We can more clearly track the role of evangelical Christianity on the formation of Australia through the *Church Acts* of NSW in 1836/39. Here, those churches of all denominations that wanted it were given government funding to build and staff local churches. Churches in Australia, as in England, became early important civic and social institutions. These local churches produced a "culture forged out of

36. Finke and Stark, *Churching of America*, 46, emphasis theirs.
37. Piggin and Linder, *Fountain of Public Prosperity*, 82–85.
38. Piggin and Linder, *Fountain of Public Prosperity*, 86–97.

Classical virtues as well as biblical values . . . Co-operation between church and state in the interests of nation-building was the norm rather than the exception in mid-nineteenth-century Australia."[39]

To express this reality in terms of the language of this book, in (and before) the mid-nineteenth century, politicians were acutely aware the values required to create a coherent and integrated society were the very same values that churches of all denominations espoused. The state and church believed in, and sought to engender and cultivate, a Christian worldview into the Australian social fabric.

Church attendance was near its peak in Australia towards the end of the 1800s. Stephen Judd and Kenneth Cable report that, in 1881, 27 percent of the New South Wales population was present at church on Sundays. Piggin believes the figure is more like 40 percent of Sydney-siders and 60 percent of Melbournians.[40] Walter Phillips concurs with this higher figure at 56 percent in 1870. Beyond New South Wales, 40 percent of South Australia and 43 percent of Victorians attended church. Atheists were yet to emerge as a force, with 95 percent of the population claiming to be Christian.[41]

We note these results are similar to New Zealand. Church attendance peaked in New Zealand in 1890, and at that time it was about 30 percent of the population. Furthermore, 90 percent of the population self-designated as an adherent of one of the six largest Christian denominations.[42]

It is also worth pausing, noting that by the late nineteenth century the church was already losing social influence. In 1875, a law was passed in New South Wales permitting a man to marry his dead wife's sister. Controversially, this state law contradicts a biblical law in Leviticus. Public transport, theaters, pools, museums and the like all began opening on Sundays. Divorce laws were weakened.[43]

Again, to express this in the language of this book, what we are seeing is the highest rates of church attendance at times where church influence is in decline. There is not a one-to-one correlation between church attendance and church influence.

39. Piggin and Linder, *Fountain of Public Prosperity*, 258.

40. Piggin and Linder, *Fountain of Public Prosperity*, 386, 410.

41. Judd and Cable, *Sydney Anglicans*, 120; Phillips, "Religious Profession and Practice," 388. See also his *Defending "A Christian Country"*, chapter 1; Foster, "Vision for the Mission," 23.

42. H. Jackson, "Churchgoing in Nineteenth-Century New Zealand, 47, 58.

43. Lawton, *Better Time to Be*, 160; Judd and Cable, *Sydney Anglicans*, 146–47.

From the late 1800s onwards, church attendance in Australia continued to decline to about 23 percent in 1950. Then in the next seven years, it jumped back up to 30 percent.[44]

Between the 1947 census and the 1961 census, the overall population grew at 2.4% per year. In this period Anglicans grew by 1.6% and added 712,000 to their number; Baptists at 2.0% and added 36,000; and Roman Catholics at 3.5% and added over one million people. As a percentage of the population, Angicans fell from 39% to 35%, Baptists remained at 1% and Catholics rose from 23% to 27%.[45]

What happened in this seven year period? The answer includes but cannot be put solely down to the 1959 crusade of Billy Graham. The fuller answer consists of a post–World War II suburban boom, where returned soldiers sought to begin new families and lives in the outer suburbs of major cities. The ambitions of this new aspirational class—stability, security, and belonging to a local community—were embodied in the local suburban church. In addition, a post–World War II influx of (mainly southern) European migrants who began attending (mainly Catholic) Australian churches, also accounts for the increase.

Since the 1960s, the Australian church has experienced a significant and continuous decline both in terms of attendance and influence. Using data from the most recent census in 2021, we can say the following. The proportion of Australians identifying Christianity as their religion has declined over the last century from 96 percent in 1911 to 44 percent in the 2021 census. Those who self-report as attending church once per month have dropped from 44 percent in 1950 to 21 percent in 2021. The decline in attendance has slowed since 1990. Those who tick the "no religion" box have also increased, from <1 percent in 1966 to 39 percent in 2021.[46]

Trends Relevant to Our Concern

Perhaps at this point you are feeling overwhelmed, or depressed by numbers. My point in this chapter is not to rehearse the decline of the Western church over the past century. This decline has happened in our lifetime, in our living memory. We know it well, and we feel it intently. We don't need statistics to point out the obvious.

44. Mol, *Faith of Australians*, 56–57.

45. Australian Bureau of Statistics, *Population, by Religion: Australia Censuses, 1921 to 1966.*

46. Australian Bureau of Statistics, *Religious affiliation in Australia,* 2021 Census.

My objectives are in fact larger, and less depressing. Without referring to the decimation of the Eastern church, we can make the following long-term observations of the Western church.

First, it has not always grown. The overall percentage of adherents across Europe appears to have remained constant between 400 AD and 1600.[47] But as I have just demonstrated, attendance shrank (in percentage terms) between 400 AD and the early 1500s declining from 50 percent to 12 percent of the population. Church attendance also shrank before the 1800s, then shrank again in the early part of the 1900s. These are declines before the one we we are currently experiencing.

Second, church attendance shrank during Christendom on at least three occasions. Just because most people in society held to a CWV does not mean that most people attended church, or that the church was always growing.

Third, church attendance has a long history of rising and falling. Attendance rose after the Reformation following a decline in the Middle Ages. Attendance likely declined in the 1700s, then rose in the mid- to late-1800s. Again attendance declined in the early 1900s and rose in the 1950s. Following the Reformation, which gave birth to denominations other than Catholicism, church attendance fell in some denominations while growing in others, all within the same historical period.

Fourth, sometimes church attendance rises at the very same time that church influence is in decline. If you read Trueman's *The Rise and Triumph of the Modern Self,* you appreciate that the shift away from a God-centered view towards a self-centered view of the universe was well underway by the late-1800s. Descartes, Rousseau, Marx, Nietzsche, and Freud have all laid the intellectual groundwork for the rise of the modern self. As they white-ant the Christian worldview, many churches experience a season of profound growth.

Fifth, the reasons for attendance growth are more complex than just asking questions about church health and evangelism. We shall consider why the church grew in the mid- to late-nineteenth century in our next chapter, but for now, we can say this. In general, churches that depart from their core message and over-accommodate, therefore becoming theologically liberal, decline.

This explanation alone is too simplistic. Remember that the Episcopalian and Congregational church in America shrank a century before theological liberalism. It is more likely that the decline initially had to do with social political factors. Episcopalian and Congregational churches carried

---

47. Barrett and Johnson, *World Christian Trends AD 30–AD 2200*, 320–28.

overtones of the British establishment, and failed to connect with the prevailing sense of revolutionary independence and frontier pioneering of the time. That the establishment churches later became liberal compounded the decline, but the decline was well underway before liberalism set in.

Sixth, just because a denomination avoids liberalism, and remains otherworldly, is no guarantee it will grow. In America, not all Baptist denominations grow. In Australia, the denomination I grew up in, the Reformed Church, has not drifted towards liberalism but its attendance rates are in long-term decline.

Seventh, a period of growth is not necessarily the result of church health and evangelistic endeavour. Consider the growth spurt in the 1950s. Sydney Anglicans may point to a conservative principal at their theological college who became Archbishop, Howard Mowll, who oversaw a decade of evangelism as the reasons for growth in the 1950s. Descriptions that refer to internal factors—we grew because we did these things—may have explanatory value, but they are often insufficient. Other denominations grew in the 1950s, with the Catholics and the Baptists growing faster than the Anglicans.[48]

If the explanation for Anglican growth in the 1950s is conservative evangelicals became intentional about evangelism, then surely a corresponding movement must be present in the Catholic and Baptist denominations to account for their growth. However, no such evidence exists. Likewise, if being evangelical and evangelistic is sufficient reason for growth, then what happened from the 1960s onwards? How do you explain the plateauing of growth? Did Sydney Anglicans become more liberal? No, they did not. The explanation for the slowing of growth was not theological liberalism.

Furthermore, why did the decade of evangelism declared by conservative evangelical Archbishop Peter Jensen (2004–2014) result in attendance decline, in an era when the population of Sydney grew? Again, the explanation for decline was not an absence of evangelistic zeal.

At this point, some may be frustrated. You may be saying, "okay, if being faithful and evangelistic is not enough to cause church growth, what is the answer then?" If you are asking this question, you are missing the point I am trying to make. Across history, on occasion, church attendance declines, even when churches are faithful and evangelistic, even when evangelism is practiced in a CWV culture that is more aligned to the gospel. We need to stop imagining that church attendance is entirely under our control, that we must be doing something wrong if the church is not growing.

48. Commonwealth Bureau of Census and Statistics, *Census of Population and Housing*, 9–10.

Conversely, across history, the church or certain denominations have come into seasons of attendance growth that cannot be explained simply by reference to faithfulness to scripture and evangelistic zeal. Again, church attendance is not solely caused by human actions and effort. It is flawed to assume that if growth occurs, it is because we are doing something right that others are not.

I am not saying that remaining true to our heritage, convictions, or scripture is unimportant. I am not saying evangelism is unnecessary. By no means. I consider myself to be a Christian of the evangelical persuasion. I am saying, sociologically speaking, that church attendance is significantly influenced by macro social trends that are beyond our control.

If you are not yet persuaded, consider this. Church attendance in every Western nation has been in decline for some time. The average decline of people claiming Christian adherence between 1970 and 2020 in Western Europe was 20 percent. Over the same period, the average decline in the Scandinavian countries was 17 percent, while in Australia, Canada, and New Zealand the average decline was 33 percent. The United States held out for longer, having plateaued in about 1980 and declined since 2000. Having said that, in the window 1970–2020 they still declined by 17 percent. Add all this together, and you have about twenty nations, all coming into significant attendance decline at about the same time.[49]

The explanation for this phenomenon that seems most probable is that, like the Eastern churches of the Middle Ages, the Western church now faces a formidable external enemy that has dealt the church a severe blow. The new worldview, modern western individualism, with its focus on the self rather than God and my neighbor, on consuming rather than serving, on short-term personal happiness rather than gaining one's life by losing it, is winning the day. The post-CWV now holds the default status of being plausible, rendering the now obsolete CWV as implausible.

All is not lost. Jesus is still king, and the gospel remains powerful. The church is flourishing in many places beyond the West. I will offer suggestions for how we might adapt to be the church that reaches out to those blinded by the charms of the PCWV. My point in this chapter is this: macro social trends beyond our control are *a*, if not *the*, primary explanation for the decline we have experienced.

49. Johnson and Zurlo, *World Christian Database.*

Simplicity on the Other Side of Complexity

1. We have a shared intuition that something is wrong in the Western church. We are living through a season of the decline of attendance and influence in the Western church.

2. We assume, for historical, theological, and biblical reasons that church growth is normal. Further, our experience in medicine, education, technology, and economics is that progress and growth are normal.

3. We assume that we can stimulate or cause growth. Conversely, when growth lags or decline kicks in, we assume someone has messed up for this to be the case.

4. The Eastern church was healthy and growing. It experienced decimation. The best explanations for this decline are not failings on the part of the Eastern church, but rather external factors, namely the rise of militant Islam and a mini ice age that caused competition and nationalism.

5. The Western church has grown, but not always. It has had seasons of shrinking as well as growth. Both seasons were present even during Christendom.

6. Even while the CWV was under sustained attack and losing its privileged status as the default position during the Enlightenment, the Christian church experienced a season of numerical growth.

7. When a church departs from its core message and over-accommodates, becoming liberal, such a move correlates with decline. This explanation carries insight, but alone is too simplistic. Churches can, and do experience seasons of decline and growth for reasons other than their theological convictions and their evangelistic efforts.

8. Sociologically speaking, church attendance is significantly influenced by macro social trends that are beyond our control.

9

Lamenting What Has Passed, Unlearning
What No Longer Works

THE FLOW OR ARGUMENT of the book this far has been this: there was a time when a CWV prevailed; when most people believed in a loving, powerful God who instilled a moral fabric into the cosmos. Jesus was the great example of how to live well in God's world. As beings made with freedom and consciousness, we can choose to live within or against God's design. The choices we make will determine our fate in this life and the next. This was a society-wide shared set of beliefs and values.

It was consistent and coherent, and it underwrote Western cultures for about 1600 years. But in the past few decades, Average Joes have abandoned, or at least radically modified, this shared and accepted CWV.

The PCWV has, or is displacing the CWV. The core feature of the PCWV is that I see my "self" as special and unique. I am the expert on me. I can listen to intuition and passions and decide what is best for me. When empowered, when I have the freedom to choose, as is my right, and when I make decisions that express my inner self, I am being authentic. When I am authentic, I will thrive. I will be the best me, and this is good for me and everyone else.

In this chapter, I would like to do two things. First, acknowledge what has been and is no more, and lament its passing. Second, tease out what happens when someone with CWV assumptions tries to speak to someone with PCWV assumptions—what is said, and what is heard.

Lamenting What Has Passed, Then Moving on

Lamenting is, I suggest, a lost art. The ancients practiced it far better than we do. Have you ever felt a profound sense of loss, then had people come to comfort you, and they are awkward, silent, and depart quickly? Or they talk too much about other things as if distracting you will somehow help. Or they try to solve your problem as if it was a riddle.

Job is the biblical account of a person (not even a Jew, just a "man") who lost everything: his ten children, his livestock, and his health. His three friends come to visit him. Later, we discover these friends lack wisdom. But before you dismiss them, marvel with me at their ability to lament. "When Job's three friends . . . heard about all the troubles that had come upon him, they set out from their homes and met together by agreement to go and sympathize with him and comfort him . . . [T]hey began to weep aloud, and they tore their robes and sprinkled dust on their heads. Then they sat on the ground with him for seven days and seven nights. No one said a word to him, because they saw how great his suffering was" (Job 2:11–13).

As I talk with many Christians, they are sad about what has been lost. They are hurting, confused, and desolate, and with good reason. They are also stuck in a forsaken place. They cannot embrace what is, because they have not let go of what was, but is no longer.

It is my inclination that some of my readers will be stuck in such a place. That for you, reading this book is like looking at photos of a much loved but now departed family member. That as I have teased out the various strands of the CWV, your heart has been stirred. That as you view the picture I painted of a previous era, you find yourself saying: "Yes, that is the world I love, take me there. That world made sense to me, and I knew how to live, how to do and be in that world. I sat comfortably in that world, whereas I sit awkwardly in this new one."

Imagine me sitting with you, in torn rags and ashes. After a protracted silence, I ask you: tell me what you loved about the CWV. Tell me. Name it up. Speak it out. Go back to the summary at the end of chapter 1, and meditate upon the list. Thank God for each of those beliefs and values.

Now, thank God for the blessings that were born and nursed in the bosom of the CWV. Thank God for learning and schools, medicine and hospitals, universal human rights, science and technology, and where they have been used to make our lives more meaningful and less mundane. Thank God for families, for a sense of purpose and direction to life, for communities that loved and cared for us, for the comfort of knowing that a good and powerful God is in control. Thank God for a world where all agreed that lying, greed, and lust were wrong, that selfishness was recognized, in the end, as hollow, and that it is better to give than receive. Thank God that you got to experience a season in history where biblical values were closer to our shared cultural values than they are at present.

If it helps, you may wish to read the book of Lamentations or some of the Psalms. Psalms of Lament are the most common type. Apparently, the Jews were aided by a hymnal full of lament psalms! Perhaps search for a musical rendition of those psalms online. Find some friends to sit with you, and share in lament.

But the time for lament will pass. Having named up, celebrated, and grieved, you may be more ready to listen for what is.

I ought to say that transitioning from one view to another, or what David Bosch in the seminal *Transforming Mission* calls a paradigm shift, is not a pleasant season. Bosch notes that for the citizens of a historical era, a paradigm acts as a frame of reference that shapes "their overall experience and understanding of reality and their place within the universe . . . and which to a very large extent has moulded their faith, experiences, and thought processes."[1]

In other words, the way we see things is in part a function of the world we grew up in. Even stronger, we assume the way we see things is normal and accurate. It has a default plausible status. Or, in Christian circles, a theological "orthodox" (literally "right beliefs") status. Given this, some will instinctively resist change. "Protagonists of the old paradigm, in particular, tend to immunize themselves against the arguments of the new. They resist its challenges with deep emotional reactions, since those challenges threaten to destroy their very perception and experience of reality, indeed their entire world."[2]

I am not suggesting that as Christians we ought to abandon everything "old," and adopt everything "new." I am not advocating for another so-called Copernican Revolution. Rather, there can (and do) remain elements of the old in the new. I have already demonstrated this regarding the idea of the dignity of all humanity. It is an idea birthed in the CWV and regenerated in the PCWV, despite having been unhinged from its foundations.

Allow me to be quite explicit and clear here. The thesis of this book is that the shared view of the world has changed or is changing. To engage in missional conversation with this world and disciple persons growing up in this milieu, we need to change. We need to adjust our messaging. I am not suggesting you must completely abandon your entire CWV. Instead, I am suggesting that you, as it is explained in the social sciences, put some temporary

1. Bosch, *Transforming Mission*, 183.
2. Bosch, *Transforming Mission*, 185.

brackets around your current beliefs. Do some mental maths outside of the brackets for now, and we will return to the bracketed stuff in time.

Bosch explains it like this. He suggests we pause "viewing my own interpretation as absolutely correct and all others by definition as wrong, [and] I recognize that different theological interpretations, including my own, reflect different contexts, perspective and biases."[3]

This does not make Bosch a relativist. Nor does it lead to the conclusion that we have detached ourselves from our anchors and are drifting wherever this tide might take us. Some theologies, readings of the Bible, and interpretations of culture will be wrong. They will be "falsifiable." It remains the task of the church to demonstrate and warn against false teachings.

To return to Neurath's boat analogy, our culture has stepped off the CWV boat onto the PCWV boat. This is a precarious place to be. As long as our feet remain firmly planted on the CWV boat, from this vantage point, we can see all the holes and flaws in the PCWV in a way that those on that boat cannot. Some Christians are shouting as loud as they can, "Don't get on that boat! It will sink!"

The problem is that those already on the other boat do not see from the same vantage point we do. Whatever we may be shouting, all they see is that we are on a sinking boat, and we have the hide to judge.

Like it or not, we are called to reach the lost people on that boat. We need to be Christians in the PCWV to reach and disciple those who inhabit this new world, not the previous one. God has called you and me to be the church of the 2020s. Not the 1960s; someone else was given that task. We need to temporarily bracket our beliefs, engage with our new surroundings, understand the contours of our new vessel, and then get back to our tasks of mission and discipleship.

Have you ever sailed on a larger yacht? There comes a time in a race when the captain calls, "prepare to tack." It's time to leave the run you are on. Your heart rate increases, your attention is focused, you prepare for change.

Listening: How It Works

What does a person who hears and thinks from within the PCWV hear when listening to someone who speaks from within a CWV? Put another way, if Christian Chris spoke, just as she did in, say, the 1960s, what will Average Joe, listening in the 2020s and beyond, hear? Before we go there, I need to share a few thoughts on how listening actually works.

---

3. Bosch, *Transforming Mission*, 187.

On the surface, listening is something we take for granted. We assume it's straightforward. I speak, you listen. You speak, I listen. In the end, we understand each other. Arriving at a shared understanding after an interaction is the goal. The listener has listened, and communication has taken place. But we all experience enough breakdown in communication to know it's not that simple.

Early theories in communication could be characterized as "linear" theories. Communication is a one-way, one-direction process, like ten-pin bowling. Linear theories imagine the goal of communication is to get a message across the gap from a sender to a receiver. The sender speaks, and the receiver listens. The sender's task is to encode her message clearly in words, and the listener's task is to hear those words and receive their meaning. If the speaker fires off a dispatch of words carefully arranged to convey a specific meaning, they will hit their target.

Christians and Christian leaders are particularly prone to supposing this is how communication works. They are drawn to this model and its assumptions because it aligns with much of their experience. God has sent a message to us, through his word. My task is to receive and understand that word. Having done so, I then sit in my study and carefully construct another word: a sermon. In the process, I choose my words carefully so as to be clear about what the Bible has said, what I am saying, and how it applies. I then proclaim or deliver that message to a congregation, or a small group, who sits "under" that word. They are the receivers whose task is to believe, meditate upon, and practice or obey that word.

Is that what happens during sermons? Are congregations passive empty vessels waiting to receive the word? Elsewhere, I have written a survey of all the research into what listeners do when listening to sermons.[4] One of the researchers, Hanneke Schaap-Jonker, a Dutch theologian and a psychologist who wrote her PhD in this field, conducted a pertinent and unsettling study in this space. In addition to asking listeners what they heard after listening to a sermon, she also attempted to clarify a listener's framework of reference by drawing upon an established theory of "God image." A God image is the experience one has of God resulting from one's emotional responses, images, and memories of God. All listeners have a pre-existing God image before the sermon begins. Some may have an image of God as someone who challenges you, others as someone who accepts you as you are, still others as a provider, and so on. Schapp-Jonker asked these persons with different God images to listen to various sermons, sometimes even the same sermon.

---

4. Rietveld, "Phenomenological Research of Listening to Preaching," 30–47.

Her research concluded that the best predictor of what listeners hear is driven by the God image they have in their head, not the sermon's content. Listeners notice and remember content in the sermon that fits with their existing God-image more than they do new material. More precisely, listeners maneuver the information they hear so that it fits within the house of knowledge they already have in their heads.

Schapp-Jonker's research is evidence that listeners do more than just receive. Listeners are interpreters and, in the very process of interpreting from within their own mental categories and frameworks, they construct first-hand meanings. They are co-creators in the communication process.

Note the prefix "co-" here. Schaap-Jonker's research, and others like it, does not necessarily conclude that listeners hear anything they want. She is not suggesting they create something out of nothing. They (selectively) hear and then interpret words, but the raw data that listeners are playing with has been brought to the table (mostly) by the preacher.[5] This is not the place to debate the ratios. It will suffice for the purposes of this book to deduce that both the "sender" and "receiver" of sermons are involved in the process of creating meaning.

Research like Schaap-Jonker's abounds, as does our personal experience that people hear things we don't think we said. Or when two people listen to you say the same words but hear you say two different things. It happens to all of us. This has given rise to new models of communication, called "constructivist models," or "constructivism." It's all the rage in communication theory and education.

Behind these two models of communication sits a profound distinction. In a communication event, where is meaning located? Christians, particularly those of an evangelical persuasion, will be quick to answer: in the biblical text. The task in a sermon, or Bible study, or evangelistic conversation, is to arrange words into a message that carries meaning. For those who hold to more constructivist assumptions, words are more so symbols. It is how people interact with those symbols that creates meaning. Meaning is located in the mind of those participating in the communication event, not in the message itself.[6]

If a linear theory could be likened to using ten-pin bowling as a metaphor for communication, what is a metaphor for a constructivist model

---

5. Listeners have also been documented as having bounced off the preacher's words, had their own thoughts, then when asked afterwards, believed their own private thoughts were spoken by the preacher. See Gaarden and Lorensen, "Listeners as Authors in Preaching," 28–45, who use the term "contemplative interaction" to describe this.

6. Hesselgrave and Rommen, *Contextualization*, 188.

of communication? Is it table tennis, or ping pong? Is communication this process of back and forth, where we take turns in being the sender and the receiver? This goes on and on, and in the process, we come closer to understanding each other.

As intuitively appealing as this metaphor may sound, it is not sufficient for capturing what is meant by constructivism. Nor is it, I suggest, an insightful metaphor for how communication works. In life, I may use a word, and you may be using the same word, and yet we have divergent meanings in our minds. Take, for instance, the word "justice." Within the Reformed Evangelical tradition, it means something close to righteousness. Within the liberal or post-Christian traditions, it means something close to social equality.

In a real-life conversation, we may think we are playing with the same word, or table-tennis ball, but it turns out in the one conversation there are two balls or definitions in play. Furthermore, in real life, the goal of communication may be to get my point across. But in the next moment, we now modify our point or try to make another, which exists in another field of knowledge, where different rules apply. The table-tennis metaphor implies there is one ball, and one table, in a fixed stadium, with no wind. Communication between people is not like that.

Em Griffin suggests communication is most like two people playing a game of charades.[7] It is a mutual game that involves interplay. Dynamic activity is going on inside one person's mind and inside the mind of the other. Whatever is going on across the two minds is similar (we use the same words, live in same culture, are discussing the same topic) and yet distinctive (each has different experiences, a different mind map with different ways of seeing things, or default neural pathways). There is overlap, but not one-to-one correlation.

Schaap-Jonker's research, the results of which support constructivism, is evidence that listening to sermons, let alone communication in general, is not like ten-pin bowling, or even table tennis. It is more complex than either of those intuitive metaphors suggest. For our purposes, Schaap-Jonker's research and the insights of constructivist approaches to communication theory have obvious parallels to our concerns.

I am suggesting that there has been a major "image" shift. Not a God image, rather a how-life-works image. What is going on inside the minds of PCWV listeners has changed. They now receive and process our words and concepts in different ways. They are on another boat. They see things from an alternative vantage point.

7. Griffin et al., *First Look at Communication Theory*, 56–58.

This presents two major obstacles to effective communication. The first I have already foreshadowed. Let's have another thought experiment. Imagine the following question.

> When Christian Chris (who holds a CWV) speaks to Average Joe (who holds a PCWV), what happens? Despite what Chris is trying to say, what is Joe likely to hear?

At this point, I need to be a little more specific about Christian Chris. For Christian Chris to still hold to a CWV in the 2020s, she is likely over fifty, is a committed Christian who goes to church regularly, and attends a Bible study. Many of her close friends are also Christians. In other words, she is integrated into a Christian sub-culture. These networks and habits will have sustained Christian Chris holding to a more traditional way of seeing the world, even though much of society/culture has moved on.

If Christian Chris, as I have described her above, tries to evangelize Average Joe, is he likely to hear her?

What if this is not the case? What if Christian Christine (let's call her that, for the sake of clarity) is a twenty-something who attended a state school and then university? What if she has many friends, some of whom are Christian, others not? What if Christine spends two hours per day on social media (below the average for her age), gets all her news online, attends church most weeks but not every week, and is in a small group made up of all young adults like herself?

If this is the case, and I know many young adults like Christian Christine, then it is likely that Christians like her will have absorbed much of the PCWV. They will agree with many of the beliefs and values as I outlined them in chapter 3.

How does Christian Christine share the gospel, when categories like God (and not you) are at the center of everything and everyone, sin, guilt, and the Lordship of Christ are not natural to her? And she knows how twenty-something Joe will react if she goes there.

> When Pastor Chris (who holds a CWV) speaks to Christian Christine (who holds a PCWV), what happens? Despite what Pastor Chris is trying to say, what is Christine likely to hear?

This second question is perhaps more disturbing than the first. Perhaps you have never considered this question with such sharpness and clarity until now.

My point is this. A changing of worldview has two significant impacts. How do we do mission? How do we communicate the gospel? How do we cross a cultural gap and speak to an audience with a different worldview, in ways they are likely to understand? I will make some suggestions in my final chapter. For now, I suggest that most of our missional tools are frameworks developed in Christendom. They assume our listeners hold to a CWV: believing in God, right from wrong, a day of judgement, and heaven and hell. Are they now, functionally speaking, obsolete? This is the concern of this chapter.

Second, how do we do discipleship? How do we disciple the next generation, those growing up inside Christian families who attend local churches, youth groups, and even faith-based schools? Despite all this, it is my observation they hold to many of the PCWV assumptions. Most of our current discipleship tools and frameworks were written by and for persons with a CWV.

Furthermore, we now have younger disciples hearing and receiving the Christian gospel framed within CWV garb, yet they hold a PCWV. What do their mental world images do with that message? Do they syncretize a new message? Do they construct a new gospel, one that is not really a gospel at all? Are there different ways and different themes we ought to be emphassiz-ing to communicate more clearly?

What Was Evangelism in the CWV?

Before we dive into this question, I have two comments. First, this is a book about how major cultural changes affect Christians and the church, and how they ought to behave in relation to the broader culture. This question has many dimensions to it, many directions in which it plays out. How we evan-gelize or disciple are but two. Both of these topics—evangelism or discipleship in post-Christendom—would fill many books! I am writing but one chapter. Part of me suspects it would be wise to avoid this topic altogether. It is too big a rabbit warren to go down, and I might not make it back. But I cannot, for the very same reason. It is too important a topic to avoid. So, I will say some things, raising as many new questions as I make observations.

Second, we have hit another topic where symbolism is at play. Each Christian tribe interacts with these symbols differently. I am speaking of the words (which are symbols) "evangelism" and "mission." In the minds of some Christian tribes, "evangelism" is a dirty word. It means something like "proselytizing." That is, it is a bombastic attack on another person's beliefs and values, and even on their personhood. It lacks respect of and dialogue with the other. At its worst, it is a contest of truth versus lies, and as such, it is about ideas and not relationships. Tribes who recoil at the term "evangelism" tend to prefer the word "mission."

When the word "mission" is used by Christians as an alternative to "evangelism," a broad definition is likely in view. "Mission" now means sharing in mission of God (*missio Dei*). God is acting redemptively in his world, bringing order out of chaos, and anything we do to participate in this movement of God is us joining in with the God who is already on mission. Mission can now include evangelism, social justice, and caring for the environment.

In response, the first tribe (evangelicals) will likely push back and note that the New Testament talks of evangelists, but it does not use the concept of "mission" as suggested above. Furthermore, to use the term "mission" in such a broad way is to confuse the "gospel" and its consequences. Caring for the poor and creation are important, but they are different to evangelism. As Stephen Neill said, "If everything is mission, nothing is mission."[8] There is a certain priority in terms of importance and as a focused category that needs to be given to inviting people to repent and trust Jesus as their Lord and Savior.

Still another clan will note that "mission" is a term that indicates crossing cultures to share the gospel. This is William Carey's definition of mission.[9] This clan fears that the mandate to go out to all the world and make disciples will be diluted if we call everything mission, including what we do to reach people near us and like us.

I note these distinctions, not because I wish to engage in this debate. As important as it is, it is tangential to the crux of this book. Instead, I acknowledge such distinctions, in part, because I do not want to lose you as a reader, in case your brain goes off on a tangent. I mention it also because the questions that drive this book call for a narrow specific use of the term "evangelism."

I shall use the term "evangelism" to mean the attempt to invite someone to believe and trust in Jesus as their Lord and Savior, when both the evangelist and the hearer of the gospel share a CWV. And I shall use the term "mission" to mean cross-cultural mission, including when a person who holds a CWV tries to share the gospel with a person who subscribes to a PCWV.

Please note I am not trying to offer a new or a theological definition of evangelism. Mine is a functional and socio-historical driven definition. There was a point where the broader culture held to Christian worldview assumptions. Christian Chris did not need to cross a cultural boundary to share the gospel with Average Joe in that era. Joe's assumptions about how life

---

8. Neill, *Creative Tension*, 81.

9. Bosch, *Transforming Mission*, 330.

worked and its purposes were similar to Chris'. Chris could talk to Joe about "sin," "forgiveness," "judgement," "God," "love," and "heaven and hell," and Joe would hear and know what Chris meant. When Chris and Joe have shared definitions of those terms, I shall call that activity "evangelism."

How Did Evangelism Work in the CWV?

If the CWV began in about 400 AD and lasted until about 2000 AD, how did evangelism work in that time? Wow—that is not a trivial question. Bosch, whose *Transforming Mission* is the go-to book in this space, argues there are four or five paradigm shifts in the period I have just mentioned, and we are in the midst of yet another. I am talking about evangelism from the time of Augustine of Canterbury (early 500s–604) and his mission to pagan England, to Billy Graham and his crusades, and everything in between. Surely I cannot be suggesting that all of these evangelistic endeavors were fundamentally the same?

Indeed, I am not. Nor do I need to. My contention is this. When a person, Average Joe, holds to a CWV, then there is a raft of assumptions within that worldview that align to believing in Jesus as your personal Lord and Savior. To paraphrase missiologist Donald McGavran, I contend it is easier to invite someone to become a Christian without having to cross worldview barriers.[10] People who hold a CWV are more attuned to hearing Christian-type answers. They are more receptive to the contours of the gospel invitation.

This is different from saying that people with a CWV are statistically more receptive to an actual invitation than those who hold a PCWV. Whether or not this is case, time will tell. The present trends in the West are not positive, but there were previous times in history when Christian adherence declined, and it did so in Christendom. In any case, questions about how easy it is to share, or how receptive people will be to invitations, are beyond our control and mandate. We are called to invite people to follow Jesus, whether or not they are likely to respond.

I assert that the Christian evangelistic message fitted more readily inside the CWV than it does in the PCWV. To demonstrate my point, I shall briefly outline three clear examples of where the themes of an evangelistic surge overlapped with core themes inherent in CWV. If this all sounds a little abstract, read on.

Consider the Great Awakening (1726–1760) in the USA and its parallel expression in the UK, sometimes called the Evangelical Revival. This

---

10. McGavran, *Understanding Church Growth*, 190-211.

historical period is often viewed as the high-water marks of effective evangelism. The revival began in a Dutch Reformed congregation in New Jersey, then spread across the east coast of the US through Jonathan Edwards and George Whitefield's ministry. The revival was led in the UK by Whitefield and the Wesley brothers, John and Charles.

Before this revival, mainstream theology emphasized the objective status of what God has revealed through his word. In comparison, Pietism emphasized the subjective nature of personal spiritual experiences. H. Richard Niebuhr summarizes the brilliance of the Great Awakening in that it brought these two together: that Scripture without experience is empty, and experience without scripture is blind.[11]

Why was this message so well received? If I may bracket theological explanations for a moment (such as revival comes after prayer, or when God wills it to come), let us consider the spirit of that age and in those locations, the *zeitgeist* as it is called.

Humanism was the philosophical movement of the fourteenth and fifteenth centuries. It caused scholars to return to fundamentals, including source documents such as Plato and Aristotle. This intellectual movement influenced Luther and Calvin, who went back to scripture, behind the Vulgate (the Latin Bible) to the Greek and Hebrew scriptures to bring underpinnings to their theological positions. They didn't look to the pope or synods. As an inheritor of the Calvinist tradition, Jonathon Edwards had a high regard for scripture, truth, and the sovereignty of God.

However, another social movement was simultaneously afoot. With Luther's Dictum ("Here I stand, I can do no other"), followed by Descartes' Dictum ("I think therefore I am"), there was a growing sense that the individual can and must appropriate truth as personal. For Descartes, the individual is a *res cogitans*, a thinking thing with a subjective experience or soul who contemplates *res extensa*, the objective physical world. This subjective *zeitgeist* explains the popularity of Puritanism at that time, with its accent on the personal. In the same period, Rousseau began publishing his thoughts, emphasizing the authentic individual.

Now we must ask, what is the timely appeal of the Great Awakening? How did it scratch where the people of that day were itching? You can have both the subjective experience of the objective God who speaks through his word. This is *the* message that answers the big question of that day.

That the themes of Great Awakening preaching does so is no accident. The CWV is precisely the one that is founded upon a Creator all-knowing God, who has created humanity in his image, capable of knowing

---

11. Niebuhr, *Kingdom of God in America*, 109.

and experiencing. Furthermore, the Christian God is personable, vitally interested in individuals. You can have a personal relationship with him, and he desires one with you.

Edwards and his peers were known for their passionate preaching. Without abandoning a belief that God's word was truth to be proclaimed, they pioneered a move away from preaching from full notes to preaching from a few notes, with greater passion, and an ability to connect with their audience emotionally. The preacher's task was to speak to the mind and the heart, to arouse so-called religious affections.

The very worldview that generates the questions is the one that has the answers to those questions within its frameworks. Edwards' evangelistic message answered the big questions of the day.

A message that you can have a personal subjective relationship with the God of objective truth has little appeal to a Muslim or a Hindu. Muslims do not yearn for a personal relationship with God; Allah is watching from a distance, and his holiness and sovereignty call for submission and obedience, not personal connection. Hindus do not imagine that a relationship with one god is sufficient. Nor does the message that you can have a personal subjective relationship with the God of objective truth appeal to a person from an honor-shame culture, or a power-fear culture. Their yearning is for a god who can bring security and safety, or a god who brings you into an extended kinship relationship rather than a personal one.

The CWV generates yearnings, or existential questions, that the Christian message answers. And so when the Christian evangelist uses ideas like a personal God, a God of truth and love, who made humanity in his image, and desires forgiveness and restored relationships, this all makes sense to a person who subscribes to the CWV.

Let us now consider the Second Awakening, which began about fifty years later in the 1790s. The view that God oversaw an ordered balanced universe (known as Classicism), was giving way to a more scientific understanding of a world governed by natural laws. Following Kant, this world is a closed world of cause and effect. God is one step removed, as the first cause, or as the source of our moral imperative, our conscience.

It was an era known as the Enlightenment. Human reason and aspiration could overcome and control the physical world. It was an era of science, invention, progress, and optimism. Having thrown off the shackles of Dark Ages superstitious-type religion, humanity was coming into its own. Isn't it amazing how much things can change in fifty years, and that was in the 1700s!

This new era of Enlightenment does not sound like fertile ground for a revivalist message of having a personal relationship with God, as happened in the First Awakening. The *zeitgeist* had changed. People were asking different questions.

The world was perceived differently, including by the Christians who resided in the Enlightenment *zeitgeist*. So a quote from William Carey that found traction in his day is, "Expect great things from God, attempt great things for God!" Carey was, of course, a (cross-cultural) missionary. He was part of a wave of optimism and progress that sought to bring the gospel to the ends of the earth. The God of progress had blessed the West with hospitals, schools, and industrialization. He is the God who created all humankind in his image, so we ought to end slavery. There is moral progress too. All of these blessings, along with the gospel, ought to be brought to the nations.

As for evangelism at home in North America, Baptist missionary Charles Chaney noted that "Not a single sermon or missionary report can be discovered that does not stress eschatological considerations."[12] What did he mean by eschatological considerations? He meant post-millennialism themes. What is post-millennialism again, you ask? It is the belief that Jesus will return after a golden era of a thousand years. Carey believes that the final stage of the kingdom of God was breaking in during his lifetime. Sin and its consequences were being overcome. The world was becoming a better place, and soon Jesus' kingdom would find expression everywhere, for a thousand years.

Evangelists of the day were now extending a different call. The God of reason and nature, who gave these gifts to humanity, invites you to be a part of his kingdom of hope and a future that is breaking in now. The kingdom is slowly breaking in; Jesus will reign here and now, on this earth for a thousand years, before he comes again.

Do you see what has happened? We are still inside the CWV, but we are in another manifestation of it. The world is now a world of reason and progress, cause and effect. The Average Joes of the early 1800s had different yearnings from their predecessors. Their sense was that progress and science were taking the world somewhere. Where is this progress taking us? Towards what, or whom? Where will it end? What are, and who sets the parameters around what represents positive progress? These are another set of existential questions that have arisen from within a CWV.

The Christian faith has answers for such questions. Reason and progress come from God, and used rightly, they will take us forward towards God and the coming of his kingdom.

12. Chaney, as cited by Bosch, *Transforming Mission*, 282.

Again, this evangelistic message of optimism and hope in a better future makes sense to those who hold a CWV, not to other world views. For the Buddhist and Hindu, history is circular. It is the world of cycles and reincarnation. It is not a linear world of progress towards a future and an eschaton. In an honor-shame culture, honor is a limited commodity. You protect and use this limited commodity for your family; you do not share it with the world. Again, the Second Awakening is an example of how another part of the Christian message raises questions within the broader culture (where is this progress heading?). This question is answered by another part of the Christian worldview (it is heading back to an all-knowing, all-powerful, personal God).

If you happen to know something of the Enlightenment, you may be wishing to push back on me at this moment. Isn't the Enlightenment the beginning of science versus God? Is this not the age of Voltaire, who, because of his scathing writings about the church, is nicknamed the Antichrist? Is this not the age where God is being marginalized as a distant deity, and the closed world of cause and effect has human causes controlling the levers of change?

Yes, to all of the above. But to quote the (non-Christian but deistic) historian Tom Holland, who reflects on Voltaire's humanistic Enlightenment vision: "Yet in truth, there was nothing quite so Christian as a summons to bring the world from darkness into light."[13] Voltaire, raised in a volatile Protestant-versus-Catholic France, desired to enlighten the world out of Christian sectarian violence by appealing to reason as the one universal source of wisdom. Again, let me quote Holland: "The dream of a universal religion was nothing if not catholic."[14]

Do you see Holland's insight? Even the nick-named Antichrist Voltaire thought in Christian categories. His solutions were Christian by nature and Christian in origin. We may wish to nuance Holland's point and say that Voltaire was part-Christian. Voltaire emphasized certain Biblical themes while he ignored or attacked other parts of it.

Voltaire and other skeptics are not the only ones who think in Christian categories. Even atheists do. Following the Enlightenment and until recently, to be an atheist in the West was to disbelieve the Christian God. The arguments of atheists attack the God of the Bible. How can God be loving and powerful and allow suffering? To imagine God as loving, powerful, and personable is to conceive of God as the CWV does. Everyone

13. Holland, *Dominion*, 375.
14. Holland, *Dominion*, 376.

inside the West, practicing Christian or not, atheist or not, operates with distinctively CWV assumptions.

When a Christian evangelizes, their message will speak in and to categories comprehensible and even appealing to an audience that holds a CWV. Despite Voltaire being the most prolific writer of his day with God consigned to the transcendent, nonetheless, the Second Awakening or revival took place in this very *zeitgeist*.

A third example. When thinking about the social phenomenon of how evangelism is practiced within its culture, I must comment on the twentieth century and its fascination with pre-packaged gospel presentations. Evangelism is not new. "The Christian faith is . . . intrinsically missionary."[15] Jesus invited people to follow him, and Christians have been following his example for 2000 years. Yet, only in the past 100 years was this practice turned into the widespread recitation of a formulaic gospel presentation.

In the 1950s and 60s, three "presentations" emerged, and in time they would come to hold the status of being a summary of the "gospel." These were D. James Kennedy's *Evangelism Explosion (EE)*, Bill Bright of Campus Crusades's *Four Spiritual Laws*, and Billy Graham's *Steps to Peace with God*. Later technological developments, such as video, TV, and data projectors on big screens would give rise to a second round of gospel courses, such as *The Alpha Course*.

Marvel with me at the sociological uniqueness of this. There have been 2000 years of evangelists. Peter, Paul, Augustine, St. Patrick, Boniface, St. Francis and the Franciscans, Edwards, Whitefield, Carey—the list could go on and on. Church history gave rise to established creeds and confessions, rigorous spiritual disciplines and methods (hence Methodism). But only from the 1960s onwards did the gospel distill into four or five core ideas that would become widely memorized and repeated.[16] As a sociologist, I must ask, why did that happen then?

Let's start by asking what the core ideas shared across the most common gospel presentations are. First, a loving God has a plan of blessing and peace for you, and eternity with him. Second, sin separates us from a holy God. Third, Jesus is the only bridge back to life. Fourth, we must personally receive Jesus by faith to find peace and blessing from God.[17]

These presentations share other common features. They focus on an individual invitation and response. They assume CWV beliefs such as that Jesus was a good man, who died for sins. These beliefs all promise a

---

15. Bosch, *Transforming Mission*, 8.

16. See Dybdahl, *Stairway to Heaven*, 32–66.

17. Dybdahl, *Stairway to Heaven*, 19–32.

good life. They are founded upon knowledge, or a series of propositions, backed up by biblical texts. They suppose humanity and God are presently separated, and that the cross is the key to forgiveness and right relationship. They all call for an immediate response.[18]

Note the significant overlap between the above presentations and the key tenets of the CWV. These presentations are basically a restatement of core ideas of the CWV with some notable twists. All begin with an invitation to a desirable good: peace, purpose, or assurance of eternal life. They all then move to announce we are sinners, out of step with God. Here we note this diagnosis is beyond the shared assumptions of the CWV. And, so Dybdahl reports, it is contrary to the self-understanding of Average Joe Americans. Most Average Joes in America think they are essentially good, and on speaking terms with God.[19]

In other words, at this point, the assumptions of Average Joe and the message of the Christian gospel diverge. The presentations must correct this widely held but nonetheless false assumption. Put another way, the gospel presentations highlight where the broader CWV assumptions are different from the diagnosis of biblical Christianity.

Having explained to listeners that they are condemned and detached from God, the three presentations can now introduce the solution. It is by believing in Jesus that one is saved. It is by grace through faith, not by being a good person (or by works).

In short, in terms of content, the twentieth-century gospel presentations affirm many of the CWV assumptions, but highlight sin as the problem that prevents attaining the shared desired good, and then highlight the cross as the solution to that problem. In terms of style, the presentations are logical, propositional, and proof texted by the Bible, which is assumed to have the authority of God behind it. In that sense, it is an Enlightenment-style argument, where the appeal is not to nature, but to scripture, as the source of pure truth. Furthermore, given that the presentation is founded upon the pure truth, it can be taught, learned, and reproduced scientifically, so we communicate the gospel correctly.

Can you see that such a style of gospel presentation is a good fit with the 1960s, particularly for evangelicals? The logical, reasoned style fits within evangelical enlightenment assumptions. The Bible as the word of God is pure "data." Its inerrancy is emphasized. Using proper exegetical tools, theology becomes a science. We can have certainty about the truth claims we

---

18. Dybdahl, "Stairway to Heaven," 32–58.
19. Dybdahl, "Stairway to Heaven," 149–50.

make about God.[20] God's offer of peace, purpose, and eternity is attainable if this gift is received by grace through faith in Jesus, not works.

Can you also see that we no longer live in the 1960s and that many assumptions behind these presentations no longer hold? As Dybdahl so succinctly puts it: "The same message falls on different ears and thus no longer remains the same message."[21]

This shall suffice in terms of a brief survey. I believe I have demonstrated that our recent practice of evangelism is of messages and methods crafted by and for people who share the same CWV. In simple terms, I have no axe to grind here. Speaking from within a culture and to culture is something I believe Jesus and Paul modelled. I conclude it is something the Bible encourages if not instructs us to do.

Having considered how cultural change affects evangelism and or missions, let us now turn our attention to the practice of discipleship.

How Did Discipleship Work in the CWV?

Jesus said to his disciples, according to Matthew's biography of Jesus, "go and make disciples" (Matt 28:19). At the end of his earthly ministry, Jesus gathered about 120 disciples who believed that he was the Son of God (Acts 1:15). Making a disciple then, involves evangelism, conversion, and ongoing maturation.

When I use the term "discipleship," I am not wishing to narrow my focus to the process of calling and/or maturing recent converts. Rather, my central concern shall be a "covenantal" approach to discipleship. That is, how do we disciple children born into Christian families or raised with strong Christian input so that they will continue to trust Jesus as their Lord and Savior when they come of age? Passing on the faith to the next generation has been the main driver of how one comes into the people of God since Abraham and Sarah raised Isaac. Discipleship of the next generation remains critical to the long-term health of local churches and the church.

As we have seen, about 30% of Australian children attend a faith based school, and almost half of Americans attend church regularly. This suggests that something in the order of 10–30 percent of children raised in Australia, or the UK, or New Zealand, or Canada, and perhaps something like 50 percent of American children will be raised in a Christian household or attend a Christian (as opposed to a church) school. Parents, care-givers, youth leaders, and teachers are all attempting to pass on the Christian faith

20. Bosch, *Transforming Mission*, 267–68.
21. Dybdahl, "Stairway to Heaven," 160.

to the next generation, with diminishing success. We need to explore how the next generation of youth who have been raised and schooled in a PCWV hear and receive the invitation to become a follower of Jesus.

Imagine that a younger person—let's call him Jack—has grown up in a Christian family. His parents believe in the key ideas of the CWV. They believe in a loving, powerful, personable God. Jack believes that Jesus is the Son of God, he died on the cross, and saves us from our sins. They believe we all have a moral conscience: we know right from wrong, and are responsible for our actions and choices. They believe that God has spoken through Jesus, and in the Bible, if we follow God's plan in life, we will be forgiven and live in peace with him for eternity.

Jack has been raised attending the local Sunday School, and he goes to Youth Group at St. James or New Hope on some Friday nights when he has nothing better to do. Jack even attends a Christian school. He spends the average couple of hours online every day with his "friends," some of whom go to church, but most don't. He used to play sport for a local club. Now he hangs out or plays games online in his downtime.

Jack has grown up in a world where the PCWV is the dominant message. He has been told by his parents, teachers, and the world that he is unique and special, that he needs to understand and express his passions. When he does this, he will enjoy an inner sense of being who he is, of being comfortable in his own skin. To feel good about yourself is essential; it's fundamental to being your best. Jack is wary of voices and narratives that tell him who he should be. Conforming to other people's expectations will leave you feeling like you are trying to be something you are not: it's fake. Jack believes he is basically a good person, who cares for and stands up for others when his internal moral compass tells him it's the right thing to do.

Jack's Christian school has a theme this year: *Spirituality that thrives!* (I did not make that up. Recently, a Christian school asked me to speak to this very theme, and I suspect they are not alone.) Let us ask two questions. First, what do you think Jack's parents and teachers understand by this theme? We shall assume that the leadership team at Jack's school are in the mid-forties and older. What did they hope to communicate when they came up with this theme? And our second question: what is Jack most likely to hear?

What are Jack's teachers (or parents or youth leaders) likely to mean when they talk of spirituality that thrives? First, they mean something to do with God. It is of the spiritual realm, not of the flesh. There will be assumptions here that "Spirit" and "Flesh" are two competing powers. Behind this assumption will be the reflection of Paul in Galatians 5, where we read that we should walk by the Spirit, and not gratify the desires of the flesh; that the flesh desires what is contrary to the Spirit (Gal 5:16–17; see also Rom 8:5–9).

Also behind these assumptions is the thinking of Immanuel Kant (1724–1804), and behind him, Stoics, and behind them, Plato. Kant divided the world into two spheres. We live in the "phenomenal" or this physical world. We experience it with our senses, whereas God and the Spirits exist in another "noumenal" realm, one we cannot have a direct experience of. The ancient Greeks called this divide the worlds of being and becoming.

Kant thought we access the noumenal world via our compulsions. The sense of "ought" that we have about morality— we ought not to murder—comes not from our senses, but from the divine. Like the Stoics, Kant thought we cannot know much of the noumenal world. This distinction, or binary, or dualism, is fundamental to the Enlightenment and (Enlightenment) Christians would agree that we cannot know much of the noumenal spiritual world, except that God has revealed himself through his Word and his Son. Jesus says that if you have seen him, you have seen the Father (John 14:9). So actually, we can know a lot about God.

When Jack's teachers talk of spirituality, they likely mean the things of God, as opposed to the desires of the flesh. What about spirituality that "thrives?" Thriving is not a theological concept; it is a word that is on-trend. When properly nurtured, not just plants, but people now are supposed to "thrive" and "flourish." According to Ngram, the use of both words has tripled since 1980.

These words tap into a nature-based metaphor. While there are external factors required, such as water and sun, for the most part, plants grow naturally, all by themselves. Plants have the systems within themselves to tap into the resources around them. You cannot make a plant grow from the outside. You can only create the environment around it where the plant might thrive or flourish.

Jack's teachers will likely see a connection to a biblical metaphor here. Jesus is the vine and we are the branches. If we remain in him, and he in us, we will naturally bear much fruit (John 15:5). Or they may think of Psalm 1, where the tree planted by streams of living waters does not wither but prospers. Or they may think of the Old Testament metaphors, picked up by Jesus, where God's people are likened to a fig tree or a vineyard.

The assumption here will be that things grow naturally but the emphasis is likely to fall on the fact that things do not grow all by themselves, but because it is God who makes things grow (1 Cor 3:7). God has established order in nature and actively sustains his universe (Col 1:17).

When Jack's teachers, youth leaders, and parents, all of whom hold to a CWV, talk to Jack about Spirituality that thrives, they mean something like:

the things of God will abound in you when you have nearby the right resources of Bible, prayer, Christian community, etc. God has created you in such a way that your spirit will remain in step with the Holy Spirit, and you will bear spiritual fruit. When you are connected into that vine, you will feel secure, at peace, as if your life has meaning, purpose, and joy.

Is that what Jack is likely to hear? Quite likely not. Because behind all these words and metaphors sits deep CWV assumptions that Jack does not entirely share. Further, Jack holds some other unspoken assumptions that means he will likely construct different meanings, even though he is hearing and using the same words.

For Jack, spirituality does not sit within a "dualism" over and against the flesh. Jack lives in post-binary world. It is not an "either-or" where spirituality is good, and of God; whereas the flesh is evil, and of this world and the devil. Jack has been exposed to plural spiritualities. Christianity is but one expression. All spiritualities have some insight, some good in them. Jack has also grown up reading *Harry Potter* and watching *Lord of the Rings*. The Spiritual realm is here in this world. It is like a fifth dimension that some cannot perceive. Nonetheless it is present everywhere (like the Eastern notion of panentheism) and somehow interacts with and influences our phenomenal world.

Jack's default mental picture of the world is not "In the beginning God . . . " Jack holds a post-Christian view of reality. God, or some divine force, sits behind the creation as the source of life. As someone raised in a Christian household, Jack believes that God made the world somehow. But Jack will differ from an Augustinian view of the world, where everything is moving from a creator God and back towards a redeeming God. For Augustine (the CWV, and most will say all of the Bible), God is the source, the solution, and the destination.

Jack will not warm or default to a view of God as some irresistible magnet drawing his chosen children back to his bosom. Jack's view of the world is self-centered (technically anthropocentric, as opposed to theocentric). To say Jack is self-centered does not mean Jack is necessarily selfish. It means Jack does not view *his* life as but one small part of a cosmic movement of all creation from God towards God. Instead, Jack sees himself as unique and special, with particular passions. Jack has to beat his own path in life, which fits with and expresses who he is. To follow the herd is to be inauthentic and under the control of others who have their own agendas. Jack believes that to understand *his* life, you must begin with Jack, not God.

When Jack hears an invitation to be spiritual, he hears an invitation to express his own unique spirituality, which outworks his particular inner passions.

When Jack hears an invitation to spirituality *that thrives*, the word "thrives" has a pre-existing meaning for him. Jack immediately assumes that he is like a plant that has an internal DNA that will draw on the resources around it, but the plant will grow *all by itself* because of its internal DNA. The emphasis will fall on the internal DNA as the driver and shaper of growth, not on God who causes the growth.

Because Jack believes he has a unique DNA, and that he is the expert on his own DNA, it is up to Jack to decide which resources he needs to tap into to become the best version of himself. It is not his parents, or his teachers, or his pastor's place to decide. Even if the pastor thinks he is interpreting and speaking God's words, Jack will not likely defer to an external authority. Others have their own agendas, and they do not understand Jack as Jack does. It is Jack's decision; he is the captain of his ship.

Of course, we need to nuance this. The Jack I have described has grown up (or been socialized) in a church, a Christian family, and attends a Christian school. Jack is happy to believe with all his heart that he was created by God. That his unique DNA was *given to him*, by God, that God knitted him together such that he is fearfully and wonderfully made.

Jack also believes there are rights and wrongs in this world, and God is somehow behind them. He believes that Jesus is God's son, who lived life as the supreme example and died for our sins. When we are not our best selves, forgiveness through Jesus is possible. Jack is happy to admit that God somehow inspired the Bible, and it is the best spiritual resource available.

Jack can and will "talk the [Christian] talk." When Jack's school chaplain explains the new school theme for the year, "spirituality that thrives," meaning the things of God will abound in you when you have around the right resources of Bible, prayer, and Christian community, Jack will agree. But Jack's emphasis will fall on his unique divine spark that he gets to nurture, interpret, and express. And when Jack chooses to access the combination of spirituality that suits his unique DNA, then he will thrive.

That is the most likely thing that Jack will hear, in a best-case scenario.

The worst-case scenario is more apparent and takes less time to outline. Let's imagine Jack has a twin brother called Oli (short for Oliver). Oli has been raised in the same family, attending the same churches and schools as his brother. But Oli hears something different to his brother.

When Oli's teacher talks of spirituality that thrives, Oli hears arrogance and judgementalism. He thinks, "You Christians think that your God is the only God. Your spirituality is better." Oli believes there is good *and bad* in all spiritualities. But Oli also differentiates between spiritualities and institutional religion. Organized religions have a way of allowing domineering people to gain and abuse power, accentuating the bad.

Further, religions try to push everyone through the same cookie cutter, failing to affirm uniqueness. We are all sinful, we all have the same basic problem, and Jesus is the one solution. Oli will likely think that what religious leaders are suggesting may work for his brother, and Jack can choose that if he wishes; that is his right. But it's not Oli. His DNA will take him down a different path, and it's his place to pursue what will see him flourish, and we ought to empower him to be who he is. We ought to validate both his right to choose, and the choices he makes.

We could imagine Jack at one end, Oli somewhere near the other, and envisage a continuum in between. Young people would likely hear or construct various messages that fall anywhere on this continuum. Can you see the conundrum? We all interpret through our lenses. Or, we are all standing on one boat or another. If worldviews create frameworks through which we communicate, and if we are living through the transition from one world view to another, then it is likely that what we are trying to say is not what is being heard.

Our evangelism presentations and discipleship tools were written in, by, and for people who hold CWV assumptions. Remember Dybdahl's description: "The same message falls on different ears and thus no longer remains the same message."[22] I contend that while our presentations and tools may have served us well in the past, it is a new day.

Before I close out this chapter, I need to address one obvious rebuttal. Am I suggesting we need to change our message? Surely the gospel is the gospel? Jesus is the same, yesterday, today, and forever (Heb 13:8). The grass withers and the flowers fall (cultures come and cultures go), but the word of our God endures forever (Isa 40:8). Are not the gospel and the Bible enduring, even eternal?

The Gospel Is the Gospel, and It Is Timeless

Some will wish to push back on my thesis, suggesting that my emphasis falls in the wrong place. While we can acknowledge that different cultures and eras are inclined to hear things slightly differently, the greater emphasis ought to fall on the fact that the gospel is timeless, above culture, and God is a clear communicator.

To ground this rebuttal, I will express this objection through a real-life situation. I was in a meeting once with a leader of a university campus ministry, an African university student, and a former cross-cultural missionary. The university campus minister asked me and the former missionary if our

22. Dybdahl, "Stairway to Heaven," 160.

church could financially support the African student who wished to be a student ministry trainee on campus in an Australian university.

This request raised questions for me and the former missionary. What did this student wish to do after her traineeship in student ministry? She was planning to return to Africa and be a missionary in her home country. This led to another question. You plan to train someone, raised and educated in Africa, to do student evangelism on an Australian university campus, reaching out to other international students. Yet, at the end of this training, they will return to their native Africa. Why don't they just go home now and train for African mission work in Africa? How will your student ministry, led by Anglo-Saxon Australians, working in Australia, train and equip an African to work in Africa?

The response of the campus ministry leader was this: "I will train this African student in the essentials and the fundamentals of the gospel so that she will be able to be effective in any cultural setting. Once she has understood the gospel message as it is, she can later translate it into and through any cultural medium."

After the university campus minister left, my missionary friend, who was himself raised, educated and a former missionary in the very African country in question, said that it does not work like that. He believed she would be less effective as an African missionary if she completed this type of training in Australia. I agreed with him. Why?

Let us sharpen the question. Do I (and my missionary friend) believe that Jesus is the same, yesterday, today, forever? Yes! Do we believe the Word of God endures forever? Do we believe the gospel is timeless, and its call is universal? Again, yes. Do we believe that God is a clear communicator who can get any message across any barriers he so wishes? Yes, absolutely! Do we believe the Holy Spirit can cause us to hear God's message, despite our lenses? Yes, yes, yes!

Do I believe that the gospel can be communicated in a way that is above or outside culture? No. Can we decode the gospel message so that it is free from its cultural trappings, and all we have left is the pure objective gospel? No, I believe that is impossible. Why?

Several reasons. First, if it was possible to distill the gospel to a pure, culture-free, eternal formula, then we must ask ourselves why did God not communicate his message like that to us in the Bible. Why did Jesus not give us the four spiritual eternal laws or the ultimate gospel presentation? If it was possible, would not Jesus have given this to the disciples before he sent them on mission? But Jesus did not.

Instead, Jesus told first-century rural agrarian stories about farmers sowing seeds, fields, and fishing when in Galilee. The northern part of

Israel was full of farmers, shepherds, and fishermen. When in the south in Jerusalem, Jesus talked more of servants, banquets, masters who call to account, bankers, tax, and tax collectors. Jesus gave time-bound, culturally specific expressions of gospel invitations, so specific, we can even note different themes between his northern first two years of ministry and his southern last weeks.

Contrast this with Paul. He did not speak of Christians being sheep, fields, farmers, or fish. Jesus used these, the Old Testament is full of them. But Paul did not feel compelled to use the Old Testament biblical agrarian metaphors when explaining the gospel (Rom 8:36 being the exception). Why not? Such metaphors did not connect with his mostly city-dwelling audience.

Paul's sermons follow the same pattern. As I shall demonstrate in chapter 11, Paul delivered a Jewish sermon to Jews in Antioch (Acts 13), an agricultural discourse to rural farmers in Lystra (Acts 14), and a philosophical lecture to the Areopagus in Athens (Acts 17). Far from following a set gospel presentation, Paul intentionally modified his content to be relevant to his audience.

When Paul quoted the Old Testament, he tended to quote the Greek version of it (the LXX), and not the original Hebrew version. Paul's use of the Greek versus Hebrew text is not a question of which text is more accurate or inspired. He chose the Greek text because this was the text his first century Hellenistic audience would be familiar with.

I have heard Christians say that the principles of the Reformation are timeless. The Reformers formulated five statements to clarify the true Christian faith. They are *sola scriptura* ("by Scripture alone"), *sola fide* ("by faith alone"), *sola gratia* ("by grace alone"), *solus Christus* or *solo Christo* ("Christ alone" or "through Christ alone"), *soli Deo gloria* ("glory to God alone"). If these are so timeless, why then did the Holy Spirit not inspire Paul to include these in his letters? I happen to find the five *solas* easier to understand than, say Romans 9–11. One could argue that the New Testament church would have been better served by receiving the five *solas*, or the Nicene Creed, rather than confusing stuff about women being saved through childbirth, or Jesus going and preaching to spirits imprisoned since the days of Noah.

However, the five *solas* are not part of scripture, nor is the Apostles' Creed or the Nicene Creed. Instead, what we have is Paul's letters with details about food sacrificed to idols. Paul used the words "circumcized/circumcision" more than he did the words "atonement," "justified/justification," and "sanctified/sanctification" combined. Peter said of Paul's letters: "His letters contain some things that are hard to understand, which ignorant and unstable people distort" (2 Pet 3:16).

What we have received in scripture is letters and writings that are very culture-specific, at times "hard to understand" and able to be "distort[ed]." We receive examples where Jesus, Paul, and others model communication deliberately encoded to make sense to the original listeners. The student university minister suggested it is possible to decode the gospel out of its culture-bound expression into a pure form. If you could do that, why did God not do it in the first place?

To return to the metaphor of Neurath's boat, you can only ever see, partially, from a vantage point. You cannot see from an objective helicopter. We are always looking through a set of cultural lenses. Objectivity was an Enlightenment myth, achieved by Kant's smoke and mirrors.

Does this cause me to be pessimistic about evangelism? By no means. In terms of philosophy (technically hermeneutics—the study of how we know and interpret), my claim is simply that messages only ever exist in encoded forms. You cannot decode a message outside of a medium into some pure form.

I am writing this message to you in English. You are reading it in English. You and I are both thinking inside categories provided by English and not another language. The type of English that we are using right now comes with culture, assumptions, history, and context. Neither of us is thinking in a language called "pure logic and reason," and then translating out of that language into English. New Testament Greek is not the language of pure logic and reason. It, too, has cultural context and biases built into it—it is idiomatic. All messages are transmitted through a medium.

Trying to communicate with someone who shares the same culture or uses the same medium as you is challenging enough. Just because we are on the same cultural boat as someone else does not mean we all see things the same. Trying to communicate across cultures is more complex. We Christians are commanded to go to all nations. For me, this means we are commanded to take a message that has been encoded in one context, attempt to disentangle it from its cultural trappings, and then re-encode it so that it makes sense to a receptor who inhabits a third context.

This aligns with what I see Jesus, Paul, Jonathan Edwards, and Billy Graham doing (even if Graham might not have known or thought that was what he was doing). Now we must work out how to evangelize and disciple those who think and listen in PCWV categories.

Charles Kraft, a cross-cultural linguist, anthropologist, and missiologist, puts it like this: "The focus of the communicator, then, should not be on the 'precise formulation of the message' but on how the receptor is likely to interpret that message."[23]

---

23. Kraft, *Communication Theory*, 32.

Clarity on the Other Side of Complexity

1. Lamenting is a lost art. Christians understandably feel a deep sense of loss. We feel less "at home" in the PCWV, compared to the CWV. We would do well to name up what was, lament its passing, and accept that God has called us to be a witness to this new world, not the previous one.

2. Listening is more complex than it appears. We all, but especially Christian leaders, assume communication is about the speaker fashioning a clear message and then sending it down the aisle. More recent communication theories have gone beyond a linear approach to a constructivist approach, which acknowledges that listeners are active participants in the co-creation of meaning.

3. Listeners refract messages through the mental images they hold. They selectively hear, recall, and interpret information in ways that align with their pre-existing assumptions.

4. Evangelistic messages have long been tailored to the questions and yearning of receptors. This reality is not new or inherently wrong. On the contrary, at its best, this approach is an outworking of Paul's command to be Jew-like to Jews.

5. Our evangelistic presentations and discipleship tools are written in, by, and for persons who hold a CWV. I suggest the time has come to re-align our messaging such that it is orientated towards PCWV ears.

6. The current generation of youth has adopted many of the assumptions and images of the PCWV. It is likely that when a person who has CWV assumptions speaks to the next generation of youth, they will hear refracted messages. They may receive a syncretized message (as Jack does), or reject the message because it is encoded in CWV frames (as Oli does).

7. The gospel itself is conveyed in culturally encoded forms. Jesus spoke as a first-century Jew, in the first instance, to first-century Jews. Paul spoke one way to Jews, another to rural farmers, and yet another to Greek philosophers. Our task is to focus not only on the precise formulation of the message but also on how the receptor is likely to interpret that message.

10

Old Testament Models of Following God When Culture Does Not

ON SEVERAL OCCASIONS I have made claims or observations that likely sit in tension with your existing theological views, or with your understanding of the biblical narrative. I have provided sociological and psychological explanations for things that may not sit well with you. I have promised that we will remove the brackets later, and allow a biblical/theological conversation between my reading of culture and my reading of scripture. Now is that time.

In this chapter we will walk alongside a few Old Testament fellow journeyers. As they encountered social and cultural changes, how did they frame their circumstances? What were their explanations for where they were and what went wrong?

What Went Wrong?

We are presently exploring the third question: what went wrong? The very framing of that question has a bias that is perhaps unhelpful. It suggests we had things right and they are now wrong. We were heading in a healthy direction and now we are not. Many older and more conservative Christians will say, this is a self-evident truth. In society at large, things have clearly gone from good to bad to worse.

There are many things about the emerging culture that unsettle me, that I sense are wrong. But there are also things about both the CWV and the church in the past that I believe were also wrong: the abusive behaviors of some leaders, the failure of other leaders to protect the vulnerable, the accumulation of wealth, the arrogance of the West and the way it colonized or oppressed other parts of the globe, the unsustainable levels of consumption and exploitation, the gap between the haves and the have-nots in terms of wealth, and power, and status, etc. There is something about human nature that is quick to forget previous difficulties and idealize the past.

There is a story in Greek mythology about the halcyon bird, which had the power to calm the rough ocean waves so she could nest. The phrase "the halcyon days" refers to an idyllic, calmer, more peaceful time in the past. The Israelites were themselves guilty of this type of thinking. When following Moses in the desert, they grumbled and wished to go back to slavery in Egypt. When the Assyrian army attacked them, they brought out the bronze serpent from centuries earlier, now called Nehushtan, and they worshipped it.

Present elements of the church are, in my opinion, at risk of idealizing and romanticizing the past. One gets this feeling when reading Trueman's *The Rise and Triumph of the Modern Self*. Personally, I find myself in two minds. On the one hand, I concur that several elements of the emerging worldview are a step beyond healthy, towards a self-absorbed narcissism. For Trueman, this inward turn is a turn away from God. Yet, as Holland demonstrates, the inward turn happens in the West precisely because it is an outworking of the CWV. To view humanity as rational, moral, with an intuitive consciousness, self-aware, implanted with a divine spark to create and produce, in ways that act out both for good and ill is a Christian view of humanity. There will remain parts of the PCWV where Christ, through his body, is redeeming this culture. Jesus's kingdom is constantly breaking in.

It is this very tension that we are exploring in the following two chapters. There will be those who have a deep intuition that "what went wrong?" is precisely the correct way to frame the question; that our culture is going to the dogs; that we need to stand up against the current social trends; that we need to, both individually, and corporately, oppose. I interpret much of the energy and support of the ACL (Australian Christian Lobby) as being directed towards these ends.

Those who hold such views would believe that they have biblical evidence on their side. Is not the Old Testament the story of God calling and blessing a people, only for them to disobey him and bring down curses on themselves? Are we not called to be like the prophets and speak up against evil? Likewise, is not the New Testament the story of Jesus and his apostles also standing up against wrong?

Yes and no. Yes, the above is a precis of biblical themes but they are only a subset of biblical themes. I suggest that the Bible is a compilation of narratives drawn from across a span of socio-historical settings, exploring diverse challenges and resolutions. There is a breadth to scripture so that we can find in it light for any path and every season.

John Robinson's famous quote, "I am verily persuaded the Lord hath more truth yet to break forth out of His Holy Word,"[1] makes this very point. Speaking to the pilgrims setting sail on board the *Mayflower* for the new world, Robinson was not saying that God would reveal new scriptures via some golden plates from heaven, as Joseph Smith and the Mormons believe. Rather, Robinson was saying that, as we encounter new circumstances in new worlds, the Holy Spirit will inspire new insights into God's Word that will shed yet more light and truth.[2]

This being the case, it follows that our task is to return to scripture not with eyes immediately drawn to the themes that the CWV caused us to notice. Such themes are there, and they remain a core part of God's word. We must hold on to those, *and* simultaneously look again to scripture, and ask the Holy Spirit to enlighten to us themes we may have overlooked or failed to notice, because they did not readily fit into the way we saw the world. But now that our new world causes us to ask new questions, perhaps other longstanding biblical themes will come to the fore.

If we reduce our social analysis to imagining that we had it right in the past, and things are going wrong now, the answer is to go back. To make the church great again, we must go back (allusion to Donald Trump intended). We cannot go back. Culture does not have a reverse gear or a reset button. Furthermore, the kingdom of God continues to break into every culture and context. God is calling us to be the twenty-first century church and witness to the twenty-first century post-Christian world.

How does the Christian behave in a world turning away from its Christian assumptions and heritage and towards a post-CWV?

How We Read the Old Testament

In this balance of this chapter, I will look to the Old Testament for some precedents, some great ones who have gone before us, and who might be able to give us clues to the way God's people can live out their kingdom citizenship when they are in the minority. My observations will be brief. They will serve as an example of how and where we might notice overlooked (by us) yet long-standing biblical themes.

Before we drill down and walk alongside two Old Testament characters, a word about how we usually approach the Old Testament. We are used

1. Bruce, "Church History and Its Lessons," 180.

2. Vanhoozer, *Faith Speaking Understanding*, 64; see also 169–206.

to reading the Old Testament as the story of God and his people living in the Promised Land, having received the Law. Israel was, politically speaking, a theocracy, a nation where the national laws and God's commandments were one and same. The variable that drives the narrative is whether or not Israel obeyed God and his laws. As is foreshadowed at the end of the book of Deuteronomy, when Israel obeyed, the nation was blessed. When Israel disobeyed, the nation was under a curse.

This is to say that we condense the essence of the Old Testament as being the story of God's people, living under God's rule, and when they do so, they are blessed, and when they do not, they are cursed.

Granted, a percentage of the Old Testament can, validly, be summarized in such a way, but not all of it. If we start counting dates with the call of Abraham in Genesis 12, the entire Old Testament spans about 1700 years. Of those seventeen centuries, the people of God spend roughly four centuries conquering the Promised Land, five to six centuries inhabiting it, five centuries in exile or slavery, and two to three centuries as homeless.

Israel's history is played out in a number of geographical, political, and social settings. The monoculture that we assume and imagine across the Old Testament says more about us than it does about Israel's history. Israel living under God's Law in the Promised Land accounts for only part of the story.

The first person we shall consider is the prophet Elijah. He is not the first prophet in Israel's history. Think of Nathan, for instance, 100 years earlier in the time of David. But Elijah is the first of the so-called Major Prophets, who prophesied to a divided Israel, to the ten northern tribes, as opposed to the two southern tribes of Judah.

The context of his life and ministry is one of transition, which is why I have chosen him. Israel began its history on the wrong foot. After the reign of King Solomon, the ten northern tribes rejected his son Rehoboam as their king. The scriptures do not portray this separation as a disagreement between two equal options. Instead we read, "So Israel has been in rebellion against the house of David to this day" (1 Kgs 12:19). Rehoboam may have been a greedy, power-hungry monarch, but he was the rightful heir to the throne. Rehoboam was in the line of David, to whom God promised, "Your house and your kingdom will endure forever before me; your throne will be established forever" (2 Sam 7:16).

Instead, Israel chose to anoint their own king, Jeroboam, a rebellious government official from the court of Solomon. Jeroboam had a major political problem. He was a king with no temple. He had no ritualistic center of worship where one might seek God's forgiveness or blessing. Jeroboam's citizens had to return to his rival's territory in Judah to worship God as his temple was in Jerusalem. Jeroboam made an obvious political move. He built two temples in his own territory. In these temples, he placed golden calves, appointed non-Levite priests, and instituted his religious festivals.

Readers of the historical narrative get the point. Israel had made an inauspicious start. From the get-go, they were turning their backs on God. More than just disobeying him, they were baiting him with symbols reminiscent of their rebellion in the desert, where they worshipped a golden calf, and overtly stated their desire to return to Egypt.

Within sixty years of Solomon's death, a fourth king came to power in Israel, Ahab. Regarding Ahab, we read, "Ahab, son of Omri, did more evil in the eyes of the Lord than any of those before him. He not only considered it trivial to commit the sins of Jeroboam, son of Nebat [that is, continue worshipping the golden cows], but he also married Jezebel, daughter of Ethbaal, king of the Sidonians, and began to serve Baal and worship him. He set up an altar for Baal in the temple of Baal that he built in Samaria. Ahab also made an Asherah pole and did more to arouse the anger of the Lord, the God of Israel, than did all the kings of Israel before him" (1 Kgs 16:30–33).

Those of us who bemoan the quick demise of the CWV in the West should take note. It's only 100 years prior, and King David reigns—the man after God's own heart. In sixty years, Israel goes from being a part of the Kingdom of David's son Solomon, worshipping the God of (the twelve tribes of) Israel, to living under a foreign queen and worshipping Jezebels' foreign gods. The people of God, called to be a light to the nations, have become just like them.

This is the context of the life and ministry of Elijah. Elements of it sound similar to ours, do they not?

Showdown on Mt. Carmel, and the Aftermath

We now come to one of the most famous Old Testament narratives: Elijah and the prophets of Baal. It's a story in every children's Bible. It's a wonderful high point of the power of God over other gods, and of the vindication of those who remain faithful to God over those who do not.

The 450 prophets of Baal cried out to their god to come down and light the offering fire. Nothing happened. Elijah mocked Baal and taunted the prophets: "Shout louder!" he said. "Surely he is a god! Perhaps he is deep in thought, or busy, or travelling. Maybe he is sleeping and must be awakened" (1 Kgs 18:27). When I tell my children this story, they love the detail that Elijah suggests Baal might be relieving himself on the toilet. Yes, that is implied in the Hebrew. The prophets cried out all day. "But there was no response, no one answered, no one paid attention" (1 Kgs 18:29).

Then it was Elijah's turn. The one last remaining faithful prophet of God, versus the 450. He asked for the sacrificial bull that was on an altar of twelve stones (not ten) to be drenched in water three times. Elijah cried out to God, who sent an all-consuming fire that disintegrated the sacrifice, stones, and water in the surrounding trenches.

"When all the people saw this, they fell prostrate and cried, 'The Lord—he is God! The Lord—he is God!' Then Elijah commanded them, 'Seize the prophets of Baal. Don't let anyone get away!' They seized them, and Elijah had them brought down to the Kishon Valley and slaughtered there." (1 Kgs 18:39–40).

What an amazing triumph, a victory for God and his prophet Elijah. This story is well-rehearsed, as are the immediate events that follow. Elijah raced off to Ahab, dethroned him, and installed a godly king. No. On the contrary. "Elijah was afraid and ran for his life" (1 Kgs 19:3). He fled. For forty days, he travelled back into the desert, the very one Israel roamed for forty years. The symbolism is highlighting Elijah's spiritual regression, his lack of faith and trust. En route, Elijah cried out, "I have had enough, Lord," he said. "Take my life; I am no better than my ancestors" (1 Kgs 19:4).

Elijah found himself at Horeb, likely Mt. Sinai. He had just witnessed the greatest revelation of God's power and righteousness, followed by a national statement of faith. We imagine this spiritual high would embolden and strengthen him. Perhaps Elijah assumed Mt. Carmel was the first of a series of great victories for God. Whatever he imagined, we are not told. What we do know is that he lost resolve. He felt alone and under attack. "I have been very zealous for the Lord God Almighty. The Israelites have rejected your covenant, torn down your altars, and put your prophets to death with the sword. I am the only one left, and now they are trying to kill me too" (1 Kgs 19:10).

The passage that follows, the self-revelation of God, is also familiar to us but, I suggest, it is often misunderstood. Correctly interpreted, this passage gives a powerful cue to those who find themselves feeling like the faithful few among the increasingly faithless many.

The biblical text reads as follows: "The Lord said, 'Go out and stand on the mountain in the presence of the Lord, for the Lord is about to pass by.' Then a great and powerful wind tore the mountains apart and shattered the rocks before the Lord, but the Lord was not in the wind. After the wind there was an earthquake, but the Lord was not in the earthquake. After the earthquake came a fire, but the Lord was not in the fire. And after the fire came a gentle whisper. When Elijah heard it, he pulled his cloak over his face and went out and stood at the mouth of the cave" (1 Kgs 19:11–13).

Many sermons and allusions to this incident have explained this passage as being about guidance. Sometimes we want God to speak in loud, clear, and audible ways like strong winds, earthquakes and fire, ways that are unmistakable. You would have to be blind and deaf to miss them. While God does speak like this on occasion, so we are told, God often speaks in a gentle whisper. If we would but modify our expectations and attune our ears, God is speaking, and we can hear him.

This explanation of the text is problematic. God has just asked, "What are you doing here, Elijah?" Elijah had no problem hearing God. Nor does the theme of hearing God fit into the broader story. Why would God give an illustration of the different ways he can speak after Mt. Carmel? Mt. Carmel is not about God being clear or unclear. It is about God being worshipped as God, and his greatness compared to other gods.

Let us consider the question of fire that Elijah saw at Mt. Horeb first. There "came a fire, but the Lord was not in the fire" (1 Kgs 19:12). We have just encountered fire on Mt. Carmel. Fire is a symbol of God's wrath and anger at sin, in this case, idolatry. God's righteous anger rightly consumes those who do not acknowledge him as God and choose to worship another. Graciously God opts to consume an offering instead of his people. Here, and elsewhere in the Old Testament, fire is a symbol of God's wrath and judgement.

What about strong winds? In the judgement of Egypt, strong winds bring the plague of locusts (Exod 10:13). Psalm 104 is a song that celebrates the sovereignty of God. There we read God "makes winds his messengers, flames of fire his servants" (Ps 104:4). In the wisdom books of Proverbs and Ecclesiastes, wind stands for the passing of time, outside of our control, but under God's authority.

Regarding mountains being torn apart, and earthquakes, it reminds one of the earth opening up and swallowing the 250 Israelites who rebelled against Moses in the desert (Num 16:1–35). In a prophecy against Babylon, Isaiah said God "will make the heavens tremble; and the earth will shake from its place at the wrath of the Lord Almighty, in the day of his burning anger" (Isa 13:13).

Let's not forget Elijah is at Horeb, or Mt. Sinai. This is where Moses received the law. On that occasion, we read, "there was thunder and lightning, with a thick cloud over the mountain, and a very loud trumpet blast" (Exod 19:14–16). Immediately before this, Israel was told that when God came down to the mountain, any person who touched the mountain must be put to death. The people had to be consecrated, wash themselves, and abstain from sexual relations for three days. The extreme weather events underscore God's holiness. Unclean people are unsafe in the proximity of a holy God.

When the Jews, the first recipients of this Old Testament narrative, heard of Elijah's experience of God at Horeb, they would have understood the fire, wind, and earthquakes to be expressions of God's holiness, anger, and judgement of sin. Here then, is the striking part of this incident. The text explicitly says, three times, "the Lord was not in the wind; not in the earthquake; not in the fire."

Elijah had just been on Mt. Carmel and seen God's righteous anger. He wanted to see more. More wind, more earthquakes, more fire—that is, more judgement. Elijah, feeling alone and abandoned, wanted to see clear unmistakable acts of righteous anger and judgement of godless people. But God said that he was not revealing himself in that way. Instead, he was revealing himself in a gentle whisper.

After this self-revelation of God, this epiphany, God once again asked Elijah the exact same question he did moments before. "Then a voice said to him, 'What are you doing here, Elijah?' He replied [with the same answer, word for word], 'I have been very zealous for the Lord God Almighty. The Israelites have rejected your covenant, torn down your altars, and put your prophets to death with the sword. I am the only one left, and now they are trying to kill me too' " (1 Kgs 19:13–14).

Elijah has missed the point. Or at least he hasn't got it yet. It can take time to see something differently. Time for Elijah, and time for Christians post-Christendom. What is the lesson for us?

In his wisdom, God sometimes intervenes and judges sin and rebellion in quick and decisive ways. There is an obvious connection between sin and its judgement, its consequences. That is what happened with those who rebelled against Moses in the desert. An earthquake and accompanying fire swallowed them up. That is how God, on occasion, reveals his holiness.

At other times, God does not speak through fire, earthquake, or wind. Rather, at times he judges with a gentle whisper. His response is understated, subdued, and easy to miss. Sin is allowed to continue without much apparent consequence or response from God. This is precisely how the biblical narrative unfolds as Elijah departs from Mt. Horeb.

Idol-worshipping Ahab remained king, and his wicked wife Jezebel remained queen. Worse, God granted Ahab victory over his enemies. In the next chapter, the gentile king of Aram laid siege to Samaria, part of the territory of King Ahab. Then we read, "a prophet came to Ahab king of Israel and announced, 'This is what the Lord says: "Do you see this vast army? I will give it into your hand today, and then you will know that I am the Lord" ' " (1 Kgs 20:13).

Did Ahab respond with a new-found reverence for God? No. Instead, he responded by stealing land from Naboth, then allowing his wife to murder Naboth. "Some time later there was an incident involving a vine-yard belonging to Naboth the Jezreelite" (1 Kgs 21:1). Note the words "some time." There appears to be a length of time with no visible response from God. This is followed in the next chapter with the news that Ahab remained king for yet another three years.

Can you imagine how Elijah was feeling towards God in all of this? Why was God so slow to judge? Why did he allow sin to continue unre-strained? Why did God bring victory to an evil king? But this is precisely what God said he would do. He would reign with a gentle whisper. He would express his righteous sovereignty in restrained and understated ways. God remains God, justice does come, but for Elijah, it's hard to see. It can feel like too little too late.

Back to the lesson for us. At various points in history, God chooses to restrain the expression of his righteous holiness. He chooses to let the wicked prosper. As we see things, the wicked "have no struggles; their bodies are healthy and strong. They are free from common human burdens; they are not plagued by human ills" (Ps 73:4–5). At times, God allows those with futile and dark hearts to sin, and then to continue to sin. "God [gives] them over in the sinful desires of their hearts" (Rom 1:24).

That this happens at all appears unjust and unfair to us. When it happens in times, like Elijah, when the majority are turning away from God and prospering, and we feel like we are the only faithful few left, that makes it worse. This, in my observation, is precisely where Western Christians find themselves.

We have experienced the swiftest of social changes. The demise of at-tendance at the local church, and the loss of respect and influence of the church as a social institution is unprecedented. How is God responding? With judgement? With clear and unmistakable signs? No. With a gentle whisper. He appears to have given worldly people over to the desires of their hearts. He is allowing the wicked to prosper, apparently unabated.

There are significant risks for us, spiritually, in this space. Like Elijah, we want God to act. The West is becoming more self-centered and con-sumerist, disregarding godly values when it comes to questions of identity, sexuality, and end-of-life considerations. Elsewhere, the wrong people are prospering: the Taliban has won in Afghanistan; Xi Jinping increases his persecution and power in China; and the military junta has reclaimed power in Myanmar.

Like Elijah, believers and followers of God can be prone to spiritual regression and depression in these seasons. We retreat into the desert. We give up hope. We ask God to bring an end to things because it's all too hard. We withdraw from fellowship, and we think we are the only ones left.

This is an understandable response. My read on Western culture as a sociologist is that Elijah's experience is close to ours. Or better, our experiences mirror his. We are living through a fast-paced, mass movement away from God and the CWV, at a time where God is choosing to speak judgement in a gentle whisper. We understandably feel disillusioned and dismayed. We withdraw.

Then God asks us, "What are you doing here?" Like Elijah, many of us have an answer, a pre-prepared one we have been rehearsing in our minds. "I have been zealous for you. But others have rejected you. Now I am alone."

That is not the answer God accepts. Nor is it an answer that addresses the essence of the question. God speaks, revealing that he is not in the wind, earthquake, or fire, but he speaks with a gentle whisper. And then he asks again, "What are you doing here?"

In these final chapters, I am trying to help you get beyond your dismay, sense of hopelessness, or anger. I will suggest some different answers beyond "I have tried, but it's all too hard, and I am giving up." For those in this space, I would wish to sit with you in sackcloth and ashes, and lament. To sit with you, silently, for days on end. But not forever.

Elijah is a powerful Old Testament character who offers an insight into the spiritual risks we face as followers of God in periods of religious decline without apparent consequence. Daniel is another.

Daniel and His Three Friends in Exile

Daniel and his three friends is another Old Testament biblical narrative that captures our imagination. Several stories from this short book take up a disproportionately large number of pages in our children's Bibles. These stories are gripping, enduring, memorable, and easy to understand. Daniel, Shadrach, Meshach, and Abednego have a super-hero-like aura. They are the original "fantastic four." It's classic good versus evil, and the good guys win because they stick to their principles and stand up for what is right.

These stories are retold and reapplied to modern readers who live in a different world. If we would abstain from unclean (not foods, but) influences and not follow the crowd . . . If we would trust in God and his promises, rather than relying on the wise men of our day . . . If we would not bow down and worship idols, but stand up for God and honor him, whatever the risks . . . If we would faithfully and regularly continue to pray to God, regardless of the consequences . . . then, like Daniel and his three friends, God would bless us with victory over our enemies. Good overcomes evil. Just trust in God, stand up for what is right, and it will all work out.

Part of the present appeal of Daniel is that, like him, we increasingly feel like we are in exile, living under the reign of ungodly authorities who tell us to stop praying in our schools, or that we can't teach religious instruction to children or students. The masses now shun or hate on us on social media pages when we suggest God's ways are higher, that he knows better. The apparent fit between Daniel's dilemma and ours is so obvious, which makes the charm of this book all the more timely.

Are you sitting down? The above reading of Daniel is simplistic to the point of being misleading, even at times wrong. When we teach our children or students these ideas, we set them up for a life of what is called "dissonance." When two musical notes do not go together, when they are out of harmony, they are dissonant. Dissonance is where your beliefs and values do not harmonize with your experience. To believe that if I overtly follow God, the result will be blessing and victory, and to then experience ridicule and hardship is dissonance. Too much dissonance is challenging to endure. It can leave us disheartened, anxious, and doubting.

So, if the book of Daniel is not a call to stand up for capital "T" Truth at every opportunity, what is it actually about? Before we go there, let us unpack the socio-historical context in which Daniel found himself.

Daniel was born almost 300 years after Elijah. He was from the two southern tribes of Judah. In part, because they had Solomon's Temple, the Levite priesthood, and the law, Judah did not need to build new temples as did the ten northern tribes, and their descent into ungodliness was slower than Israel's. Judah had a few better kings in their history as well. But descend they did. The northern kingdom fell to Assyria in 722 BC. The Babylonians defeated the Assyrians just over 100 years later. As part of the expansion of their empire, the Babylonians defeated Judah, and Jerusalem fell in 586 BC. Daniel and his three friends were taken into exile.

I agree with popular readings and scholarship about the question that drives the book of Daniel. Namely, does God reign outside of Israel? Or has Israel's God been superseded? Do the local gods, or the local king, Nebuchadnezzar, reign? This question drives the book of Daniel.

The answer to that question is in no doubt. From the very mouth of King Nebuchadnezzar we read that "the Most High is sovereign over all kingdoms on earth and gives them to anyone he wishes and sets over them the lowliest of people" (Dan 4:17). Daniel reaffirmed this conclusion in chapter 5:17, when he reminded the next king, Belshazzar, that his father Nebuchadnezzar lived as an animal "until he acknowledged that the Most High God is sovereign over all kingdoms on earth and sets over them anyone he wishes" (Dan 5:21).

However, if we invert the driving question, "Does God reign outside Israel?," and ask the same question but from an existential perspective, "How does one live as a child of God outside Israel?," it is at this point where I begin to diverge from the popular readings. Let us continue to sharpen the question before I answer it.

Life within Israel was highly regulated by the Torah, the law. Israel was a theocracy. It was not a democracy, where the people (*demos*) rule. It was a theocracy, where God's (*theos*) rule was enshrined in law. There were God's decreed commandments to obey, rituals to practice, unclean items to be avoided. But the Law(s) of Moses were not the laws of Babylon. Nor was there a temple in Babylon where one could go and make sacrifices before Yahweh. How do you continue and mediate a relationship with God without a temple or a Levitical priesthood? The Torah was written to be practiced and obeyed by individuals living within an entire nation under God within the Promised Land, not in exile.

Very quickly behind the obvious question and answer, "Does God reign outside Israel?—Yes," comes the question, "How do you live as a citizen of God's Kingdom in a foreign land?" The popular answer, the Sunday School answer to this question is: "By standing up for capital 'T' Truth." If the food is not clean in Israel, it's not clean anywhere, so we won't eat it in exile. If we are commanded not to bow down and worship idols, or pray to them in Israel, then idolatry is wrong everywhere, so we won't do that in exile. In short, this approach advocates that we behave as if nothing has changed. God is God, inside and outside Israel. Obey him, and he will bless and protect you. Nothing has fundamentally changed, so it's business as usual for God's people.

For the sake of shorthand, and to mix my two testaments, I wish to demarcate this approach with two capitals. First, a capital "C" to represent a proud Christian who is unashamed of their allegiance to Christ. Second, a capital "T" for Truth. To suggest that every believer is to be an uncompromising person who stands up for Jesus and the Truth at every opportunity, we shall demarcate this approach as "ChrisTian."

We all agree that God reigns outside Israel. He reigns in Babylon and in America, Australia, Russia, China, and even North Korea. Is the point of the book of Daniel that it matters not when and where we live, God reigns, and we are called to live as "ChrisTians?"

Let us return to the text. In Daniel 1, we meet Daniel, Hananiah, Mishael and Azariah. They are "young men without any physical defect, handsome, showing aptitude for every kind of learning, well informed, quick to understand, and qualified to serve in the king's palace." They are to learn "the language and literature of the Babylonians." They have been assigned "a daily amount of food and wine from the king's table." Furthermore, we read "the chief official gave them new names: to Daniel, the name Belteshazzar; to Hananiah, Shadrach; to Mishael, Meshach; and to Azariah, Abednego" (Dan 1:4–5, 7).

Daniel and his three friends did not wish to defile themselves with "royal food" in Babylonian terms, but "unclean food" in Jewish terms. So the four asked to be given nothing but vegetables and water for ten days. "At the end of the ten days they looked healthier and better nourished than any of the young men who ate the royal food. So the guard took away their choice food and the wine they were to drink and gave them vegetables instead. To these four young men God gave knowledge and understanding of all kinds of literature and learning" (Dan 1:15–17).

Regarding unclean foods, the text reads as if they abstained. God blessed their conscientious objection with good health, and further blessed them with knowledge and understanding. No disagreement from me so far.

Before the refusal to eat royal food, recorded in Daniel 1:8–16, three other aspects of their new life in Babylon have been revealed to us.

First, in verse 4 we read that they were educated for three years in the "language and literature of the Babylonians." What do you think is contained within the wisdom literature of the Babylonians? In the next chapter, Nebuchadnezzar called together the wise men of Babylon, and asked them to recount and interpret his dream. The wise men responded that this was outside their remit as magicians, enchanters, and astrologers. Among other things, Daniel and his three friends were schooled in magic, chants, and astrology.

How do you think God will respond to Jewish boys agreeing to learn foreign magic? You might anticipate he is displeased. We might expect Daniel and his friends to reject sitting under this instruction. Instead we read, "To these four young men God gave knowledge and understanding of all kinds of literature and learning" (Dan 1:18).

Second, in verse 5 we read that, following their training, they were earmarked "to enter the king's service." They were going to work for the foreign king, an enemy of God's people, who at times believed himself to be a god. They entered a regime of training that would see them employed in the continuance of this despotic empire.

As I have revealed previously, my heritage is Dutch. My four grandparents and my wife's four grandparents all lived in occupied Holland during the Second World War. My two grandfathers were captured. One escaped from a concentration camp, and another jumped off a moving train bound for a labor camp. Some of my extended relatives even participated in the activities of the Resistance.

My father-in-law was an adolescent during the war. His family home was strategically placed on the corner of the entrance to town, at the canal crossing. The Nazis occupied the bottom floor of the home, while the family lived upstairs. They couldn't prevent the Nazis taking over their house using it for opposition purposes. At times, they even had to cook and clean for the invading enemies. Is this betrayal? How would their fellow countrymen feel towards them?

My grandparents despised not just Nazis, but all Germans, till the day they died. After the war, the Dutch rounded up all Nazi sympathizers and punished them. Can you feel this intense ethically reinforced loathing of your captors? Why would anyone have cooperated with the Nazis?

Daniel, Shadrach, Meshach, and Abednego agreed to do something similar. They worked within the court of Nebuchadnezzar. They were, in essence, colluding with the enemy, cooperating with the Nazis. These are all tensions being played out in the biblical narrative.

Third, in versus 6–7 we learn of the names assigned to Daniel and his three friends. Their original names, clearly mentioned, had powerful meanings. Daniel means "God is my judge," Hananiah means "The Lord shows grace," Mishael means "Who is like God," and Azariah means "The Lord is my helper." The meaning of these names is surely no accident. They are prophetic. They speak into the very questions that drive this book. They affirm that God reigns outside Israel, that he is without rival, and that his people ought to both continue to fear him as judge, and look to him for grace and help.

Daniel and his three friends were given new names. The exact meaning of these names is disputed, but likely Belteshazzar means "Marduk protects his life," Shadrach likely means "under the command of Aku," Meshach likely means "Who is what Aku is?" and Abednego likely means "servant of Nebo."[3]

How could Daniel, Hananiah, Mishael, and Azariah allow themselves to be called by these new idol-worshipping names? Why did they not object, as they did with their diet? How could they let go of these prophetic, God-honoring names?

Do you hear the progression of the first chapter of Daniel? God delivers Judah into the hands of Nebuchadnezzar (v.2). Daniel, Hananiah, Mishael, and Azariah are carried into exile. They allow themselves to be educated in foreign magic, serve a foreign power, and take names that honor foreign gods.

---

3. Wright, *Hearing the Message of Daniel*, 33.

While you are thinking about that, let us return to the text. To read Daniel 1 as a chapter of no compromise does not do justice to the entire text. It would be more accurate to conclude that Daniel, Hananiah, Mishael, and Azariah made one stand regarding unclean food after making three concessions. And then we read that God blessed all of their choices.

Before we deal with how we resolve this tension or apply this new and more nuanced reading of Daniel, let me complicate matters just a little more for you. In chapter 10, Daniel has a dream. He takes time to contemplate upon this revelation. We read "At that time I, Daniel, mourned for three weeks. I ate no choice food; no meat or wine touched my lips; and I used no lotions at all until the three weeks were over" (Dan 10:2–3).

Allow me to speculate for a moment that Daniel may not have had the capacity to source kosher meat and wine in Babylon. In other words, it is possible that Daniel, later in life, chose to eat unclean Babylonian "choice food." If he did, this further confounds our dilemma.

Theologically speaking, why might Daniel stop obeying Mosaic food laws? The reasons God forbade certain foods were twofold. First, it demarcated his people as different, as set apart, as his. Second, it mediated against mixing with the nations. If you cannot eat with others, if you don't share "table fellowship," then it's challenging to form meaningful relationships. It prevents others from becoming a person of influence in your life. Inside a theocracy, this makes sense. In Babylon, this logic is stretched, if not broken. It is possible Daniel came to appreciate that he was called to be different in Babylon, but not as set apart as he was when in Israel.

I freely admit at this point my reflections entail some speculating. It is possible that somehow Daniel could source kosher wine and meat, and that he remained a law-abiding Jew. There were thousands of other Jews in exile, perhaps as many as 18,000 (see 2 Kgs 24:14, 16; Jer 52:28–30). This may have created sufficient demand to see a kosher meat supply line established. This text opens a possibility but is inconclusive. Either way, the fantastic four have made three (if not four) serious concessions.

Daniel then, is not simply the book of no compromises, ever. Granted, it still contains the narratives where Daniel would not cease praying; where Shadrach, Meshach, and Abednego would not bow the knee and worship an idol. They stood up and stepped out in faith, they risked their lives, and God honored and protected them. It still contains dreams and apocalyptic material, the interpretations of which reaffirm that Yahweh alone is God.

Yet even here, a closer look at the dreams and apocalyptic half of the book of Daniel leads us to a more nuanced reading. The best known of these more apocalyptic dreams is Nebuchadnezzar's dream of a statue with a gold head, chest of silver, thighs of bronze, legs of iron, and feet fused with iron and clay. This vision of Daniel 2 mirrors the visions in the less read chapters 7 and 8. These visions have consecutive animals that fight for dominion over the earth. Without undermining God's sovereignty—his capacity to place anyone whom he wishes over them—Daniel and his readers are to anticipate centuries of foreign empires that will rule over the Israelites.

God remains God, inside and outside Israel. But this does not mean God will soon re-enthrone kings who acknowledge him, or seek to bring godly wisdom and justice to bear in their kingdoms, or that this season of living under oppression will only last seventy years, as prophesied in the book of Jeremiah, and then God will make Israel great again. Nor do we get the impression that it becomes the core task of Daniel, his peers, and any future Jewish administrators to try to subversively overcome these kingdoms, to get our man on the throne or even to be a significant influence in these forthcoming kingdoms for good.

The dreams in the book of Daniel give the impression that forthcoming evil kingdoms are to be endured. The resolution will come when "the God of heaven will set up a kingdom that will never be destroyed." Future judgement is symbolized in a crushing "rock cut out of a mountain, but not by human hands" (Dan 2:44–45). The parallel external solution in Daniel 7 is the "Ancient of Days."

To summarize the theme of the book of Daniel, framed in ways pertinent to our deliberations, God is sovereign everywhere and at all times. Yet this does not lead to Daniel anticipating a short exile and a return to a theocracy under a David-like king. The answer is not a better version of the good old days. God is foreshadowing, perhaps even ordaining, centuries of foreign violent and oppressive empires. These times are to be tolerated, patiently. After this, God will send a new king who will judge the nations and rescue his people. The answer is a future kingdom, under this king.

In the meantime, Daniel is called to endure, to trust in God, standing firm on some fronts, and making concessions on other fronts. God remains God, but how one lives as a citizen of his kingdom has changed. In a theocracy, one serves God directly and indirectly: directly, as a child of God, and indirectly, by serving a human king who is himself a servant of God. The two coalesce; the young Daniel was born a child of God, as a citizen of a God-honoring nation. In exile, a new possibility arises. How does one remain totally loyal to God as an individual while serving the (ungodly) state and king, installed by God?

Debate will now ensue about exactly where we draw the proverbial line in the sand. I suggest I have done enough to validly conclude that, with regards to Daniel at least, a new context calls for new expressions of following God. I have demonstrated that, within the biblical canon, texts offer us alternate lenses to how we live when we are not in power, but in exile; that life as a citizen of the kingdom of God is expressed differently inside and outside a theocracy.

And the Meaning for Us Is . . .

The application flowing from this more nuanced reading of Daniel is profound. Daniel was born in Israel, in a theocracy. I am not proposing that Christendom was a theocracy. But the CWV was founded upon a subset of Christian beliefs and values. There was within the CWV a shared belief in an all-knowing God, who created a universe with a knowable moral fabric. Jesus' teachings and life represent the high point and exemplary model. There was a shared belief in an afterlife, an eternal destiny determined by one's choices in this life, and the graciousness and judgement of a just all-knowing God.

In a loose sense then, Western countries vote in democratically elected governments, but they voted in parties like the Christian Democratic Union of Germany. No American president has been an overt atheist, and the vast majority have been practicing Christians. Even in much more secular Australia, in his book *In God They Trust*, Roy Williams demonstrated that Christians are significantly over-represented among our prime ministers when compared to the general population. The Netherlands (Holland) in 1901 elected as its prime minister Abraham Kuyper, whose career before politics was as a noted theologian and founder of a Reformed Church denomination. Western countries have historically been led by democratically elected politicians who possess a CWV, who see themselves as somehow accountable to God as a higher authority and the source of the great virtues that underwrite our nations.

In this context, we have been attuned to "notice" or, to put it another way, certain themes in the book of Daniel have been more salient to us. We have read Daniel as a no-compromise book, which calls us to be "ChrisTians," to take a stand for Truth in favour of prayers and chaplains in schools, prayers in parliament, freedom of conscience in religious schools and welfare agencies; to take a stand for Truth against abortion, euthanasia, and same-sex marriage.

To return to my earlier comment, we read the book of Daniel just as we read the rest of the Old Testament. We assume that to be the People of God always means to live under his laws in every context. When you do, you are blessed; when you do not, you are cursed. We imagine that Daniel was blessed because he took a stand and we jump to the conclusion that if we would make a stand, just as Daniel did, we would be blessed and vindicated by God.

I suggest this is not a balanced reading of the book of Daniel. Rather than condensing the Old Testament to one basic plot, we need to appreciate that it contains narratives set in various contexts and that within these different contexts there are profound variations as to how the themes play out.

This insight will help us appreciate that the changing contexts we are living through may invite us to consider if variations to the themes are called for in our times. The goal posts of being disciples who make other disciples has not moved but the playing field of where and how we do that has.

A more nuanced reading of Daniel opens a new possibility. Outside of a theocracy or Christendom, or when in exile, the book of Daniel advocates for some concessions. At various points, we may oppose the state. At other times we may choose not to agree, and yet not object. The book of Daniel may be inviting us to us to pick our battles or, to borrow a phrase from Jesus, to be shrewd. Daniel does not defend every bridge, and perhaps we need not either.

How to decide when to stand up and when it is discerning for us to keep our heads below the parapet is a vexed question. It is a discussion we are close to, but not yet ready for. There remains one piece of the puzzle I shall explore. What clues, what precedents do we get from Jesus and the early church about how we live and express kingdom citizenship when we are in the minority?

For now, we reaffirm the insight from the book of Daniel. Life in exile is somewhat different. It calls for discernment. We stand out and speak up in some circumstances but on other occasions it might be wise and appropriate for us to adopt a more understated posture, to endure and wait.

Combined with the insight from Elijah, namely that at various points in history God's judgement of individual and national rebellion is understated, I am suggesting that these are trying times to live in as a citizen of God's kingdom in an increasingly foreign land. Many of us are already feeling that.

Clarity on the Other Side of Complexity

1. There is a temptation to idealize the past, believing we had it right, and what is going on now is wrong. We can even read the Bible this way. The Bible is a complex book, composed across diverse eras and circumstances, and has within it light and truth for every age.

2. We are used to reading the Old Testament as a theocracy, where God's commandments are enshrined in the national laws. We condense the essence of the Old Testament as being the story of God's people, living under God's rule, and when they do so, they are blessed, and when they do not, they are cursed.

3. The Old Testament is written across varied political settings: a theocracy in the Promised Land; in exile or slavery; amid centuries-long warfare; and of homelessness and wandering.

4. Elijah lived through a season of national turning away from God and towards idolatry. Elijah imagined that God would judge Israel's unfaithfulness but God's judgement was more understated and reserved than Elijah might wish. This gave rise to depression and hopelessness in Elijah.

5. I suggest we are living through a season of a culture-wide abandoning of the CWV and replacing it with a more selfish post-CWV. God does not appear to be judging this as clearly or decisively as we might presume. This may leave twenty-first century Christians prone to dismay and despondency, as it did for Elijah.

6. The book of Daniel is often read as encouraging us to make a stand, as Daniel did. If we do, God will honor us, as he did Daniel and his three friends.

7. A closer reading reveals that Daniel and his friends at times made a stand, and at other times made a series of compromises. They did this in response to their modified context because God's authority was not recognized in Babylon as it was in Israel.

8. Daniel appears to have believed, because of a prophecy in the book of Jeremiah, that the exile in Babylon would last seventy years, and then things would return to some sort of normal. The dreams in the book of Daniel suggest that following the downfall of the Babylonian Empire, other empires would rise, and there would be multiple forthcoming evil empires for God's people to endure for centuries.

9. I suggest that living as a Christian in Christendom somewhat parallels how the people of God were called to live in a theocracy. Likewise, I suggest that there are some parallels between living as a Christian in post-Christendom and Daniel who lived in exile in Babylon. If so, the book of Daniel may be inviting us to us to pick our battles, to be shrewd, to not die on every hill, and to endure.

11

Jesus and His First Followers as a Minority

How did Jesus position himself when he was at odds with the powers-that-be? Jesus stood up for the Truth, did he not? He overthrew the money changers' tables in the temples and declared God's house a house of prayer. He repeatedly healed on the Sabbath, right under the noses of the Pharisees. He cursed, pronouncing the teachers of the law and Pharisees as hypocrites, blind fools, whitewashed tombs, and snakes and vipers. Jesus took a stand, it is argued, and so ought we.

Just as there is a simplistic reading of Daniel, I suggest there is a simplistic reading of the gospel accounts of the life of Jesus. The simplistic reading renders Jesus as a radical, with no fear and no regrets. To be a follower of this Jesus—to take up your cross and follow him—involves embracing the ridicule and shame he did. Followers of this Jesus are called to be radicals, or what I demarcate as "ChrisTians."

In this one chapter of a book that aims to hold an interdisciplinary conversation between sociology, history, and ecclesiology (that is, how we be and do "church"), I cannot do justice to the vast amount of ink spilt on the topic of who Jesus was and how he lived and interacted with his context. My aim in this chapter is much more limited, more humble. My aim is to contrast the simplistic view of a Jesus who stands up for Truth, no matter what, with some critical incidents of his life as revealed in the gospels. I will explain why the simplistic view of Jesus is appealing and why this view held sway and fitted into our corporate mind maps. Or, sociologically speaking, why it was functional and plausible during Christendom.

I will also highlight how this simplistic view is less effective as a mission strategy in the post-Christian West. How a more nuanced reading of the gospels, and even some bits of the Acts of the Apostles too, offer us some additional strategies for how we might behave as faithful followers of Jesus in an increasingly antagonistic era.

The simplistic view of a Jesus who opposes all wrongs is appealing for two reasons. First, it is easy to understand. You can get your head around it and remember it. It's almost intuitive. To use a slightly technical term, it is mono-causal, or mono-factorial. That is, its power to explain involves or is dependent upon one factor.

People love mono-factorial explanations, not just Christians—everyone does. Migrants take our jobs, so stopping illegal migration protects local employment. Cheap imports do the same, so tariffs are good for our nation's economy. If we keep all infected people out of our state, we will be disease-free. People have a right to make personal choices, so any form of birth or death control is wrong. If two people love each other, that's all that matters, whatever their gender. They should be allowed to marry, because marriage is about love. Sexism is a form of discrimination, so we should impose gender quotas in politics. Banks are greedy, and we need to regulate them. Religions cause war. The church abuses power, so any step that removes power from the church is a step in the right direction.

These are all simplistic mono-causal or mono-factorial explanations, which have a popular appeal in mainstream culture. But each of them is simplistic to the point of being unhelpful. Migrants do take jobs, but they also increase demand and production. Tariffs, in the long run, can facilitate local producers being inefficient and non-competitive. Tariffs drive prices up and quality and innovation down. Abortion and euthanasia are more complex than just personal choice. Marriage is about family, the best place to raise the next generation, *and* love. Banks can be greedy, but an economy needs a banking sector for investment and growth, and managing finances incurs costs. War is usually about the control of resources, religion is often used (or abused) as the banner under which to march. At times, the church has exploited power, but more often it uses its power to bring public good, like education to the masses and access to health care.

You get my point, I trust, even if you are debating with me in your head about one or more of the above-listed examples. One-factor explanations are appealing and even compelling. You can make a meme, a tweet in less than 140 characters, or a political slogan around mono-causal explanations. But you cannot do justice to a complex issue, let alone the entire dynamic of a person's life, with reference to only one factor.

The second reason we are drawn to a radical Jesus who stands up for Truth is because this view is supported or reinforced by "evidence" and experience. Jesus stood up for the Truth, and he was persecuted, ultimately crucified. Jesus made statements like, "If the world hates you, keep in mind that it hated me first" (John 15:18). Likewise, "Whoever wants to be my disciple must deny themselves and take up their cross daily and follow me" (Luke 18:23).

Given this, we should expect opposition when we stand up for traditional marriage, or for religious freedoms, or against the sexualization of adolescent females. And when we make a stand, what happens? We are persecuted, like Jesus. If the world is against us, then we must be aligned with Jesus. This argument sounds logical, compelling, and we have experience and evidence to support it.

This argument contains a flaw in logic. It's an easy mistake to make. So many people make this mistake that philosophers of logic have a name for this flaw: affirming the consequent. If I follow Jesus (P), then I will be persecuted (Q). I am being persecuted (Q), therefore I must be following Jesus (P). Let's take the emotion out of the argument. If P, then Q. Q therefore P.

Now let's try the argument elsewhere. People who have COVID-19 cough. She is coughing, so she must have COVID-19. If I have a heart attack, I will experience shortness of breath. I have shortness of breath, therefore I must be having a heart attack. Quick! Call an ambulance! No wait—there could be all sorts of other reasons why one has shortness of breath. You may be unfit. You might be exercising.

Likewise, there can be all sorts of reasons why Christians are experiencing persecution or opposition, other than because they are following Jesus. If I started communicating that the Bible teaches a flat earth, I would experience ridicule. If I teach that the Bible endorses racism and slavery, I would experience scorn and opposition. If I posted these thoughts online, I would get hated on. We could even say that I would be persecuted for my beliefs about the Bible. But it does not follow that my persecution would be the result of me following Jesus.

Now we have a real dilemma. If you follow Jesus, at some points you ought to expect opposition. Having said that, there will be times where individuals, and even groups of Christians, will experience persecution, and they will interpret that persecution as evidence that they are following Jesus. But this may not be the case. Their persecution will, on some occasions, be a result of their lack of wisdom, however honorable their intentions might be.

The question for Christians who live in this time of transition out of Christendom, and into a post-Christian West, is how much of our persecution is because we are following Jesus? And how much of our persecution is because we are following Jesus in outmoded ways, non-essential to being one of his disciples, in ways that made sense in a widely held CWV, but do not make sense in a post-Christian setting? That's a tough question and one that will elicit a diverse range of answers, but it's a conversation we must have, and we must have it now because our changing context requires it.

Simplicity is, at this point, an enemy of productive conversation. I have highlighted what I believe are the two primary reasons why Christians are drawn to a simplistic picture of a Jesus who always stands up for the Truth. There are, of course, other reasons. The best explanations for this are also multi-factorial. I will now add another. We readily see a Truth-announcing Jesus because this is a picture or interpretation of who Jesus was that we have inherited. It has held sway for centuries, because it worked (or functioned) within a CWV culture.

Of course, I affirm that Jesus did stand up for Truth. Sometimes. I will contend that Jesus, like Daniel, also made compromises. He did not die on every hill. He died on some hills, and literally died on one in particular. Some things are as important as life and death, but not all things. Jesus let some things slide. We will consider where he was prepared to make concessions in a moment.

For now, the point I wish to highlight is that we are more positioned to notice the Jesus who made a stand. In the CWV, it was the role of the church to name up good from evil, and ground moral conversation in God's word and not just opinion. Following Jesus's example, it was also our task to provide for the poor and care for the sick. Always taking a stand is a learned way of seeing Jesus with 1600 years of history.

Why Did Standing up for Truth as a Christian Fit in the Past?

We have previously noted how the early church grew from 120 people in Acts 1 to about half the empire in 350 AD. The rise of Christianity can be linked to a parallel political problem within the empire. By the end of the third century, the empire was disparate, lacking unity. The peoples were a conglomeration of tribes and nations that traditionally fought against each other. Furthermore, the government was divided by two languages: Latin in the West, and Greek in the East. From 285 AD onwards, the empire was formally divided into two parts, leading to two rival emperors.

One of those rivals was Constantine. The night before a decisive battle in 312, he was "converted." He instructed his soldiers to paint crosses on their shields. The following day he defeated Maxentius in the Battle of Milvian Bridge, a decisive victory that would lead to Constantine becoming the sole Roman Emperor.

Constantine took control of Rome. In 313, in the following year, he issued the Edict of Milan, a decree that granted religious tolerance to all religions, including Christians. In 324, he defeated the last of his military rivals. In 325, he convened an empire-wide church council, the Council of Nicaea. The council wrote the Nicene Creed, which brings uniformity of belief to the church. Christianity, the religion of the emperor, became the belief system, the view of the world that brought unity to the disparate Roman Empire. In this regard, it is without peer.

Christianity in the West retained this privileged position until recently. Historians and the like will argue over the dates and markers of its rise and demise. Here is the crux of the matter. For something in the order of 1600 years, the CWV was *the* social glue, *the* belief system that unified any given Western culture. The church as a social institution played a necessary role. It served a function within that culture. Among other things, it was the custodian of moral objectivity. The church interpreted the Bible and applied its moral codes to individual and collective dilemmas. They were the messengers of divine-inspired Truth, proclaimed for the common good.

Within that frame of reference, Christians who read the gospels will be attuned to notice when Jesus stood up against the powers-that-be, and spoke inspired Truth for the common good. They will notice a Jesus who stood up for the blind, the poor, and the widows. They will notice a Jesus who stood against the abuse of power, and institutional corruption. Who stood and preached the Truth, and invited others to believe in and follow him. As followers of Jesus, the church and ChrisTians will believe it their calling to do what they notice Jesus doing.

Our culture no longer looks to the church or the CWV for moral guidance. On the contrary. The church has been rejected as a power-hungry institution that exploits its authority to amass wealth and protect its own. Any attempt by Christians (now viewed as influenced by the church) to bring biblical insights to bear on a conversation is dismissed as a power play; an attempt to perpetuate or reinstate a view of the world that was an unfair playing field; a view of the world that gave the church an unmerited amount of influence. Whether or not this reading is accurate does not matter. It is widely held; it is the new consensus. It is assumed, not even open for debate anymore.

Christians feel this long-held moral compulsion to stand up and speak up, believing they are following Jesus in doing so, but it is not well received by culture. What do we do? Stand up anyway? Even if it leads to persecution?

What I am proposing is that Christians have Christendom lenses through which we have read the gospels. These lenses highlight certain themes and obscure others. They frame what we see. We need to, quite deliberately, lay these glasses to the side, and put on another pair of lenses that ask, with intent, did Jesus always stand against every evil? And if not, what posture did Jesus adopt when he chose not to take on evil and evil doers? When did he choose to divest himself, or not avail himself of his power?

Before I go there, I fear I have just distressed some readers. You may have heard me say something like: readers can read into the text whatever their lenses will let them see. There is no such thing as an author's intention, or an objective meaning in a text. That conclusion is nonsense. Authors, especially God speaking through his Word and Spirit, can and do convey meaning. In short, my position is this. The biblical text is God's inspired revelation. God, by his Word and Spirit, can and does get across any message he so desires. This statement does not nullify the parallel reality. In the very process of reading, a reader interprets meaning. Readers, who belong to interpretive communities, are prone to notice some truths and overlook others, depending on the cultural glasses they wear.

A Turn in the History of Interpretations of Jesus

We are by no means the first readers of the gospel to suggest that prior readings of Jesus have been unbalanced, biased by a set of lenses. Martin Luther and John Calvin believed the Roman Catholic Church misinterpreted the Bible. Another notable precedent of this was Albert Schweitzer (1875–1965). He was educated under scholars such as William Wrede, who argued that the gospel accounts of Jesus reveal more about the early church's attempts to divinize Jesus than they do about Jesus the man. The gospels are constructs of early church authors more so than biographical accounts of Jesus' life.

Schweitzer came to disagree. For him, the historical Jesus of the gospels was a radical. He concluded that "it is a good thing that the true historical Jesus should overthrow the modern Jesus, should rise up against the modern spirit and send forth upon earth not peace, but a sword."[1] Jesus was an eschatological prophet. After John the Baptist "comes Jesus, and in the knowledge that He is the coming Son of Man lays hold of the wheel of the world to set it moving on that last revolution which is to bring all ordinary history to a close. It refuses to turn, and He throws Himself upon it."[2]

Schweitzer leaves two legacies relevant to our concern. First, he was convinced that the biblical text is historically reliable. The gospels are biographies of Jesus, more so than constructs of the early church. Second, to understand Jesus, you must make sense of his eschatological aspirations. It

1. Schweitzer, *Quest of the Historical Jesus*, 403.
2. Schweitzer, *Quest of the Historical Jesus*, 370–71.

is said you can divide the history of scholarship about Jesus into two camps: those who think Jesus came to Jerusalem to preach; and those who think he came to die. Schweitzer's view is that Jesus was clear about what was going to happen to him. "When the days drew near for him to be taken up, he set his face to go to Jerusalem" (Luke 9:51 ESV). He came as the Son of Man, prepared to die, in the greatest of spiritual showdowns.

Part of the legacy of Schweitzer is that Jesus is often viewed as a revolutionary, a radical. You may have seen the meme with a Che Guevara-like Jesus and the words underneath "Meek. Mild. As If." One may hold this view out of Reformed Evangelical convictions (that is, Jesus knew he is fully God and fully man and must die to atone for the sins of the world), or out of more social gospel convictions (that is, Jesus intended to bring in a new kingdom order of peace and justice, and his death somehow inaugurated and inspired the sacrifice required for such a noble cause). Either way, it is common to view Jesus as a radical.

Who and What Jesus Stands Up against

Let us take a moment to consider the interactions in Mark's gospel where Jesus might be construed as rebellious. You will find a full account of all the interactions in Appendix 1. I have divided them into three categories. First, instances where Jesus was a provocative radical, confrontational towards others. Second, instances where Jesus was compliant towards authority. Third, instances where Jesus was guarded, coy, or silent before an authority figure that he was likely at odds with.

The moments where Jesus was provocative and confrontational towards authority are well known to us. He ate with sinners and tax collectors, healed on the Sabbath, taught against the Pharisees and teachers of the law as hypocrites, and accused them of self-aggrandizement. Beyond these well-rehearsed instances, I will single out two particular interactions.

Mark 8 is a turning point in the gospel. A blind man receives partial, then full sight. This is symbolic of the disciples, who have begun to see, but do not yet fully appreciate Jesus for who he is. Peter then confesses Christ. Jesus begins to teach that the Son of Man must be rejected by the elders, the chief priests, and the teachers of the law, and that he must be killed (Mark 8:31). Jesus identifies the particular Jews who will reject him. But he remains vague about the role of the Romans, and fails to mention Pilate or Herod. Mark 10:32–34 follows the exact same pattern.

Mark 12:1–12 is another key passage that sums up the ministry of Jesus. New Testament scholar N. T. Wright described this parable, the

parable of the tenants, as the one that most captures the essence of Jesus' ministry incarnate.[3] Israel's leadership is likened to tenants plotting
against their landlord by rejecting his messengers (prophets) and killing
his son. Core to the ministry of Jesus is that he comes to Israel's leadership
with all the authority of the Son of God. He calls Israel to give his Father,
their God, the obedience and honor due to him. They must overtly reject
Jesus and kill him to disqualify themselves as the children of God. It is
Israel, not Rome, who kills the son.

     In all instances where Jesus was confrontational, as in the cases just
highlighted, Jesus focused his harshest criticism, his most provocative critique, on Israel's religious leaders. They were the bad guys he targeted.

     By way of contrast, when Jesus referenced Roman political leader-
ship, he was vague. In addition to the two instances mentioned above,
notice Jesus' actions when he heard John the Baptist had been beheaded
by Herod. He said nothing (Mark 6:14–29). In Matthew's account, "he
withdrew by boat privately to a solitary place" (Matt 14:13). Luke's account
is similar: Jesus withdrew.

     Likewise, note Jesus' response to the murder of John the Baptist. In
Mark 9:12–13, Jesus teaches specifically that the Son of Man must be rejected by Israel, just as they rejected Elijah. Jesus was at this moment speaking
in code. Elijah is a reference to John the Baptist, and the phase "they have
done to him everything they wished" is an allusion to John's beheading by
Herod. Jesus avoided being confrontational; rather he was coy. He did not
mention Herod by name, or beheading as the crime.

     At the risk of over-stating my case, Jesus' guarded critique of Herod
is in contrast to John the Baptist's. John's prophetic voice spoke explicitly
against Herod and his unlawful marriage. It is for this reason Herod and
his daughter imprisoned and killed John (Mark 6:17–28). If John the Baptist was a prophet in the line of Elijah, then Jesus' silence on a topic that
cost John his life is noteworthy.

     We see the discreetness of Jesus again when he was asked an inflamma-
tory question regarding paying imperial taxes. Jesus responded, "Give back to
Caesar what is Caesar's and to God what is God's" (Mark 12:17). This could
have been a clear moment for Jesus to affirm that Caesar Tiberius was not
the son of a divine god, as was inscribed on Roman coins. Jesus might have
confirmed that he was Lord and not Caesar. But Jesus did not go there.

     In short, what I am proposing is that Jesus had two sets of adversar-
ies. First, there were his antagonists. In literary analysis, an antagonist is
the villain, who directly opposes the main character. In the gospels, the

---

3. Wright, *Jesus and the Victory of God*, 565–66.

leaders of Israel antagonize. That is to say, the Pharisees, the elders, the chief priests, and the teachers of the law directly opposed Jesus. Then there are the gentile powers-that-be, namely Herod, Pilate and his soldiers, Caesar, who claims to be Lord, and Rome. On the surface, the non-Jewish powers-that-be found Jesus politically annoying and dangerous, but Jesus avoided directly provoking them. The gentile powers do not function as antagonists in the narrative.

This is not to downplay the role of Herod, Pilate, and Rome. Both groups were active in Jesus' crucifixion, as players in the greatest spiritual showdown. Both were the face of evil and opposition. Both were expressions of the work of the Devil against the purposes of God in this world. Yet Jesus directly opposed one group, and avoided confrontation with the other.

This observation, while not common, is not entirely new. Usually, we account for the difference of response with a theological explanation. In ways similar to N. T. Wright, we highlight the ministry of Jesus in coming to Israel as tenants, as children of God, as inheritors of his promises. Jesus first "came to that which was his own," and they must reject him, or "not receive him" (John 1:11). The Jews are the incumbents, not the gentiles and Romans. It is the Jews who must first reject Jesus, so that the gospel can then go out to all the nations.

I agree. This is all true. But none of this precludes another explanation being equally true. If we consider the political dimension to all of this, let's imagine Jesus chose to antagonize the gentile powers as John the Baptist did. What would happen if Jesus spoke against unlawful marriages, or the entrenched slavery system, or the common practice of the gentiles exposing unwanted children to the elements and leaving them to die, or the entrenched sexism of Roman law that gave women few rights? Surely Jesus was against all of these? Why did he not oppose them?

The answer is complex, but part of the explanation is because Rome was not a democracy. It would not listen. Jesus would be branded an insurrectionist and crucified or beheaded. He would die before his time and perhaps on the wrong hill. Jesus was following the advice he gave to his disciples. When one comes before not only (Jewish) local councils and synagogues, but also (gentile) governors and kings, one must "be as shrewd as snakes and as innocent as doves" (Matt 10:16–18).

What I am proposing is this. It is too simplistic to suggest that Jesus was the first ChrisTian who also stands up against every evil and injustice, and to be a follower of Jesus means we must do the same. This explanation is flawed on two fronts. First, it does not fit with or take into account all the biblical data. Clearly there are times where Jesus did not oppose evil.

Scripture does not record him as directly opposing slavery, or sexism, or exposing unwanted children.

Second, Jesus is the Son of God, who is uniquely positioned in the unfolding drama of salvation history. Only he could challenge Israel's leadership with the authority of being the Messiah. Only when Israel rejected the very Son of God did they disinherit themselves as a nation and open the way for gentiles to come into the Kingdom of God. Jesus as the Son of God must speak truth to religious entrenched power, so it rejected him, in ways exclusive to him as the incarnate Messiah.

The focus and intensity of Jesus' challenge to Israel is unique, not transferable one-to-one to us. He had to make a stand as the son of God who came to reclaim his father's vineyard. That was a once-in-human-history moment. We are never in that situation as Jesus was. His stand was unique.

Working from Mark's gospel, we have identified the theme of Jesus selectively making a stand, and that his stand was in some ways unique. Matthew's gospel has similar themes. Regarding the purpose of Matthew, Wright says, "Matthew is quite clearly offering a *manual* for discipleship, for a church living as a minority group in a hostile majority culture."[4] The invitation to inherit the kingdom through meekness, being peacemakers, and turning the other cheek, written in times when believers were being persecuted, is striking.

I am not suggesting Jesus and his disciples never opposed. To understand how Jesus' followers balanced the themes of when and against whom they chose to take a stand, and when to be more subversive, we must turn our attention to the very early church as we find it in the book of Acts and beyond.

Who and What the Early Church Stands Up against

Peter followed the pattern as set by Jesus regarding who he opposed. In his speech on the day of Pentecost, he was unequivocal in implicating the Jews of Jerusalem as those who "put [Jesus] to death by nailing him to the cross" (Acts 2:23). Likewise, en route to the temple in Jerusalem, Peter said, "Fellow Israelites . . . You handed him over to be killed . . . " (Acts 3:13). Before the Sanhedrin, Peter said, "Rulers and elders of the people! . . . It is by the name of Jesus Christ of Nazareth, whom you crucified . . . " (Acts 4:8–10).

Peter was direct and combative in his assessment of Jewish guilt. Regarding the Romans, he was altogether different. In his speech on the day of Pentecost, Peter said that the Jews killed Jesus with the help of lawless

---

4. Wright and Bird, *New Testament in Its World*, 589, emphasis theirs.

men (Greek *anomos*). The Romans are described as those without the guidance of the Old Testament law. In Acts 3:13, Peter partially exonerated Pilate as one who, independent of Jewish pressure, had decided to let Jesus go. In the Acts 4 speech before the Sanhedrin, there is no reference to Pilate or otherwise.

Stephen's speech in Acts 7 was similarly critical of the Jews as those who have always persecuted the prophets. Stephen neither mentioned nor referenced the Romans.

Acts 11 represents a turning point. Acts follows a geographical pattern outlined in Acts 1:8. The Apostles will bear witness to Jesus in Judea, Samaria, and then to the ends of the earth. Antioch was the first gentile mission beyond Judea and Samaria. Granted, there were Jewish diaspora communities in many of the cities Paul visited. Still, his mission was now fulfilling the mandate of reaching beyond Judea and Samaria, that is, beyond traditional Israel.

A brief survey of Paul's first three sermons reveals something of the transition in the second half of Acts. His first sermon was in the synagogue at Antioch. While Antioch was a large Hellenized city of about 300,000 people, Josephus the Jewish historian recorded two thousand Jewish families who called the city home.[5]

Paul's sermon began by retelling the story of Israel's salvation history (Acts 13:16–37). He reached his climax when he declared Jesus as the long-awaited Jewish Messiah. "Therefore, my brothers, I want you to know that through Jesus the forgiveness of sins is proclaimed to you. Through him everyone who believes is justified from everything you could not be justified from by the law of Moses" (Acts 13:38–39). Paul concluded with an exhortation (Acts 13:40–41) inviting his audience to "take care" to avoid making the same mistakes as those in Jerusalem: unbelief.

This sermon, preached to a Jewish audience, contains similar themes to those of Peter and Stephen. The Jews of Jerusalem are described as those who did not recognize Jesus, but instead condemned him. The Jews "asked Pilate to have him executed" (Acts 13:28). Paul portrays Pilate's role as somewhat passive. Paul's exhortation to avoid unbelief then follows. In all this, there is a subtle yet profound shift. The Jews in Jerusalem were in error, but Paul did not blame Diaspora Jews. He invited the Jews in Antioch to respond more appropriately to the good news of the Messiah's coming.

Paul's second sermon, as recorded in Acts, is not set in a synagogue among fellow Diaspora Jews. He was now in Lystra, a Roman colony,

---

5. Josephus, *Ant.* 12.3.4; Josephus, *J.W.* 7.3.3.

among what a Greek historian calls "a prototypical mountain dwelling tribe of primitive rustics . . . "[6]

What is not said in this sermon is as noteworthy as what is said. There is no mention of the God of Israel, the Law, the Messiah, sin, or forgiveness. There is no blame attached to Jesus' crucifixion. There is even no mention of the cross. We must acknowledge, though, that the account of the sermon is truncated by the arrival of hostile Jews from Antioch. Instead, this address highlights a monotheistic living God of all nations, who leaves a testimony to himself through the rain, crops, food, and joy (Acts 14:15–17). Paul constructs a sermon that targets gentile farmers, not law-abiding Jews.

Much ink has been spilt on Paul's third sermon to the Areopagus in Athens. My observations will be brief and focus on details relevant to our line of questioning. Athens, in Paul's day, was a shadow of its former self. Once the center of Alexander the Great's empire, it was now a superseded university town of about 25,000 with a Jewish contingent. Its status was more symbolic than real. Whereas Rome represented the political and military center of the empire, Athens represented the heritage of Greek philosophy and thought that underwrote the Roman Empire.

Three big names dominate Greek philosophy: Socrates, the founding father of philosophy; Plato, his most famous student, who in turn taught Aristotle (who tutored Alexander the Great). Socrates was brought to trial before the Areopagus, which was an open-air forum that functioned as a court that heard and judged the teachings of thinkers. Socrates was found guilty of corrupting young minds towards impiety. That is, he was guilty of disrespecting the gods and the prevailing belief system. He was sentenced to death and drank the legendary poison hemlock. *The Power of One* is a movie of a more recent rehearsal of the same themes. (Readers, be wary of undermining the prevailing belief system of a culture!)

Luke carefully scripted his account such that Paul was positioned with allusions to Socrates as a herald of new or strange divinities, addressing the leading philosophers of his day. The audience was initially skeptical of his ideas. Paul spoke in the symbolic intellectual and religious capital of the empire, using both simple and more complex rhetorical conventions. As Witherington remarks, Luke had been "building a portrait of Paul who can stand toe to toe with the great intellectuals of the age, even in Athens."[7]

Paul began by seeking to build common ground between himself and his audience, highlighting their religiosity, their desire to worship even an unknown god. From here, I am most persuaded by the view represented by

6. Strabo, *Geographica*, 12.6.5.
7. Witherington, *New Testament Rhetoric*, 68.

C. K. Barrett, that outlines how Paul used a series of "proofs" used by the Stoics and Epicureans. He used their arguments, sometimes with them, and sometimes against them.[8]

Commencing with reference to an unknown god is a tipping of the hat to the Stoics. Yet Paul was not in total agreement with Stoicism. He challenged the Stoic thought of an impersonal yet all-pervasive *divine logos*. Instead, he talked of a creator God who is transcendent above and judges over creation. Nor did he endorse the Athenians' belief in their racial superiority. Paul asserted that this one creator God made all men equal, descending from one man (Acts 17:26). His thinking, in conjunction with his critique of idolatry, was, at this point, Jewish. Here is the brilliance of Paul. He did more than just play the Stoics off against the Epicureans and vice versa. Rather, his arguments were a mixture of Hellenistic, Jewish, and Christian thought, all designed to sound familiar at times, yet still strike out against pagan polytheism.[9]

Similar observations can be made regarding Paul's quotation of the Greco-Roman poets. He moved his audience from the known and shared, then used these authoritative voices in his dialogue to critique pagan polytheism and contend for a relational, knowable god.

In both his Athens and Lystra speeches, three phenomena are relevant to our concerns. First, gone are the quotations of Old Testament scriptures of his synagogue sermon in Antioch, not because Paul believed they lacked authority, but because Paul believed they held no authoritative status in the minds of his audience. Second, gone are the indictments. Paul was not standing up against wrong. Whatever critique he offered, it was not framed as a confrontation between truth and falsehood. It was about removing obstacles to faith. Third, Paul spoke the language of his audience. He appealed to natural laws, or he quoted Greco-Roman thoughts and sayings as part of his proofs, precisely because they were part of the accepted wisdom of his listeners.

Again, it is beyond the scope of this book to conduct an entire biblical theology of when and how God's people confront ungodliness. I sense I have done enough analysis of the biblical text to convey my thesis. In short, it is this: Jesus, Peter, and Paul confronted God's people (initially Jews, but later already converted believers from any ethnicity) head-on. However, when there was godlessness present among gentiles or non-believers, it was not directly or specifically challenged.

---

8. Barrett, "Paul's Speech on the Areopagus," 75.

9. Flemming, *Contextualisation in the New Testament*, 79.

All this begs the question. Am I suggesting that Jesus, Peter, Paul, and the gospel were politically neutral? That Paul and hence Christians are only concerned with converting people and saving their souls? To use Augustine (and Luther's) categories, am I suggesting that governments are concerned with the City of Man or the Kingdom of this World, whereas Christians ought to be concerned with the City or Kingdom of God? Let the government do their thing, and we will do ours.

Whenever the topic of Christians and politics comes up, we immediately head to Romans 13. There we read, "The authorities that exist have been established by God . . . For rulers hold no terror for those who do right, but for those who do wrong" (Rom 13:1, 3). Governments are (or were) seen as God's instruments to maintain order. When our politicians and leaders held to a CWV, national laws more or less affirmed the shared Christian worldview morality. We could just let the government maintain law and order while we focused on the Kingdom of God.

Two things have changed, so that this view is less sustainable than it once was. First, biblical historians such as N. T. Wright have highlighted how Caesar Augustus instituted an emperor-worshipping cult, in which Caesar claimed to be lord, the son of god, who brought peace and justice. Having appreciated this, it follows that the introduction to many of Paul's letters involve rival claims that Jesus is Lord, son of the one God, who calls even gentiles to obedience. Second, Western Christians can now foresee a time when we will fear political authorities, even if we do right (the scriptures reported just that development: Peter; book of Revelation).

I am not suggesting that Jesus and Paul were apolitical or that they were concerned only for souls, not politics. A better reading of Jesus and Paul and their relation to politics is this. Jesus' claim to be a king of a new kingdom was always a political claim. Paul's letters called people to enthrone Jesus, not Caesar, as Lord. Both Jesus and Paul were always political, but they were subversive in how they went about it. Neither chose to be directly confrontational to Rome with their subversive claims. I am not saying they hid it, but they did not adopt the path of direct confrontation and rebellion, as some would have encouraged them to do so. Instead, the early Christians set about being a different people who lived by a different code following a different king and establishing a different kingdom without looking for a fight with the powers-that-be.

And it worked. Not only were thousands of souls saved, even up to half of the entire empire, but Christians also changed the social fabric for the better. As I observed earlier, none of the New Testament leading characters and teachers directly confronted sexism, slavery, or exposing unwanted children (usually girls) and leaving them to die. Rather, they modelled and taught that women, children, and slaves would be treated differently within the Christian community.

Jesus had disciples, not immediately among the twelve but within the wider group, who were female. He affirmed Mary's place when she adopted a non-traditional role listening to his teaching. Some scholars claim women are among the seventy who were sent on mission.[10] Women were present in critical roles in the four gospels and Acts. For instance, Elizabeth, the mother of John the Baptist, was the first person in Luke's gospel to be named as one "filled with the Holy Spirit" (Luke 1:41). Then she was the first to prophesy.

Paul twice, and Peter once, in their letters, include what scholars call a "household table" (Col 3:18—4:1, in Eph 5:21–6:9, and in 1 Pet 2:18–3:7). These tables outline the appropriate relationships and behaviors within Christian households. Slaves were to be treated with respect. They were in some sense equal sons and co-heirs in the kingdom. Conversely, Paul also described free persons as all equally prisoners of Christ Jesus (see also Phlm 9). Women and children were to be esteemed, loved, and not mistreated. Whatever position one holds, we are called to use our freedom to serve God, and he will judge us all equally, without favoritism.

The early Christians embraced and lived out this radical social order with profound consequences. Stark notes that women born, raised, and married in Christian communities were advantaged at every step. Female infants born to Christians were less likely to be exposed. Further, Christians even rescued the abandoned daughters of others and raised them as their own. Teenage Christians were married later than their peers. They were less likely to be forced to have an abortion, which was often fatal for the mother. In marriage, they were more financially independent, stable, less at risk.[11]

This meant that women were attracted to Christianity. In an era where eligible females were significantly outnumbered, Christian women were a significant factor, so Stark argues, in the conversion of both their husbands and eventually by slow accumulation, the empire.

Slavery is another example of where Christians began by adopting different practices within their own communities that eventually led to radical social structural change. First, a note about slavery: slavery is common. It is normal. Every culture has a history of competing for limiting resources, leading to war, winners and losers, and the losers being enslaved.

Mention the word slavery today and two pictures immediately come to mind for your average Westerner: the African-American Atlantic slave

---

10. Forbes and Harrower, *Raised from Obscurity*, 104–5.
11. Stark, *Rise of Christianity*, 95-127.

trade of the seventeenth and eighteenth centuries, and the sex slave trade that is present in pockets of South East Asia, Eastern Europe, indeed in much of the modern world. We view slavery as occasional and exceptional. For the most part, we imagine nations have co-existed without institutional slavery. Not so. Sadly, slavery is normal and universal. But I will have to make a case to convince you.

The story of William Wilberforce and the Clapham sect has often been told, but it is worth briefly recapping. Wilberforce was born in 1759 in England, when the slave trade was well established. Ships would bring goods from Britain to Africa. British goods were traded for African slaves, who were then brought to the West Indies and the New Americas. The slaves would be traded for cotton, sugar, tobacco, molasses, and rum, all produced by slave labor. These goods were then transported back to Britain. This was a highly lucrative and established trade route, condoned by many, and critical to the British economy.

A former slave trader, John Newton, was converted, repented of his former ways, and went into the ministry. He became Wilberforce's pastor and spiritual advisor. Between 1789 and 1807, Wilberforce and others from the Clapham sect championed anti-slave trade legislation in the British parliament. It was not until 1833 that the Slavery Abolition Act passed in the British House of Commons. By this time, anti-slavery was becoming seen as progressive, moral, and popular, not just in Britain. In 1842, an American diplomat defined the slave trade as a "crime against humanity."[12]

In the same year, the British consul-general to Morocco sought to raise the anti-slavery case with the Islamic sultan. The sultan replied that slavery was a matter "on which all sects and nations have agreed from the time of Adam".[13] That slavery is immoral is a view that took hold in the West from 1800s onwards. Before that, most people, like the sultan, perceived and experienced slavery as the norm.

Even a cursory reading of the Bible shows that slavery was an organized and established part of the Egyptian, Assyrian, Babylonian, and Roman Empires. In Jesus' day, up to 30% of the empire's population was a slave, depending on where you lived.[14] The legal system formally recognized the right of slave owners to treat their slaves as possessions.

This is the better-known account of when the CWV voice managed to end systemic slavery. There was a prior occasion, in the so-called but misnamed Dark Ages.

12. Wheaton, as cited by Holland, *Dominion*, 414.

13. As cited by Holland, *Dominion*, 415.

14. Wright and Bird, *New Testament in Its World*, 148.

Christian emperors after Constantine inherited an empire and economy founded upon slavery. Over time, some became uneasy about this. Charlemagne, who re-united the empire in the eighth century, opposed slavery, but it was Christians and the church who brought an end to systemic slavery. First, slaves were permitted to receive the sacraments. Then slaves were admitted into the priesthood. Then the church allowed slaves to marry free people. Note it is the church taking the initiative, in its own domain. It demonstrated that in Christ there is no slave or free person. In time, slavery became untenable. By the eleventh century, slavery was banished from Christendom.[15]

Jesus', Peter's, and Paul's failure to stand up against Rome and directly oppose slavery appears to be a moral failure to our modern ears. Instead, they model and teach that slaves are equal in the Kingdom of God. Slowly but surely, this strategy works. Not once, but twice, Christians alone undo the injustice of systemic slavery.

And the Meaning for Us Is . . .

If we take a step back, what ground have we covered in this chapter? I highlighted how Jesus stood up against injustice and evil within Jewish culture, but balanced this observation by noting his lack of confrontation against Roman wrongdoing. This trend continued. In the early church, the apostles were hard on sin inside the Christian community, such as when Ananias and Sapphira lied about how much money they had donated to others in need. When in Jerusalem and Judea, the apostles confronted the Jewish leaders and populace with their rejection of Jesus as the Messiah. From Acts 11 onwards, such confrontation is replaced with attempts to find more common ground with Diasporan Jews and then gentiles as a footing from which to share the gospel.

Both Jesus and his disciples, then later the apostles and the early church, lived under totalitarian regimes. They did not have democratic rights. Their capacity to influence the socio-political injustices of their day by direct confrontation was zero. Speaking truth to power was a death wish.

Instead, a different approach was adopted, a more subversive one. If a lack of power and influence means confrontation was likely to be counter-productive, as an alternative the twelve and the early church chose to live by a different code. They were neither zealots wishing for a political and military revolt, nor Essenes who withdrew. Rather, they chose to be in,

---

15. Stark, *Triumph of Christianity*, 247–48.

but not of the world. And it worked. In time the entire empire changed for the better.

My thesis is this. The CWV is passing or has passed. ChrisTians who stand up for the Truth, contending that Christian values be retained as mainstream are ridiculed, mocked, and hated on. Such voices are critiqued as wishing to maintain power and privilege to tell others what to do.

Technically, in a democracy, everyone has power, rights, and the capacity to participate in the public debate, but when Christians nowadays try to exercise that right they are quickly judged, misunderstood, and rejected. The dominant ethos of the West is intuitively suspicious, cynical, and dismissive of Christianity. We have been there, tried that, and it failed.

Christians are perceived to be loud, arrogant, and opinionated. The church is yesterday's bully who needs to be put back in its box, the sooner, the better, for everyone. In such a context, it is socially acceptable to be discourteous and impolite to assertive Christians. Platforms are granted to those formerly disempowered and discriminated against, but former bullies are shouted down and cancelled out of the public discourse.

I can't help but conclude that it is shrewd to change tack in this new social context. I suggest we behave more like Jesus, the twelve disciples, Paul, and the early church when they found themselves under suspicion and without power. Direct opposition and taking a strong stand may be a counter-productive strategy that elicits hatred and misunderstanding. Our CWV message is falling on different ears; hence it is not heard as the same message.

Simplicity on the Other Side of Complexity

1. We have a default picture of Jesus as a radical who stood up against every evil and injustice. Jesus was persecuted for doing so. We believe Jesus calls us to follow him and stand up against all evils. We interpret all persecution we receive as bearing our cross as Jesus bore his.

2. It is flawed logic to assume that, if Jesus suffered for doing wrong, any time we are suffering, it is because we are like Jesus. Parts of our suffering may be because we have made unwise decisions about interpreting and expressing Christian life.

3. Jesus directly opposed the Jewish leaders, namely the Pharisees, the elders, the chief priests, and the teachers of the law. In turn, they directly opposed Jesus; they were his protagonists.

4. Jesus was more coy and elusive in his comments about gentile leaders and their actions. The non-Jewish powers (Pilate, Herod, Rome) found Jesus politically annoying and dangerous, but they did not antagonize him.

5. Peter and Stephen also directly opposed and blamed the Jews, and were vague or failed to mention the actions of Rome.

6. Paul intentionally framed his message so that it appealed to his audience. He, too, blamed Jerusalem's Jews. But Paul invited his fellow Diasporan Jews to accept Jesus as the fulfillment of the Old Testament promises as one who can forgive sins. He invited Lystran farmers to trust in a kind God who brings rain. He revealed to Athenian philosophers their unknown God as knowable in Jesus.

7. Rather than standing up confrontationally against the powers-that-be, the early Christians set about being a different people who lived by a different code, following a different king, establishing a different kingdom. And it worked. The rights of women, children, and slaves were enhanced, and thousands came to follow Jesus as their king.

8. After 1600 years of Christians and the church holding a privileged position of power and voice, we now find ourselves in a social setting more like that of Jesus, Paul, and the early church. Post-Christendom has similarities to pre-Christendom. It may be shrewd for us to notice Jesus' and Paul's non-confrontational posture towards Rome, and adopt a similar posture going forwards.

PART FOUR

What Is The Solution?

WE REACH THE FOURTH and final section of our journey. In part one, we explored where are we now. As a culture, the West is shedding its Christian beliefs and values. Evangelism, discipleship, and being the local or institutional church all took a certain form within the CWV. The world is changing. Our CWV heritage is being displaced by a post-Christian set of beliefs and practices.

In part two, we traced how we got here. We tracked some of the historical, philosophical and cultural shifts that have transpired. We contrasted where the West now sits with other cultures to bring a sense of perspective.

In part three, we considered what went wrong. Church attendance has declined, as has the standing of Christianity. This does not lead to the conclusion that it is all our fault. Scripture provides some perspectives for how we might frame our present realities. God is still sovereign and working out his purposes, even when it looks like his followers are not 'winning' the day.

God calls his people to be salt and light in whatever social setting and circumstances they find themselves. Now we can ask: what is the solution? How ought we live as followers of Jesus in this new context in which we find ourselves?

12

Being Christian after Christendom

FINALLY, I HEAR SOME of you sigh, we get here. Finally, you will share your reflections about how Christians, local churches, and the (institutional) church might posture in the most winsome and relevant way in a post-Christian Western context.

I trust you have run the entire race and not rushed ahead in an attempt to cherry-pick the candy. I began this book by suggesting that simplicity on this side of complexity isn't worth a fig. Because we are in a season of worldview change, this book is about how we think about challenging our unspoken assumptions about how to be a public Christian, what the church is, what the world is, and our place in it. This book struggles with our new reality. We are standing on the deck of a new boat and observing from a fresh vantage point. Even if our calling remains fundamentally unchanged, this book is about how we do what we do: adapt.

What Does It Mean to Defend the Faith?

Christians have a deep-held conviction that we are called to defend the faith. Perhaps this notion has biblical undertones, given that God defends the fatherless and widows (Deut 10:18). It certainly has historical associations. Pope Leo X called King Henry VIII a defender of the faith after Henry wrote a tract in favour of Catholicism and against Protestantism. Leo later revoked this title, but the idea that the English monarch is a defender of the faith still has traction today.

Implicit in the idea of defending something is the notion that you presently control it. You can only defend ground you already hold. The notion of defending assumes, to use a military metaphor, that we are the occupying force.

Greg Sheridan, until recently one of the editors of the newspaper *The Australian*, tells us otherwise. "Christians in the West now live in exile."[1] To extend the military metaphor (which I borrow from Sheridan), we are no longer the occupying force. Any ministry or mission campaign strategy that suggests we must defend every bridge is now outdated.[2]

A clear example of this transpired in 2017 in Australia. The government called for a plebiscite on legalising same-sex marriage. The majority of the church saw this as a bridge that must be defended. This was an attack on the Christian view of marriage. Given that marriage is ordained by God and the foundation of any society, we ought to defend it.

Putting aside the specifics of whether or not it was wise for Christians and the church to defend the hetero-normative view of marriage, let us play out the insight of the "we must defend every bridge" metaphor. Christians spent huge amounts of energy, time, and resources defending this bridge and we still lost.

As Western culture pivots away from some of its Christian values, other bridges will be attacked. The obvious ones are abortion, euthanasia, or voluntary assisted dying, and the right of religious institutions to employ staff who share their core values. There are attacks on many of our bridges. Some will be direct attacks, such as the proliferation of gambling, decriminalizing drugs, legalizing prostitution, the availability and de-shaming of pornography. Others will be more subtle, such as the rights being grounded in the individual, consumerism as the expression of selfhood, and self-love preceding love for others.

If the church tried to mount a defense against all of these attacks, as we did the same-sex marriage plebiscite, we would exhaust all of our energy, resources, and personnel. Our efforts would likely only delay the inevitable, but not stop or change anything.

Vanhoozer puts it like this: "the church's mission is not to conquer territory or even to Christianize society; that way Christendom lies. The church is called rather to make disciples and present Christ."[3] While both Vanhoozer and Sheridan would perceive that Christendom had its faults, both would also lament much of its passing. Yet we cannot bring back

1. Sheridan, *God Is Good for You*, 317.
2. Sheridan, *God Is Good for You*, 325.
3. Vanoozer, *Faith Speaking Understanding*, 176.

Christendom by defending every bridge. What is called for is to further extend the military metaphor of "situational awareness".[4]

Situational awareness is the ability to see, to gain perspective despite being deep in the trenches, while bullets are flying past your head, and realize that the battlefield has shifted. Ground has been lost, and it's time to change strategy.

Before we consider the substance of our new strategy, I will move outside of metaphor into the more concrete. I do not suspect it is possible for the church to prevent more abortions, or the legalization of euthanasia, or the decriminalization of marijuana and perhaps other substances, or the normalization of polyamorous relationships. Furthermore, I suspect that if we invest all our efforts defending those bridges, we will deplete our resources. Our reputation will be affirmed as nay-sayers who are against all things and bitter about the fact that we have lost our privileged position of power and voice.

A Guerrilla Offensive

If it is not possible or shrewd for us to sustain a defence on every front, this does not lead to the conclusion that we throw in the towel. We may feel like it. Elijah sat under the tree and asked God to take his life because he believed he was not making a difference. The twelve disciples withdrew to a room and locked the doors after Jesus was crucified. Such responses feel natural when we sense momentum is against us. To quote Sheridan, "Nothing is more debilitating than a mistaken belief that you represent the majority."[5] Yet with fresh situation awareness comes the ability to re-imagine who we are and see new opportunities for offensives.

While we are not the occupying majority on the new battlefield, the speed and dynamism of social change suits minorities. Other minorities, such as the Greens, LGBTI+ people, or some Eastern religions, have found and grown a niche. It is easy to overstate the case, imagining that if the church followed the political playbook of the Greens or the gay lobby, we could have their levels of influence. The West is inoculated against Christianity. The consensus is they have been there, tried that, and moved on. Conversely, the minorities mentioned above have the advantage of being perceived as the formerly persecuted, and it is now just to stand up for and give voice to those groups.

4. Sheridan, *God Is Good for You*, 318.
5. Sheridan, *God Is Good for You*, 324.

Nonetheless, I maintain there are advantages to understanding ourselves and posturing as a minority. We can re-group, clarify, and affirm our identity. I will say more about how we can do this in a moment. For now, let us agree we can re-group, and then boldly and confidently state who we are.

We are, of course, the people of God, indwelt by Christ through his Spirit. We bear and are called to reflect God and to live out his story. God's story is compelling, whether or not it happens to be in alignment with or in contrast to the dominant narrative of any given culture. As a minority, we can proclaim this positively *without* arguing that our view is right and should be the dominant shared consensus.

Allow me to illustrate. The Christian view of marriage is a picture of the love and faithfulness that exists between Christ and his church, between God and his people. Marriage is in that sense indissoluble. In Christendom, Christians would have applied this understanding of marriage as indissoluble, concluding it our task to oppose no-fault divorce. However, the CWV is no longer the consensus. No-fault divorce is a bridge we have lost and cannot win back. Western culture is increasingly one that embraces serial monogamy, including same-sex relationships, and is drifting towards polyamorous relationships.

The minority or guerrilla approach to marriage would be to liberate ourselves from the compulsion to try to influence or control the world's practices. Instead, we should focus on the fact that, for us, we value life-long faithfulness and exclusive commitment to the other. As our liturgies remind us, marriage is for better for worse, for richer for poorer, in sickness and in health, till death us do part. We are the people who celebrate milestone anniversaries and invest in growing healthier, long-term relationships. If you are looking to be part of a community that affirms and supports your marriage so it might go the distance, come and do life with us.

I was at the bar after soccer practice, sharing a beer with my non-Christian team mates the other day. The conversation topics can be narrow and base. There is usually someone in my team in some kind of relationship breakdown, seeking another partner. Relationships are about sexual liaisons. This night, the details of an elderly couple (both almost 90 years old) who still walked down the road everyday hand-in-hand came up. Intuitively, all admired if not envied the deep companionship of this relationship. The length, depth, and exclusivity of this elderly couples' relationship was of a different order than the aspirations and experiences of my non-Christian friends. I was able to tell them this couple came to my local church.

In addition to being the pro-healthy marriage people, we ought to be pro-life, not the anti-abortion and anti-euthanasia faction. When first-century Christians went down to the river and rescued exposed baby girls, they expressed pro-life. When early Christians cared for those infected by the Antonine Plague (165–180 AD) or the Plague of Cyprian (249–262 AD), instead of fleeing to the hills as everyone else did, they expressed pro-life. Stark agues this orientation was part of the great appeal and hence the growth of early Christianity.[6]

There is an advertisement on TV at the moment that has an older person saying, "When you get over a certain age, you become invisible." We live in an aging era, and yet culture celebrates youth and marginalizes the aged. During Christendom, Christians cared for the sick, orphans, and the aging before the welfare state existed. To some extent, in the PCWV, the state has taken over that responsibility. We need to find ways for our local churches to embrace and express pro-life, because we believe everyone is created in God's image, not just the presently fashionable minorities.

We are also the people of reconciliation. Forgiveness is a piece of the puzzle that has gone missing. Our culture is quick to blame, hate on, and cancel those who commit unforgiveable sins. As I write, a member of the Australian Cricket team is caught up in a sexting scandal. Before him there was the ball-tampering incident. To be found to have made a racist or sexist post, even if it was years ago, is a social death sentence. Culture has replaced the old ethical code with a new version of the seven deadly sins, but we have not replaced the cross as a symbol and means of forgiveness and reconciliation. Being overt about forgiveness and re-inclusion will increasingly be a Christian distinctive virtue and practice.

Having been relieved, or relieving ourselves of the duty to Christianize all of society (to use Vanhoozer's phrase), we can instead focus on being who we are. As our culture distances itself from its Christian heritage, we will look increasingly unique. There is an opportunity for us to be bold, creative, confident, and focused in acting as light and salt in the world.

Guerrilla warfare also has the advantage in that it can target, or be strategic. If we don't have to fight every battle, we can now ask ourselves which battles are we most likely to win. This can all sound Machiavellian, cunning to the point of being unscrupulous. Again, allow me to illustrate.

In the southern Australian state of Victoria, where I was once the senior pastor of a Baptist Church, attendance at Baptist weekend services has plateaued. On the surface one might say, well at least they are not in decline. Dig a little below the surface and this is what you find. Attendance by Anglo-Saxons in Victorian Baptist churches remains in decline but there is growth in Victorian Baptist churches in ethnic, non-English-speaking congregations. Most notably, growth is occurring in Chinese (Mandarin and

6. Stark, *Rise of Christianity,* 73–128.

Cantonese speaking), Myanmar (Chin and Karen), Korean, Persian (Farsi), African, Indian, and Pacific Islander congregations.

Research informs us that migrants and refugees are more open to conversion than are those whose residency and nationality remains stable.[7] Something about life disruption makes one more open to other changes in your worldview.

If this is the case, then would it not be prudent for us to target our evangelism towards recent migrants? To reach out to those who are more likely to be receptive? If dislocated groups of people are more receptive, what other groups might be more open?

We know, for instance, that females are more religiously active than males. Females appear to have a higher spiritual I. Q. What about targeting women? My present church has a thriving craft group attended by over 100 women , most of whom are retired and do not regularly attend church. We also run a fortnightly café church for females only. This service is interactive and conversational. There is also a social media messenger group of women who pray and encourage one another online.

This outreach strategy targets and fits a receptive demographic: females with disposable time, who are looking for friendship and support networks, as they offer maternal care to their children and grandchildren in disruption. They are looking for relational networks, a space (our church has a café), and a positive outlet (the craft group makes personalized quilts for people in need). They seek a "congregation" they can be part of that does not meet on a Sunday morning and where they won't feel awkward if their husbands are absent. Dozens of women have come to faith through this group. It is effective, niche-market evangelism. Or guerrilla tactics.

In addition to asking what groups of people are more open to exploring faith, we can also ask at what life stage people are more open to exploring changing their beliefs and worldviews

I remember taking an acquaintance of mine through a gospel course. We played on the same soccer team, he had an Orthodox religious heritage and desired to get his children christened. He was also a partner in his law firm. He was re-married, and had a blended family with multiple children spanning more than a decade in age.

Together we watched a presentation that summarized the gospel. When we came to the end of the course, I asked him what he thought about the claims of Christianity about there being a God, about sin, repentance, etc. He said he believed most, if not all, of these claims. He then quickly

---

7. Akcapar, "Religious Conversions in Forced Migration," 61–74.

added that the problem for him was not unbelief, but an inability to re-arrange his life to fit God and church in.

Put into the vocabulary of this book, my lawyer friend was saying that he had a particular worldview, with beliefs and values and practices. He was focused on his firm, his children's education, and the complexities of parenting a blended family. Even if he had an inclination that there was a God, and he was somehow not presently right with God, he was unwilling to change his present worldview and the priorities it committed him to.

This is a key observation: people do not readily change worldviews. I shall return to this observation in a moment. For now, it is shrewd for us to ask when are people more open to changing their beliefs and practices. One answer is in life-stage transitions. When people leave home, attend university, get married, begin having children, when they become empty nesters, when they retire, or when they begin to face the end of life, they are more open to change.

It is possible to have a targeted evangelism strategy that reaches out to groups of people when they are in transition. Examples would include new university students, couples planning to get married, parents asking to have their children baptized, recent retirees taking up new hobbies, or older people entering nursing homes. Focused evangelistic efforts in such settings are not new, of course. With hindsight, you are perhaps thinking, yes, these mission types have been more effective in the past. I suggest we focus even more on people in transition moments into the future.

Sociology of Conversion Literature

A key insight in this book is that beliefs and values have a strong social dimension. We see things the way we do because we are part of a community or a culture that understands them as so. Knowledge is communal. We need people around us who reinforce and sustain our shared worldview. This being the case, there is something compelling about a belief or value when it has the status of being the default position. Conversely, there is an obstacle to overcome when a belief system is outside of the norm, and considered implausible.

All of this causes us to ask how a person changes their mind or worldview. How is it ever possible for an individual who has adopted the consensus position, and is integrated into a broader culture and its prevailing worldview, to "convert" to another way of seeing the world?

As it turns out, some sociologists explore this very question. Indeed, Rodney Stark, who is most known to Christians as the author who explains how and why Christianity grew in the first few centuries AD, wrote his doctoral thesis on the sociology of conversion. Stark was perhaps the world's leading sociologist of religion at the time of his death in 2022.

His thesis researched the rapid growth of Mormonism, which parallels the growth rate of the early church, hence his interest as a sociologist, not a historian, in the early church. Stark's initial research, however, considered how and why presently people are converting to Mormonism.

Stark's thesis is one of a number in this field. Helpfully for us, Scot McKnight has surveyed all the research and compiled his findings into a book: *Turning to Jesus*. He suggests there is no one-size-fits-all account of conversion. He outlines several possible paths, though it must be said his definition of converts includes those raised within the Christian faith who then choose to remain within the faith.[8]

The most helpful part of the book for our purposes is where McKnight outlines the stages of conversion most common when a person converts from one faith to another, or from one worldview to another. It is informative to note the progression between the stages. They are as follows:

Context

It is vital to appreciate that everyone has an existing context, which is a set of beliefs, assumptions, and networks that agree with and support that shared worldview. Those seeking to evangelize others need to be aware of the contours of the potential's context. Put another way, people are not converted from unbelief to belief. Rather, they are converted from one belief system to another. An appreciation of a person's current belief system and its support structures is helpful when evangelizing someone.

Disruption

A person's current worldview has a default and stable status, and that equilibrium needs to be disrupted. Would-be converts tend to experience a tension that requires resolution. This can either be a negative disruption—for example, my default system is broken and cannot explain what is happening in my life—or it can be positive—for example, I have encountered another worldview (in another person) that works better than mine, and I cannot explain that from within my current worldview.

8. McKnight, *Turning to Jesus*.

Advocate

An "advocate" (think "witness" or "evangelist") is a person who walks alongside a would-be convert as they encounter and attempt to resolve the new tension that follows a disruption. The advocate must be able to both deconstruct the old worldview and persuasively portray the Christian alternative. Attempts to persuade may be cognitive, affective, pragmatic, or relational. I think of the advocate as a personal spiritual tour guide who asks questions like: Did you notice this? What do you make of that? Have you thought about it this way? The process of advocating is a dialogue, but must manifest into an appeal at some point in time.

Connect

The would-be convert must move beyond a one-to-one engagement or relationship with an advocate, and somehow become encapsulated within a new network. That is, new relationships of people who hold to the new worldview, new rituals and rhythms that sustain and invigorate the new worldview, new rhetoric and vocabulary that explains, affirms, integrates, and internalizes the new worldview.

Commit

The convert comes to belong inside and believe the new meta-narrative. This involves making a decision. It may be one big decision or a series of gentle nods of the soul. The convert must surrender the old narrative and the privileged status of the voice of the previous community of belief that reinforces that worldview. The new and most significant voices in the convert's life now come from within the new faith community. The convert belongs to the new community and gives witness to the new narrative as the story that shapes and makes the best sense of their life. In sociological terms, conversion happens when most of the significant other voices in a person's life belong to the new narrative, and the voices of the old narrative are now in the minority.

If you are used to reading Christian literature, not sociology, you will likely experience an urge to correct some of the above. You may want to counter that conversion is spiritual and the work of God. You may want to reinforce that an "advocate" must talk about repentance and the cross. If you sense that compulsion, I understand that. It is both possible and appropriate to explain conversion in those categories. Sociological and theological explanations need not be viewed as mutually exclusive. Ask this question instead: What insights from the above-outlined conversion process might be harnessed as we seek to evangelize those who hold an established non- or post-Christian worldview? I have played with these ideas in my last two churches for almost ten years now, with quite some success. Here are my reflections to date.

Applying New Insights into the Twenty-First-Century Church

Appreciate that people you are seeking to evangelize have an existing belief system, with practices, communities, and support structures that reinforce it. Appreciate that people have a way of seeing the world, and they believe that the world is as they see it. They are not about to walk away from that lightly.

In the past, when most people held to a CWV and there was much overlap between the dominant worldview and core Christian beliefs, it made sense to consider non-Christians as non-believers, or people without faith. They did not believe in God, judgement, or heaven and hell. They did not put their faith in Jesus. Now, the dominant worldview is other than Christian. It is more proper to consider that non-Christians are people who have different beliefs and a different faith. It is unhelpful to imagine they simply need to come to faith or come to believe. Rather, they need a two-staged conversion. They need to convert away from their existing beliefs, practices, and communities that sustain and share that same faith before they can convert to a new faith.

Let us put the shoe on the other foot for a moment via another thought experiment.

Imagine that the Masonic Lodge down the road gets a new leader. He is a younger family man. Under his leadership, the Freemasons repaint the building, open a pre-school, launch a new website, and host a free family fun day with a jumping castle and fairy floss. You happen to drive past the lodge on Saturday morning en route to the shops, and your kids talk you into letting them go on the jumping castle. Given the changes, are you about to become a Freemason? No. Not even close. You have an existing belief system and community that you feel no inclination to abandon.

In the CWV, most people assumed there was a personable God who created humans with a purpose, there was right and wrong, life after death, and God somehow decided where we spent eternity. If a person holds to those assumptions, you have sufficient grounds to begin a conversation about a person's lifestyle and its consequences, and about how they might find certainty and peace regarding their future. But we do not inhabit that world. That world has passed and is deemed implausible.

Instead, we live in a world where a person's default is to believe that "I am special, and have a unique combination of passions and gifts. If I can get in touch with those, and express them, I will become my best self, and make the world better for me and others around me. It is your place to affirm and empower me to become my best self." This is the world we now inhabit. This worldview does not give you sufficient grounds to begin a conversation about God, or eternity, or forgiveness. If you try, you will look arrogant, judgemental, and non-supportive. Trying to evangelize in this method is, humanly speaking, likely to be as effective as the local masonic lodge handing out free fairy floss.

Does this mean we ought not to evangelize anymore? Does this mean we are loving and compassionate, withholding comment until people ask us about our faith? No. That is not where it takes me.

Instead, I am looking for people in disruption. I befriend as many non-Christians as I can. I am polite, interested in them, and open but not pushy about my faith. Then I wait until I see God bringing disruption into their life. I encourage my parishioners to use the same technique.

Returning to the Bible for a moment, let's take this new lens of "disruption" and think about the converts we read of in scripture. Marvel with me that many had a disruption experience prior to conversion: Rahab in Jericho was about to have her walls come down; Ruth married and lost her Jewish husband; Paul's experiences on the road to Damascus; those who are miraculously healed.

Disruption causes people to question their existing beliefs. My world used to make sense when I believed and acted this way, but now that "x" has happened, my world no longer makes sense. My belief system cannot explain how or why this happened or what I am to do about it.

In the past few years, I have personally experienced four people I have closely walked alongside through this process. These were not conversions that were a result of my role as a professional minister. Two were positive disruptions: non-Christians who became a close friend of a Christian, and found in that person a life and hope beyond their own. I had the joy of being an advocate as we unpicked their old worldview, and explored another.

Two were negative disruptions. I had a friend in one of my sporting teams. After every game, the team shared a beer. This man was married. I came to learn that he and his wife could not have children, so they adopted. They went to great lengths to love this child as their own and include some of his cultural heritage as part of their family's values. Then things went amiss.

The son ran away from home, blocked contact from his parents, and got involved with the wrong crowd and illegal drugs. The parents believed that if they were loving, accepting, compassionate, open-minded, and inclusive, their son would respect them back, and they could enjoy being the ideal happy family. It turns out those assumptions were flawed. They also believed they had been good parents, and the government welfare arms would support them. Those assumptions were also flawed. Social workers took the view this boy was an individual who could decide for himself, and if he felt the need to "individuate" himself from his parents, that was his right.

This disruption meant two things. First, my friend and his wife began asking profound questions about life that they could not answer from within their existing worldview. Second, they were open to befriending me (and others) who had an alternate take on life, parenting, and family. Again, I became an advocate, a spiritual tour guide, who asks questions and engages in dialogue.

At this point, I did not invite my friend to church. Instead, I asked him to dinner, along with others who shared connection points with him, who had challenging children or an interest in the same hobbies as him. That is to say, I intentionally built connections and community around them. This new community of people all shared a Christian worldview.

Eventually, this man and his wife started coming to church and made a commitment. They experienced a conversion. To be completely transparent, this particular conversion did not last, as far as I am aware. Sometimes the seed falls on rocky ground. But you can see the stages of conversion unfolding in his story.

One of the positive stories involves a sixteen-year-old boy who transitioned from a state school to a Christian school for the last two years of his high schooling. The disruption was twofold. First, coming into a new school community that had a different set of values and culture than his previous school. This was not a school where it was cool to be a Christian; Christians were a minority of the student body. However, the school leadership team and most of the teachers were overt Christians.

The second disruption was that he took a liking to my daughter. Her response was that she did not date boys who did not share her faith. But, given that he lived up the road from us, and being the two new students into an otherwise stable year group, did mean the two became friends.

This positioned me to become the coach of my daughter as his main advocate, and an advocate myself. They travelled to school together, and studied and shared notes for final year exams. The connections took place across three fronts. Seb (his name) would often find himself at our home, and got to share in an extended family experience that was different to his own. He began attending the lunch-time Christian group at school. In time, he also attended our evening church service, where he encountered still other Christian youth and young adults.

After about twelve months at church, Seb was asked to attend an Alpha course. He agreed, and even brought his grandmother along. Seb made a commitment, and his grandmother had a reawakening of her dormant orthodox faith. I still see Seb regularly; he is now my son-in-law.

Both of those anecdotal stories are about where mission is decentralized. Conversations begin long before anyone darkens the door of a local church. I will now share an illustration of implementing this mission strategy within church programs.

New Peninsula Baptist has its own incorporated caring arm: New Peninsula Community Caring. For years, even before my time as the senior pastor, Community Caring ran an outreach program where local church members were connected with someone from the community who was doing it tough. The church volunteer functioned as a life coach. Community Caring social workers would train, equip, support, and resource local church members to be life coaches.

In addition to this coaching program, Community Caring also ran two food-hamper distribution services and an op shop. Although Community Caring saw hundreds of clients per year and had regular engagements and an ongoing relationship with those who repeatedly accessed our services, we saw very few conversions. As I became aware of the conversion pathway, we began to reflect on what might be missing. A one-to-one coach relationship was positive, facilitating meaningful engagement but the opinions of the coach remained a minority lone voice. Furthermore, we realized that, while the participants had access to a support program, there was no community to belong to.

We decided to run a weekly dinner followed by a church service (of sorts). The philosophy of this meal and service was heavily informed by what is called "strength-based practice" in social work. It means that you encourage participants to get in touch with their strengths and bring them to the corporate problem-solving table. Participants do not just access programs and receive support; they actively participate.

The dinner was prepared and served by participants. Church people could help, and we paid for the food, but a local community member, a resident in the public housing estate, drove the catering. Likewise, the church service had devotions shared by participants, participant-led music, and their fellow participants prayed for each other. Often, someone would have a personal disaster. They might blow all their welfare payments on gambling or drugs and alcohol. Their car might break down, or they may have a mental health episode. Rather than the middle-class, wealthy Christians stepping in to solve these problems, the social workers would ask how we could solve these problems from within the group. They would then pray for each other. The next week, we would check in and celebrate wins. Devotions would be illustrated with personal stories about how God answered prayers.

Soon we began to see conversions. Every year we would baptize a dozen people or more. In a Baptist Church, baptisms are a big deal. Why did we begin to see conversions? What had changed?

First, we encountered people who were in disruption and open to challenging their beliefs, practices, and worldviews. Second, the social workers behaved as advocates. Furthermore, they trained the recent converts to become advocates. After about twelve months of running the dinner followed by a service, we started a discipleship group before the dinner. Here, participants would be trained in how to lead, share a devotion, pray, *and* be a person who helps others within the community to explore and solve problems in new ways.

We also created a community to which one could belong where the belief system was that God is real, he cares, he loves, and he asks us to serve others just as Jesus came to serve us. This was not a network of fellow clients of welfare programs. It was a community, complete with its own beliefs, rhythms, rituals, and vocabulary. Last, this community invited people to commit to following Jesus and joining his body.

As I think about the successes of the craft group reaching out to retired women in my current church, I see all the same key factors at play. Disruptions in family and life, advocates who walk alongside and offer to pray, connections and integration into a community, followed by a commitment. These learnings have caused me to reframe how I disciple my local church members in their personal evangelism. Here is a short version of what I tell them.

First, be a loyal, generous, compassionate, not pushy but openly Christian friend. By all means, when you can, share your faith.

Second, wait and watch for life changes. In my experience, you don't have to wait long. It's everywhere, for those who have eyes to see it. The old adage that God loves us too much to leave us the way we are is true not only for his prompting of Christians, but not-yet Christians also. I even suggest it is acceptable to be proactive in disruption. Go above and beyond in your support. Shout beers after soccer more often than is your turn. What is likely to catch people off guard is not that you notice them experiencing disruption, but that you care enough to lean into their disruption and offer genuine support. When you see disruption, your spiritual antennas ought to be on alert.

A further word about what constitutes a disruption. As I explain this concept to people, their first assumption is disruptions are moments of suffering or loss. Often they are, but not always. Disruptions may be changes to life stage or location. When people move suburbs, they may feel socially isolated; or if they start dating someone of faith, and come into an entire new friendship network; or they retire and start playing golf, or cycling regularly; they make a new group of friends. An abnormally thoughtful friend can be disruptive. Disruptions can take various forms.

Third, part of how I must equip my congregation is coaching them how to be an advocate for Jesus in the twenty-first century marketplace. This will not look like sharing a gospel presentation from start to finish. However, it may be appropriate to use parts of one. It may be appropriate to re-tell a parable, or share their experiences and struggles. Such content is shared within a dialogue, leaving others with questions to ponder. Changing worldviews, and evangelism that asks people to change their worldviews, takes time. It is a cumulative process. If you are looking for a resource in this space, try Sam Chan's *How To Talk About Jesus, Personal Evangelism in a Skeptical World* or Jeff Vanderstelt's *Gospel Fluency.*

Fourth, where are the communities we invite people into before we invite people to church? If you happen to follow the literature, they are often called a missional community. This is a welcoming, intentionally inclusive community. It may gather around an interest, location, or life stage. Food is usually critical. These gatherings attempt to envelop seekers into the experience of Christian community before they convert. If you don't have these in your church, you might consider expanding the brief of your small groups. Ask them to hold a missional community type event once per term. Extend the brief of your infant's playgroup to see itself as a missional community, or coach people to gather others around their friends to whom they advocate, as I did with my friend and his wife.

Last, there needs to be an invitation at some point in time. Conversion is increasingly a process, but it remains both process and a point in time. Tools such as Alpha align with many of the above insights. Let us assume that a disproportionate number of people who agree to come to Alpha are in disruption. Alpha is conversational and communal. That, in my opinion, is the great value of the weekend away. For non-Christians, choosing to go away with someone for a weekend means those relationships go beyond acquaintances and fast tracks them into the "friends" category. Finally, the Alpha course gets participants to the point of invitation and decision.

What I value about the above process, which I call a missional pathway, is that it is not just another evangelistic tool. Rather, it is a process that fits with how evangelism might work when Christians are a minority. It is built on the observation that others have a pre-existing worldview, and that worldview has its own rhythms, rhetoric, reasoning, and support structures. To my non-Christian soccer mates, their worldview seems logical to them, and mine seems implausible. Humanly speaking, it is highly improbable I can just persuade them that following Jesus is better. As I perceive Paul to be doing, I have an obligation to share the gospel in ways that make sense to them, to be receptor orientated in my communication.

Speaking beyond personal evangelism, I think this missional pathway also has insights and applications for other Christian agencies. Disruptions happen in Christian schools, and in church-run nursing homes and hospitals. In such settings, there are opportunities for training and coaching advocates and creating intentional community. I suggest mission as a one-to-one activity of the professional chaplain is a Christendom model that requires revisiting.

Discipleship as Raising Children and Youth within a Sub-Culture

As previously noted, changing worldviews creates a communication gap. We must cross a cultural gap to evangelize those who hold to a PCWV. In addition, we must be conscious of the cultural gap as we disciple the next generation of youth and children. How does Christian Chris, who attends New Hope or St. James, disciple her children? If she is a school teacher at a Christian school, how does she lead devotions and encourage children from Christian families in their faith development?

In this space, I have noted some concerning shifts in the vocabulary of youth and young adults in my church. I have heard comments like: "I am stepping back from (worship or youth) ministry. It's just not my passion at the moment. I'm waiting to see if God gives me another passion." When I talk on a controversial topic, young adults are increasingly likely to process their responses online with friends who think as they do. They see my view not as a theological or biblical position to be contemplated, but as the voice of the institution seeking to maintain its power.

As I outlined in chapter 11, those who listen through PCWV ears will likely refract the message in ways that align with their pre-existing opinions. This is an obvious challenge to those of us who are seeking to disciple the next generation. However, there is another, slightly less obvious challenge.

Our discipleship methods are materials that were developed during Christendom, by and for persons who hold a CWV. They are built upon CWV assumptions. For instance, they assume that belief in God is opposed to believing in no God. They were not written in a pluralist context where observations about the Christian God can be made by contrasting him with other gods. They assume that a person's moral conscience aligns with and is guided by biblical ethics. They were not written in times when people trusted their own intuitions over sacred texts. They assume that biblical principles eclipse personal experience. Yet, personal experience now eclipses biblical principles. For instance, I often hear younger Christians say something like, "The Holy Spirit clearly speaks through Jane, so women must be able to preach to men." A "theological" position is arrived at by reference to personal insights alone.

We can no longer take it as given that children and youth hold to CWV assumptions, even those in Christian homes and schools. To think that Jesus knows me better than I know myself, and Jesus knows what is better for me than I do is not an innate thought pattern of younger people. Nor is the idea that my pastor or my parents understand biblical ideas and morality as it applies to me better than I do.

In my experience, Christian-raised youth often have a hybrid worldview. They believe in God, but they are at times suspicious of what the church says about God. They respect Jesus; he was loving, non-judgemental, and inclusive. They believe God is hyper-personable; he is vitally interested in them, because he has made them unique and special. His Spirit is inside them, guiding their inner intuitions and passions. They have a limited sense of the redemptive power of suffering and their need for repentance because they are not fundamentally evil. Rather, their intentions are good. They believe they are the best judge of their intentions. Of course, God has eternity in mind for them. God is loving, not judgemental; and they are good, and eminently forgivable when they are not their best selves.

How then do we disciple the next generation in ways that result in fewer of them walking away from belonging to the body of Christ and those that stay having a more robust, less flaky faith? I cannot give a complete answer in this book. Instead, I shall offer two framing suggestions that flow out of the central thesis of this book. Given we are living through a change of worldviews, we ought to own that our beliefs and values are increasingly distinctive. Second, we must re-articulate our beliefs and values against the new backdrop of the PCWV.

I shall expand upon my first suggestion using another metaphor. I suggest we need to raise and disciple our next generation as part of a sub-culture, not the dominant culture. The dominant culture is now post-Christian. We must intentionally teach our youth that we are different from and disagree with parts of the world's ways of seeing things.

I gather you have detected by now that I was raised in a Dutch sub-culture. My parents were both born in the Netherlands. I attended a Reformed church, along with other first and second-generation Dutch migrants. I attended a Christian school started by Dutchies. I played soccer for a mostly Dutch soccer team. I married someone whose parents were also Dutch, as did my siblings, all of my wife's siblings, and almost all of our forty-odd cousins.

At one point in time, I lived in Kingston, just south of Hobart, in Tasmania. Kingston was the most pure Dutch community anywhere outside of The Netherlands. There was a street in Kingston with over 300 Dutch people living on it, all of whom attended the same local church I did. Our street adjoined that street, and four out of eighteen homes belonged to Dutchies. One building company, Laver construction, employed about half of our church either directly or as sub-contractors. The biggest festival in town was called the Olliebollen festival. Olliebollen are Dutch donuts.

We were a very clearly demarcated sub-culture. We had our own soccer, basketball, and netball teams. At various points, I even experienced racism. I have been spat on and even physically assaulted because I was Dutch. I went for a haircut once, and asked for an under-cut, only to be told by the hairdresser that was too radical a choice for a Dutchie.

We knew we were different. We knew Aussies played footy, but we played soccer. We ate salted liquorice. We ate olliebollen, not donuts. We did not go to the shops on Sunday. We were frugal, hardworking, and practical, inclined towards small business ownership, had working bees and helped build each other's houses, and were on average wealthier than the Aussies. We knew and understood their worldview, and even lived in their country. But we could name up why our world was different, and in our mind, better. Our allegiance to our heritage was stronger.

I am suggesting we need to disciple our next generation children and youth as if they are sub-culture. They do live in the post-Christian West. They inevitably breathe the air of this culture. But we need to do three things, intentionally.

First, name up the idols of our culture. What does the post-Christian West worship? Choice, self-actualization, empowerment, tolerance, rights, and experiences that please the senses. Why do we not worship these? How are they false idols? How are they dangerous, or perversions of God's good plan? How can we affirm what is good in these, without making them our first love? Our discipleship of our youth needs to equip them so that they can see this for themselves.

This will involve more than just the occasional opportunistic push back. We need to get behind the flash points: the debates about rights, or who has voice, or abuses of power. We need to explain the logic and assumptions that underwrite the PCWV. We need to demonstrate where the PCWV is inconsistent, or incoherent, or unworkable. Richard Rorty says "Truth is what our peers will let us get away with saying."[9] We need to be the voices in our teenagers' ears that push back against what everyone else allows to pass as truth.

Second, if we do not align with the world's vision of what it means to be a person, precisely what then do we live for? We need to clearly articulate and teach who we are, if we are different from everyone else. Just as I knew what it meant to be a second-generation Dutch migrant, as opposed to an Australian, we need to present a clear, compelling picture of our view of the world, and how we inhabit it. In Christendom, we could assume that everyone would absorb a belief in God, right and wrong, life after death, with Jesus as the exemplar human being.

In the PCWV, we can make no such assumptions. In the CWV, evangelicals preached on the next book of the Bible, mainstream church taught what was topical, successful churches inspired, and liberal progressives shared Jesus' love for the marginalized. No-one ever had to teach the Christian way to understand the world. Now we do. In addition to exegetical, topical, or inspirational preaching, or whatever else we do, we need to intentionally communicate the central tenets of our worldview in coherent and compelling ways, and contrast it with the prevailing PCWV.

Third, building upon the insight that knowledge is social, not just propositional, we need to create a stronger sense of kinship within and around our children and youth. There needs to be a tangible experience that my Christian children and youth are part of an extended family; that we are more joined to each other than we are to the world. Children's and youth ministries are places where we express and encounter the joy and pride of being "us," where we rehearse and retell why we are as we are, and we are different from others.

Sub-cultures have more than just distinctive beliefs and values. They have rituals and rhythms, unique vocabulary, narratives, and boundary markers that affirm and sustain those beliefs and values. This was the social consequence of food laws in the Old Testament (and in Islam), and communion as a love feast in the New Testament. There is a correlation between the number and strength of the social practices and structures that gather/define/affirm a community and the ability of the sub-culture to sustain its unique identity against the dominant narrative.

9. Rorty, *Philosophy and the Mirror of Nature*, 176.

To be very concrete, I will make some practical suggestions about what this might look like in a present-day youth ministry. It means camping ministry is critical, the ability to get away from the world and its influences, and not just give a series of talks, but be an alternate community who marches to the beat of a different drum. It means community identifiers and symbols are critical. These may be captured on T-shirts, or jewelry, or some other accessory. It means chat rooms and online forums where the community can connect, "friend" each other, and "like" behaviors that we value. It means facilitating face-to-face social gatherings beyond youth-group programs. It means having unique vocabulary, just as the Jesus People used the phrase "one-way" and raised their index fingers in the 1960s. It means gathering around food—the ministry of hospitality is critical. It means having a physical space that is home away from home. Sometimes people call this a third space. Home is your first space, work is your second, and your third space is your happy social space.

All of these are more than trappings or fluff. They are part of how to create a sub-culture that sustains a younger person holding onto a different worldview than the dominant one their culture is socializing them into. Or, to use biblical language, they are part of how you facilitate someone living as a citizen and an ambassador of a different kingdom, following a different king.

And, of course, it means clearly and succinctly articulating your unique beliefs and values in ways that are memorable, repeatable, easily re-called, re-affirmed, and rehearsed, so that they can define one's identity and behavior. All of this is how you create and sustain a social kingdom movement when it is in the minority.

You see elements and echoes of this in the New Testament and the early church such as pithy creeds like "Christ died for our sins according to the scriptures, that he was buried, that he was raised on the third day" (1 Cor 15:3–4); the way communion is practiced, crossing established social and cultural boundaries; regular social gatherings and sharing, as in Acts 2:42–47 and Acts 4:32–36; the cross, or the fish, or the *Chi Rho* as symbols that identify one as a member of a community; the way they treat slaves and women; the sacrificial generosity for your people, even if it is a collection for others you have never met (2 Cor 8–9). The New Testament church was a social movement, as well as a gathering of believers.

It is time for a new wave of dialogues and books about how to be Christian and raise Christians in a post-Christian world. If you are looking for an example of this, read Andrew Root's books about faith formation, congregation, or pastoring in the secular age, or Stephen McAlpine's *Being the Bad Guys*.[10]

Succinctly Restating Our Beliefs and Values

What then is the content of our unique beliefs and values that we need to communicate to the next generation of disciples? What is the position we advocate for? What is a concise version of the worldview we are asking the disrupted to believe in?

Is it the gospel? Is it as simple as Christ died for our sins according the scriptures, was buried, and has risen? Yes—those beliefs are essential and fundamental. But no—that is not sufficient. As I have demonstrated, when refracted through the mind of someone who believes in a PCWV, one can make a short creed like the one we find in 1 Cor 15 mean something else. Average Jack can, and likely will arrive at a hybrid or a syncretized gospel, that is perhaps no gospel at all.

We need to restate and rehearse our beliefs and values as an entire worldview. Pithy short creeds are shorthand for longer articulations. Our new creeds must function as a lens through which we can correctly hear Jesus' words and reject the false teachings of our day.

Am I advocating that we go back to the CWV as I summarized it in chapter 1? After all, it is *the* Christian view of things, is it not?

I would willingly sign my name underneath every point of the CWV as I have outlined it. I believe all of those statements reflect truths as revealed in God's word. But no, I am not suggesting we can simply continue to restate the tenets of the CWV as they were framed in Christendom. Why not?

This is a very complex question, but I will attempt a brief answer. The Bible is a complex book, written in multiple contexts, addressing multiple themes. Of course there is one God, one Lord, and one Spirit who sits behind all scripture, and brings a fundamental unity to its message. But this unity does not negate the breadth and depth of scripture.

Furthermore, the gospel incarnates itself and expresses itself in culture. As opposed to the Koran, which is ideally read and recited in Arabic, the Bible is translated into different languages. In the process, the message is also being translated into a culture to speak in and to that culture.

When I am in Asia, or speaking to Asian cultures, I intentionally accentuate the honor-shame themes already present in scripture. When Adam and Eve sinned, they felt ashamed. They were cast out of the family

---

10. Root, *Congregation*; Root, *Faith Formation*; Root, *Pastoring*; McAlpine, *Being the Bad Guys*.

home and system. They were naked and vulnerable when isolated. God ought to disown children who bring shame upon his family. Instead, Jesus came and scorned the shame of the cross, sits at his father's right hand, and invites us to join them at the banquet.

When I am in Africa or preaching to African congregations, I intentionally accentuate the power-fear themes of scripture. Adam and Eve chose to entrust themselves to Satan and self, not to God. The consequences of trusting self and Satan are being banished from God, his good garden, and his blessing. Adam and Eve were exposed and at risk. Israel failed to trust God and live as his people, and ended up in exile. The cross is Satan's attempt to win, to demonstrate his power and superiority. Satan tells us you can win with lies, and bribes, and being a traitor, and aligning yourself with the powerful. But precisely when Jesus appears weak, he trusts himself to God, and is vindicated and raised to new life. God is stronger, and Jesus defeats sin and death and Satan. Trust Jesus.

Notice what I did not accentuate in either case. I did not emphasize Adam and Eve as disobedient, and therefore guilty and condemned. I did not highlight Israel as breaking the law. I did not accentuate Jesus's death as paying the price for my guilt and sin, and that he brings personal forgiveness. Does this mean I did not preach the gospel?

No. I am attempting to demonstrate that the gospel message has a multiplicity of themes. No one presentation of the gospel captures every dimension of it. How then do we know which parts to communicate? The answer to that is twofold. We communicate the focal elements that are consistently present across and regularly reaffirmed within scripture. And we communicate the parts that speak in and to and against the receptor and their culture. We must do both. Paul did both. Jesus did both. Edwards did both. Carey did both.

Don Richardson, in his book *Eternity in their Hearts,* makes a similar observation, but from the perspective of a cross-cultural missionary. Richardson documents how various cultures have been "prepared for the gospel" by God, in that there are themes and yearnings embedded into a culture. The gospel speaks to these deep yearnings. There are yearnings and openings present in the PCWV that the gospel speaks into. There are themes that harmonize with the message of Jesus, as well as themes that grate.[11]

This insight presents us with a conundrum, an almost unsolvable riddle. The missionary must share the essence of the gospel, but in ways that dialogue with the receptor culture. Which then, are the focal, recurring, and unfolding essential themes of scripture? Those of us raised within a CWV will be quick

11. Richardson, *Eternity in Their Hearts.*

to answer: it is that Jesus died for our sins so that we can be forgiven. Who is giving that answer? The person who is reading scripture as it is or the person reading scripture from within a guilt-innocence CWV? I suggest the answer is both, perhaps even more so the latter.

Can we not get beyond our lenses and read scripture as it is? We must go back to God and his word, and we must ask the Spirit of truth to remind us of what Jesus has said, and guide us into all the truth (John 16:14–15). But, this side of glory, there is a sense in which we can only ever see in part, only a reflection as in a brass mirror (1 Cor 13:12).

I am sure you can tell by now I am given to using metaphors. I shall use another. Is not God's word truth, and a sure and certain anchor through which he reveals things that we could not otherwise know? Yes, it is. Let us call that an anchor. But here is the problem. I am standing at sea, on the deck of a cultural boat, seeing things from the perspective of that boat. The anchor is fixed onto something more substantial than just my opinion.

When we live through the experience of a worldview change, it is as if the tide changes and the boat moves. Some of what we assumed to be fixed, or certain, shifts. Does this mean the anchor has given way? No. The certainty that there is an anchor and that it is secured to a seabed remains. But there is movement on the surface. The changing of tides and the shifting of our boat gives us occasion to reconsider and reframe what we believed was certain and has remained, versus what we believed was certain and has shifted.

I am contending for a position known in hermeneutics (the study of how we know and interpret) as critical realism. I am not suggesting that all we can see is our perceptions, or that what I see is relative to my sensitivities. Critical realists believe there is real world: a big "R" reality. There is God, who has spoken and revealed things we can know. There is an eternal gospel that is true. We are not just adrift on the high seas of relativism. There is solid ground. But, I cannot know Reality without accessing it through my perceptions. My lenses, my perspective, my assumptions affect what I see. I see through a dim mirror, not directly as things are. My analogy is an attempt to capture the "both-and" of critical realism.

Furthermore, I believe we have biblical grounds to acknowledge the reality that human perceptions limit people's ability to see clearly. In addition to the texts I have cited, we could add the observation that the Israelites could not hear Ezekiel because they were stiff necked. Satan placed scales over people's eyes. The disciples could see only as a blind man who sees people as trees (Mark 8:24). Matthew and Mark both have a curious phrase: "let the reader understand" (Matt 24:15; Mark 13:14).

To return to my opening question, can we restate our beliefs and values clearly and succinctly? Yes, and we must. But our recent efforts were construed assuming that both the speaker and the listener shared a CWV. Now we must go back to scripture, standing on the shoulders of those who have gone before us, but reimagine our beliefs and values as they will be heard by people living in a PCWV. What themes will be salient to them? What is the existential angst of this culture, and how does the gospel address that? What are new myths to be countered, as well as the new insights to be redeemed? What new truth is yet to break forth out of his Holy Word, as we find ourselves in a new world?

This is the task of a missionary. That is what we now are, missionaries, crossing out of the CWV and into another world. The paradigm of us as evangelists who share a message from within a CWV to Average Joe who holds the same worldview has passed.

Just as Edwards and Whitefield spoke to an audience increasingly conscious of their feelings and invited them to express their religious affections for God; just as Carey invited progress-minded Enlightenment thinkers to attempt great things for God and bring education, healthcare, and the gospel to the new world; just as the Australian church of the post–World War II 1950s spoke to the aspirations of returned servicemen looking for community and stability in the suburbs, we must find ways to speak out the parts of the gospel and to live out the parts of the kingdom that harmonize with the aspirations of the post-CWV. We must also name up and reject the idols of the post-CWV, more so than the idols of the previous era.

It would be both premature and counter-productive for me to announce a final succinct summary of our beliefs and values when stated over and against the PCWV. I say premature in the sense that we are still in transition and the PCWV is still emerging. Or perhaps we have reached a state where everything changes so fast, so constantly, that being in flux is the new normal. I say counter-productive in that this is a journey that post-Christendom Christianity must take. It will be a journey with many voices. Those voices are emerging. But would-be prophets beware, for prophets are rarely embraced.

We can say something decisive about what Average Joe is receptive to. Average Joe now imagines his world with his "self" at its centre. It is Joe's calling to be the best Joe, not just Average Joe. Joe's gospel is one where he must better himself. If God exists, spiritual beings assist Joe in self-betterment. Any gospel explanation that begins with what God has done through Jesus will intuitively sound flawed.

Can the gospel be faithfully yet creatively explained in a way that will grab Average Joe, initially, at least? Some will say no. The gospel is about what God has done in Christ, so we read in Romans 1:1–5. Others will say yes, and Jesus does. To the question of what must I do to be saved, Jesus's answer revolves around what the rich young ruler must do. Likewise, Jesus can say, "Do you want to get well?," "If you knew . . . you would have asked [me]," "What do you want me to do for you?" (John 5:6; 4:10; Luke 18:41).

Much ink will be spilt over this topic. Attempt we must. Go we must. For as the Father has sent his Son, so Jesus has sent us to be his disciples, as witness to the twenty-first century post-Christian West.

Simplicity on the Other Side of Complexity

1. Christians have a deep-held conviction that we are called to defend the faith. Defending assumes we are in control; we are the occupying force. We no longer are.

2. If it no longer makes sense to defend every bridge, we are free to employ other approaches to mission. A guerrilla offensive metaphor facilitates us thinking about which parts of our message might prove most appealing, and where we are most likely to find receptive ears.

3. Average Joes have an existing worldview, with beliefs, values, practices, and support mechanisms and relationships. One does not abandon one's worldview lightly or easily.

4. The sociology of conversion literature highlights four stages that an average person transitions through when they convert from one worldview to another. This includes a *disruption* of the existing equilibrium; an *advocate* who walks alongside a would-be convert; forming significant *connections* with a web of people who hold to the new worldview; and finally a *commitment* or decision to surrender the old narrative, and adopt the new narrative as the story that shapes and makes the best sense of their life.

5. The sub-culture metaphor helps us appreciate that we must disciple our children and youth as those who inhabit a dominant post-Christian narrative, and must come to understand ourselves as living in but not of that world.

6. We must find new ways to succinctly restate our beliefs and values. Our old ways were not wrong, but they were framed in and against tenets of the CWV. We must find vocabulary, frameworks, rituals, and rhythms that highlight where the gospel harmonizes, and where it opposes the beliefs and values of the post-CWV.

7. We must do this, because God has sent us to reach not the twentieth century CWV West, but the twenty-first century post-CWV West.

Appendix

Jesus's Behaviors in Relation to Authority Figures

Where Jesus Is Provocative and Even Confrontational

Mark 1:22 Jesus teaches in the synagogue with an authority beyond the teachers of the law

Mark 2:5 Jesus pardons sins, whereas the teachers of the law think only God can do this

Mark 2:15 Jesus eats with sinners and tax collectors

Mark 2:18 Jesus' disciples ignore the fasting festivals

Mark 2:23 Jesus' disciples pick grain on the Sabbath

Mark 3:5 Jesus heals on the Sabbath

Mark 3:34 Jesus dishonors his mother and brothers, and calls the disciples his family

Mark 5:13 In a gentile region, Jesus drives demons out of people and into pigs

Mark 7:2 Jesus' disciples do not ceremonially wash their hands

Mark 7:6–13 Jesus teaches against the Pharisees and teachers of the law as hypocrites

Mark 8:15 Jesus teaches to the twelve against the yeast of the Pharisees and of Herod

Mark 8:31 Jesus teaches that the Son of Man must be rejected by the elders, the chief priests and the teachers of the law, and that he must be killed, but makes no mention of Herod, Pilate, or Rome

Mark 9:50	Jesus infers that Israel and its leadership are salt that has lost its saltiness
Mark 10:33	the chief priests and the teachers of the law will condemn Jesus to death, and they will hand him over to the unnamed gentiles
Mark 11:14	Jesus judges the fig tree, a symbol for Israel
Mark 11:17	Jesus clears the temple, calling its incumbents a den of robbers
Mark 12:1–11	Jesus tells the parable of the tenants, where Israel's leadership is like tenants plotting to dispose the land owner by rejecting his messengers (prophets) and killing his son
Mark 12:38–40	Jesus describes the teachers of the law as self-aggrandizing
Mark 14:48–49	Jesus criticizes a crowd sent by the chief priests, the teachers of the law, and the elders for arresting him at night, and not in the day time in the temple courts.

Where Jesus Is Compliant and Agreeable

Mark 1:44	Jesus tells the healed man to go show himself to the priest and offer sacrifices
Mark 5:38	Jesus heals the daughter of a synagogue ruler
Mark 10:5	Jesus' clarification about divorce to the Pharisees is not overtly confrontational
Mark 12:17	Jesus says, "Give back to Caesar what is Caesar's and to God what is God's."
Mark 12:28	When answering what appears to be a genuine question about the most important law from one of the teachers of the law who is not far from the Kingdom of God

Where Jesus Is Guarded, Coy, or Silent

Mark 6:14–29	Regarding the beheading of John the Baptist. In Matthew's account "he withdrew by boat privately to a solitary place" (Matthew 14:13). Luke's account is similar, Jesus withdraws.
Mark 9:12–13	Jesus teaches that the Son of Man must be rejected by Israel, just as they rejected Elijah. But Jesus speaks in code. Elijah is a reference to John the Baptist, and the phrase "they have done to him everything they wished" is an allusion to his beheading.

Bibliography

ABC News. "Gay Former Rugby League Star Ian Roberts Feels 'Sorry' for Israel Folau." May 4, 2019. https://www.abc.net.au/news/2019-05-05/israel-folau-gay-kids-in-suburbs-killing-themselves-ian-roberts/11081230.

Akcapar, S. N. "Religious Conversions in Forced Migration: Comparative Cases of Afghans in India and Iranians in Turkey." *Journal of Eurasian Studies* 10, no. 1 (2019) 61–74.

Asian Pacific Institute on Gender-Based Violence. "Pacific Islanders and Domestic & Sexual Violence." (2018). https://www.api-gbv.org/resources/dvfactsheet-pacificislander/.

Australian Bureau of Statistics. "Schools." https://www.abs.gov.au/statistics/people/education/schools/latest-release.

Banks, Joseph. *Journal of the Right Hon. Sir Joseph Banks during Captain Cook's First Voyage in H.M.S Endeavour in 1768–71.* Edited by Joseph Dalton Hooker. 1896. Reprint, Cambridge: Cambridge University Press, 2011.

Barna Research Group. "State of the Church 2020." https://www.barna.com/research/changing-state-of-the-church/.

Barrett, C. K. "Paul's Speech on the Areopagus." In *New Testament Christianity for Africa and the World: Essays in Honor of Harry Sawyer*, edited by E. Glasswell and E. W. Fasholé-Luke, 69–77. London: SPCK, 1974.

Barrett, David, and Todd Johnson. *World Christian Trends AD 30–AD 2200.* Pasadena: William Carey: 2003.

Bosch, David J. *Transforming Mission: Paradigm Shifts in Theology of Mission.* New York: Orbis, 1991.

Brierley, Peter. "Church Attendance in Britain, 1980–2005." http://www.brin.ac.uk/figures/church-attendance-in-britain-1980-2015/.

Bright, Bill. *Have You Heard of the Four Spiritual Laws?* N.p.: Campus Crusades for Christ, 1965.

Bruce, F. F. "Church History and Its Lessons." In *The Church: A Symposium*, edited by J. B. Watson, 178–95. London: Pickering & Inglis, 1949.

Burge, Ryan. "Does Education 'Cure' People of Faith? The Data Says No." https://religionnews.com/2022/11/10/does-education-cure-people-of-faith-the-data-says-no/

Commonwealth Bureau of Census and Statistics. *Census of Population and Housing, 30 June 1966, Commonwealth of Australia, Volume 1. Population: Single Characteristics, Part 7. Religion.* 1970.

Chan, Sam. *How To Talk About Jesus (Without Being That Guy): Personal Evangelism in a Skeptical World.* Grand Rapids, MI: Zondervan Reflective, 2020.

Chesterton, Andrew. "Australian Car Market." https://www.carsguide.com.au/car-advice/australian-car-market-car-sales-statistics-and-figures-70982#:~:text=Again%20according%20to%20data%20from,number%20was%2035%20per%20cent.

Christianity.com. "The Explosion of Christianity in Africa." April 28, 2010. https://www.christianity.com/church/church-history/timeline/2001-now/the-explosion-of-christianity-in-africa-11630859.html.

Dawkins, Richard. *The Selfish Gene.* Oxford: Oxford University Press, 2016.

Dewey, Caitlin. "A Stunning Map of Depression Rates around the World." *Washington Post*, November 7, 2013. https://www.washingtonpost.com/news/worldviews/wp/2013/11/07/a-stunning-map-of-depression-rates-around-the-world/.

Dickson, John. *Bullies and Saints: An Honest Look at the Good and Evil of Christian History.* Grand Rapids, MI: Zondervan, 2021.

———. *Humilitas: A Lost Key to Life, Love, and Leadership.* Grand Rapids, MI: Zondervan, 2011.

Dybdahl, P. B. "The Stairway to Heaven: A Critique of the Evangelical Gospel Presentation in North America." PhD diss., Andrews University, 2004.

Field, Clive D. "A Shilling for Queen Elizabeth: The Era of State Regulation of Church Attendance in England, 1552–1969." *Journal of Church and State* 50, no. 2 (2008) 213–53.

———. "Counting Religion in England and Wales: The Long Eighteenth Century, c. 1680–c.1840." *The Journal of Ecclesiastical History* 63, no. 4 (2012) 693–720.

Finke, Roger, and Rodney Stark. *The Churching of America, 1776–2005: Winners and Losers in our Religious Economy.* New Brunswick: Rutgers University Press, 2005.

Flemming, Dean. *Contextualisation in the New Testament: Patterns for Theology and Mission.* Downers Grove, IL: InterVarsity, 2005.

Forbes, Greg W., and Scott D. Harrower. *Raised from Obscurity: A Narratival and Theological Study of the Characterization of Women in Luke-Acts.* Eugene, OR: Pickwick, 2015.

Foster, T. "A Vision for the Mission and Message of the Australian Church after Christendom." Unpublished D.Min thesis, Fuller Theological Seminary, 2005.

Gaarden, Marianne, and Marlene Ringgaard Lorensen. "Listeners as Authors in Preaching: Empirical and Theoretical Perspectives." *Homiletic* 38, no. 1 (2013) 28–45.

Gaustad, Edwin S., and Philip L. Barlow. *New Historical Atlas of Religion in America.* New York: Oxford University Press, 2001.

Graham, Billy. *Steps to Peace with God.* Garland, TX: American Tract Society, 1997.

Griffin, Ledbetter, et al. *A First Look at Communication Theory.* Boston: McGraw-Hill, 2009.

Harris, Sam. *Waking Up: A Guide to Spirituality Without Religion.* New York: Simon & Schuster, 2014.

Hewings, Grant, et al. "The Facts of Loneliness." https://www.campaigntoendloneliness.org/the-facts-on-loneliness/.

Hesselgrave, David John, and Edward Rommen. *Contextualization: Meanings, Methods, and Models*. Pasadena, CA: William Carey Library, 2013.

Holland, Tom. *Dominion: The Making of the Western Mind*. London: Little Brown, 2019.

Hofstede, Geert, et al. *Cultures and Organizations: Software of the Mind*. London: McGraw-Hill, 2010.

Jackson, Hugh. "Churchgoing in Nineteenth-Century New Zealand." *New Zealand Journal of History* 17, no. 1 (1983) 43–59.

Jenkins, Philip. *The Lost History of Christianity: The Thousand-Year Golden Age of the Church in the Middle East, Africa, and Asia—and How It Died*. New York: HarperOne, 2009.

Johnson, Todd M., and Gina A. Zurlo, eds. *World Christian Database*. Leiden, Neth.: Brill, 2021.

Jones, Jeffrey. "U.S. Church Membership Falls Below Majority for First Time." *Gallup*, 2021. https://news.gallup.com/poll/341963/church-membership-falls-below-majority -first-time.aspx;.

Josephus, Flavius. *Antiquities of the Jews*. https://www.perseus.tufts.edu/hopper/text?do c=Perseus%3atext%3a1999.01.0146.

———. *History of the Jewish War*. https://www.perseus.tufts.edu/hopper/text?doc=Per seus%3atext%3a1999.01.0148.

Judd, Stephen, and Kenneth Cable. *Sydney Anglicans*. Sydney: AIO, 2000.

Kennedy, D. James. *Evangelism Explosion*. Wheaton, IL: Tyndale, 1970.

Kraft, Charles. *Communication Theory for Christian Witness*. Maryknoll, NY: Orbis, 1991.

Lawton, W. J. *The Better Time to Be: Utopian Attitudes to Society Among Sydney Anglicans, 1885 to 1914*. Kensington, NSW: University of NSW Press, 1990.

Livingstone, Hart, et al., eds. *Evangelicals and Science in Historical Perspective*. New York: Oxford University Press, 1999.

Lobodov, B. "Alcohol and Illicit Drug in Russia." https://nida.nih.gov/international/ abstracts/alcohol-illicit-drug-in-russia-current-situation-possible-solution

Mallaby, Sebastian. "How Economists' Faith in Markets Broke America." *The Atlantic*, September 2019. https://www.theatlantic.com/magazine/archive/2019/09/nicolas- lemann-binyamin-appelbaum-economics/594718/.

Mangalwadi, Vishal. *The Book That Made Your World: How the Bible Created the Soul of Western Civilization*. Nashville, TN: Thomas Nelson, 2011.

Manson, Mark. *The Subtle Art of Not Giving a F****. New York: HarperCollins, 2016.

Marx, Karl. *A Contribution to the Critique of Hegel's Philosophy of Right: Introduction*. Cambridge: Cambridge University Press, 1994.

McAlpine, Stephen. *Being the Good Bad Guys: How to Live for Jesus in a World that Says You Shouldn't*. London: The Good Book Company, 2021.

McGavran, Donald. *Understanding Church Growth*. Grand Rapids: Eerdmans: 1970.

McKnight, Scot. *Turning to Jesus: The Sociology of Conversion in the Gospels*. Louisville, KY: Westminster John Knox, 2002.

Mol, Hans. *The Faith of Australians*. North Sydney: Allen & Unwin, 1985.

Neill, Stephen. *Creative Tension: The Duff Lectures, 1958*. London: Edinburgh House, 1959.

Niebuhr, H. Richard. *The Kingdom of God in America*. Middletown, NY: Wesleyan University Press, 1959.

Nouwen, Henri. *Adam: God's Beloved*. New York: Orbis, 1997.

————. *Sabbatical Journey: The Diary of his Final Year*. New York: Crossroad, 1998.

Pepper, Miriam, and Katha Jacka. "Highly Educated Churchgoers on the Rise." https://www.ncls.org.au/articles/highly-educated-churchgoers/.

Pew Research Center. "Religion and Education Around the World." December 13, 2016. https://www.pewresearch.org/religion/wp-content/uploads/sites/7/2016/12/Religion-Education-ONLINE-FINAL.pdf.

————. "Return to Religion, But Not to Church." February 10, 2014. https://www.pewresearch.org/religion/2014/02/10/russians-return-to-religion-but-not-to-church/.

Phillips, Walter. *Defending "A Christian Country": Churchmen and Society in New South Wales in the 1880s and After*. St Lucia: University of Queensland Press, 1981.

————. "Religious Profession and Practice in New South Wales, 1850–1901: The Statistical Evidence." *Historical Studies* 15, no. 59 (1972) 378–400.

Piggin, Stuart, and Robert D. Linder. *The Fountain of Public Prosperity: Evangelical Christians in Australian History 1740–1914*. Clayton: Monash University Publishing, 2018.

Richardson, Don. *Eternity in Their Hearts*. Minneapolis, MN: Bethany, 2005.

Rietveld, David. "A Survey of the Phenomenological Research of Listening to Preaching." *Homilectic* 38, no. 2 (2013) 30–47.

Root, Andrew. *The Congregation in a Secular Age: Keeping Sacred Time Against the Speed of Modern Life*. Grand Rapids, MI: Baker Academic, 2021.

————. *Faith Formation in a Secular Age: Responding to the Church's Obsession with Youthfulness*. Grand Rapids, MI: Baker Academic, 2017.

————. *The Pastor in a Secular Age: Ministry to People Who No Longer Need a God*. Grand Rapids, MI: Baker Academic, 2019.

Rorty, Richard. *Philosophy and the Mirror of Nature*. Princeton: Princeton University Press, 1979.

Roser, Hasell, et al. "War and Peace." https://ourworldindata.org/war-and-peace.

Rousseau, Jean-Jacques. *The Social Contract*. Translated by Maurice Cranston. 1762. London: Penguin, 1968.

Ruscio, Hallion, et al. "Cross-Sectional Comparison of the Epidemiology of DSM-5 Generalized Anxiety Disorder Across the Globe." *JAMA Psychiatry* 74, no. 5 (2017) 465–75.

Sandler, Rachel. "Jeff Bezos Just Gave Away Nearly $120 Million." *Forbes*, May 6, 2022. https://www.forbes.com/sites/rachelsandler/2022/05/06/jeff-bezos-just-gave-away-nearly-120-million/?sh=25499b1a1010.

Satter, David. "100 Years of Communism—and 100 Million Dead." *Wall Street Journal*, November 6, 2017. https://www.wsj.com/articles/100-years-of-communismand-100-million-dead-1510011810.

Scarisbrick, J. J. *The Reformation and the English People*. Oxford: Basil Blackwell, 1984.

Schweitzer, Albert. *The Quest of the Historical Jesus: A Critical Study of Its Progress from Reimarus to Wrede*. London: Black, 1954.

Secretariat of the Pacific Community for Ministry of Women. "Solomon Islands Family Health and Safety Study: A Study on Violence against Women and Children." Suva, Fiji: Star Printery, 2009.

Sedauskas, Andrew. "Percentage of Aussie Taxpayers Giving to Charity in Decline." https://www.fpmagazine.com.au/percentage-aussie-taxpayers-giving-charity-decline-report-359440/.

Sheridan, Greg. *Christians: The Urgent Case for Jesus in Our World*. Crows Nest, NSW: Allen and Unwin, 2021.

———. *God Is Good for You: A Defence of Christianity in Troubled Times*. Crows Nest, NSW: Allen & Unwin, 2018.

Smith, Adam. *An Inquiry into the Nature and Causes of the Wealth of Nations*. London: Strahan, 1776.

———. *The Theory of Moral Sentiments*. London: Strahan, 1759.

Stark, Rodney. *The Rise of Christianity: How the Obscure, Marginal Jesus Movement Became the Dominant Religious Force in the Western World in a Few Centuries*. San Francisco, CA: HarperCollins, 1997.

———. *The Triumph of Christianity: How the Jesus Movement Became the World's Largest Religion*. San Francisco, CA: HarperOne, 2011.

Stark, Rodney, and Roger Finke. "American Religion in 1776: A Statistical Portrait." *Sociological Analysis* 49, no. 1 (1988) 39–51.

Stephan, Andre, and Robert Crawford. "Size Does Matter." *The Conversation*, 2016. https://theconversation.com/size-does-matter-australias-addiction-to-big-houses-is-blowing-the-energy-budget-70271.

Stolyarova, Galina. "Russia: Mental Illness on the Rise as Economic, Social Instability Grow." https://www.rferl.org/a/1096839.html.

Strabo. *Geographica*. https://www.perseus.tufts.edu/hopper/text?doc=Perseus%3atext %3a1999.01.0198.

Trueman, Carl. *The Rise and Triumph of the Modern Self: Cultural Amnesia, Expressive Individualism, and the Road to Sexual Revolution*. Wheaton, IL: Crossway, 2020.

——— *Strange New World: How Thinkers and Activists Redefined Identity and Sparked the Sexual Revolution*. Wheaton, IL: Crossway, 2022.

Vanderstelt, Jeff. *Gospel Fluency: Speaking the Truths of Jesus in the Everyday Stuff of Life*. Wheaton, IL: Crossway, 2017.

Vanhoozer, Kevin J. *Faith Speaking Understanding: Performing the Drama of Doctrine*. Louisville, KY: Westminster John Knox, 2014.

Vogel, Klaus. "Sphaera terrae—das mittelalterliche Bild der Erde und die kosmographische Revolution." PhD diss., Georg-August-Universität Göttingen, 1995.

Weber, T. P. Review of *The Churching of America*, by Roger Fink and Rodney Stark. *Fides et historia* 26, no. 1 (1994) 138–40.

Williams, Roy. *In God They Trust: The Religious Beliefs of Australia's Prime Ministers 1901–2013*. Sydney: Bible Society Australia, 2013.

——— *Post-God Nation: How Religion Fell Off the Radar in Australia and What Might Be Done To Get It Back On*. Sydney: ABC, 2015.

Witherington, Ben, III. *New Testament Rhetoric: An Introductory Guide to the Art of Persuasion in and of the New Testament*. Eugene, OR: Cascade, 2009.

Wood, Stella. "A Spiritual Wilderness." *History Today* 69, no. 10 (2019) 78–83.

World Health Organization. *Depression and Other Common Mental Disorders: Global Health Estimates*, 2017.

Wright, Christopher J. H. *Hearing the Message of Daniel: Sustaining Faith in Today's World*. Grand Rapids, MI: Zondervan, 2017.

Wright, N. T. *Jesus and the Victory of God*. Minneapolis, MN: Fortress, 1997.

———. *The New Testament and the People of God*. Minneapolis, MN: Fortress, 1992.

Wright, N. T., and Michael Bird. *The New Testament in Its World*. London: SPCK, 2019.

Yancey, Philip. "Holy Inefficiency of Henri Nouwen." *Christianity Today*, December 9, 1996.

Printed in Great Britain
by Amazon

27211149R00159